blue
rider
press

THE MOST
FAMOUS WRITER
WHO EVER
LIVED

ALSO BY TOM SHRODER

*Old Souls: Compelling Evidence from
Children Who Remember Past Lives*

Acid Test: LSD, Ecstasy, and the Power to Heal

*Fire on the Horizon: The Untold Story
of the Gulf Oil Disaster* (with John Konrad)

*Seeing the Light: Wilderness and Salvation —
A Photographer's Tale* (with John Barry)

BLUE RIDER PRESS

New York

THE MOST
FAMOUS WRITER
WHO EVER
LIVED

———

A True Story of My Family

TOM SHRODER

blue
rider
press

An imprint of Penguin Random House LLC
375 Hudson Street
New York, New York 10014

Copyright © 2016 by Tom Shroder

Grateful acknowledgment is made for permission to reprint from the letter of Ernest Hemingway
to MacKinlay Kantor dated May 16, 1952. Copyright © Hemingway Foreign Rights Trust.
Reprinted with the permission of Scribner, a division of Simon & Schuster, Inc.

Frontispiece photograph by Tim Kantor. Photograph of John M. Kantor (center, page 7 of photo insert)
courtesy *Baltimore Sun*. All other photographs are from the author's personal collection.

Library of Congress Cataloging-in-Publication Data

Names: Shroder, Tom, author.
Title: The most famous writer who ever lived : a true story of my family / Tom Shroder.
Description: New York : Blue Rider Press, 2016.
Identifiers: LCCN 2016016448 | ISBN 9780399174599 (hardback)
Subjects: LCSH: Kantor, MacKinlay, 1904–1977. | Kantor, MacKinlay,
1904–1977—Family. | Authors, American—20th century—Biography. |
Authors, American—20th century—Family relationships. | Shroder, Tom—Family. |
BISAC: BIOGRAPHY & AUTOBIOGRAPHY / Editors, Journalists, Publishers. |
BIOGRAPHY & AUTOBIOGRAPHY / Literary. | BIOGRAPHY & AUTOBIOGRAPHY / General.
Classification: LCC PS3521.A47 Z84 2016 | DDC 813/.52 [B] —dc23
LC record available at https://lccn.loc.gov/2016016448
p.   cm.

Printed in the United States of America
1   3   5   7   9   10   8   6   4   2

Book design by Gretchen Achilles

This book is dedicated to my mother,

who never let me forget. I wish she could

have lived long enough to read this.

KANTOR FAMILY TREE

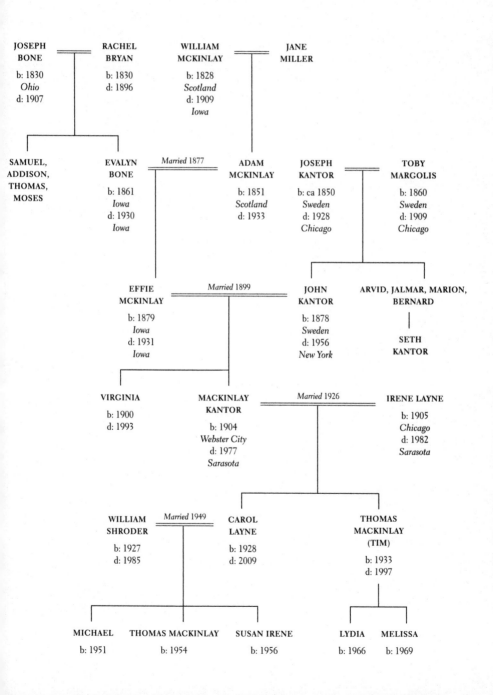

JOSEPH BONE
b: 1830
Ohio
d: 1907

RACHEL BRYAN
b: 1830
d: 1896

WILLIAM MCKINLAY
b: 1828
Scotland
d: 1909
Iowa

JANE MILLER

SAMUEL, ADDISON, THOMAS, MOSES

EVALYN BONE
b: 1861
Iowa
d: 1930
Iowa

Married 1877

ADAM MCKINLAY
b: 1851
Scotland
d: 1933

JOSEPH KANTOR
b: ca 1850
Sweden
d: 1928
Chicago

TOBY MARGOLIS
b: 1860
Sweden
d: 1909
Chicago

EFFIE MCKINLAY
b: 1879
Iowa
d: 1931
Iowa

Married 1899

JOHN KANTOR
b: 1878
Sweden
d: 1956
New York

ARVID, JALMAR, MARION, BERNARD

SETH KANTOR

VIRGINIA
b: 1900
d: 1993

MACKINLAY KANTOR
b: 1904
Webster City
d: 1977
Sarasota

Married 1926

IRENE LAYNE
b: 1905
Chicago
d: 1982
Sarasota

WILLIAM SHRODER
b: 1927
d: 1985

Married 1949

CAROL LAYNE
b: 1928
d: 2009

THOMAS MACKINLAY (TIM)
b: 1933
d: 1997

MICHAEL
b: 1951

THOMAS MACKINLAY
b: 1954

SUSAN IRENE
b: 1956

LYDIA
b: 1966

MELISSA
b: 1969

ONE

——

My mother once told me that when she and her brother, my uncle Tim, were growing up, their father led them to believe he was the most famous writer who ever lived.

This was an absurdity, of course, but not to the degree it may at first seem. My grandfather MacKinlay Kantor wrote innumerable works of fiction, including thirty-one novels, one of which, *Andersonville*, won the Pulitzer Prize. Another novel, *Glory for Me*, was the basis for the movie *The Best Years of Our Lives*, which took seven Oscars, became the highest-grossing film since *Gone with the Wind*, and is often ranked among the greatest American movies of all time. These successes played out over more than three decades, during which Mack, as everyone called him, rose from near-starvation poverty to considerable wealth, performed on popular television shows, and made cameo appearances in movies. He "discovered" Oscar-winning actor and folksinger Burl Ives, mentored the crime novelist John D. MacDonald, and hung out with the likes of Grant Wood, Gregory Peck, Stephen Vincent Benét, Carl Sandburg, James Cagney, and Ernest Hemingway.

My first clear memories of my grandfather are from the late 1950s, when he was still at the height of his fame. He was fifty years old in 1954, the year I was born, already acclaimed on the front of *The New York Times Book Review* for having reinvented the historical novel and two years away from his Pulitzer. When he came to visit us in our suburban New York home, often between long sojourns in Europe, he arrived in a limo. Maître d's in swank New York restaurants fussed over him and gave him primo tables. I was mightily impressed, both with the chauffeur-driven limos and the kowtowing factotums, but also painfully uncomfortable when, after the third or fourth cocktail, he would grow loud and demanding, and could be counted on to make a profanity-laced scene if some product, service, or individual fell short of his expectations.

We all knew that he had overcome a difficult childhood. We'd been told the story in bits and pieces, which I'd always suspected were a little too lurid to be entirely true. They added up to this: His father, my great-grandfather John Kantor, was a con artist who had abandoned his family (Mack, his sister, and their mother) before Mack was born, barely staying ahead of the sheriff, rose to wealth and power in corrupt political machines in Chicago and Montreal, hobnobbing with characters out of a gangster film, and ultimately did time in Sing Sing prison for one or more of a series of scams. My grandfather talked often of his bitter hatred for the man, who continued to hold out the possibility of love and support throughout Mack's youth, only to betray his hope over and over. But to us great-grandkids, John Kantor was merely a splash of spice on the family tree, an object of curiosity and irony, an off-color genealogical punch line. We didn't take him seriously, just as, in the years to come, we wouldn't take Mack—his bluster, his fame, or his literary accomplishments—entirely seriously.

When we were young, he was simply Grandpa. Once each winter, my parents; my brother, Michael; my sister, Susan; and I would board a train at Pennsylvania Station in New York City and make the overnight trip down the East Coast and through the swampy wilds of Central Florida to Sarasota on the state's southwest Gulf Coast, where we would be met by Mack and my grandmother Irene Layne, a petite woman with dyed-blond hair who was a fairly accomplished amateur painter and still daintily pretty well into her fifties. They would pull into the gritty small-town train station in a late-model canary-yellow Lincoln Continental. Grandma, dressed in pastels, would enfold me in a hug smelling of gardenias, oil paints, and the little cigarillos she smoked and kiss the top of my head while Mack stood back, puffing on his pipe. When the cuddling was out of the way, he'd stick out his chest and offer a firm handshake, man to man.

We'd load the luggage into the trunk and Mack would whisk us off to Siesta Key and the rambling beach house he'd built in 1936 with the proceeds from his first big literary success. As he drove, he took long sips from the cocktail glass parked in the custom-made cup holder he'd had installed on the dashboard—this was long before the days when such things came standard. The house, built with termite-proof pecky cypress lumber and a pair of coquina rock fireplaces, was hidden down a long shell driveway on three acres of beachfront jungle. We'd park in the carport and my sister, brother, and I would burst from the backseat and race through the open, airy house, out the sliding glass doors, through the screened patio, across the palm-studded lawn of prickly Bermuda grass, and straight down to the beach. We'd toss off our city shoes and splash into the gentle swells rolling from the Gulf of Mexico into Big Pass as Mack mixed drinks for the adults.

Most days after that he spent in his study with the door closed, and woe be to any child or canine (of which there were always one or two) whose boisterous vocalizations disturbed him. But when the study door, just off the living room, opened at precisely five p.m.—cocktail hour—we were free to explore the big room with its book-lined walls and eclectic museum of mementos. The very atmosphere altered when we entered. The air seemed stiller, somehow, infused with an intoxicating bouquet of pipe tobacco, sea salt, seasoned wood, and the musty aroma given off by hundreds of bookbindings slowly decaying in the unconditioned Florida humidity. Hanging above the volume-crammed shelves and on every bare wall was a *Boys' Life* fantasy of artifacts: black-and-white photos of bombing runs taken from the bombsight of a B-17, the impact of the bombs evident in a trail of tiny black mushrooms erupting from the distant surface; rough-and-tumble group shots of louche pilots lounging before sheet-metal hangars—the men of the bomber groups he flew with in World War II and Korea; framed *Saturday Evening Post* covers featuring his short stories; a photo of the bronze plaque containing a poem he'd written embedded in a wall on the eighty-sixth-floor observation deck of the Empire State Building; Nazi spoils of war, including German helmets, a dummy potato masher, uniform insignia, and, most intriguing, a bullwhip; original prints of Civil War battle scenes; a red, white, and blue sign that said FUCK COMMUNISM; and a scale model of a B-52 jet bomber perched atop a metal stand, which I coveted most of all.

His mahogany desk backed up to a picture window overlooking the deep green lawn, which was studded with palms draped in long links of sausage-like cacti that made excellent targets for the archery sets Mack bought for us, much to my mother's horror. The cacti's juice-filled segments clung to the spiky palm trunks and threw out fragrant white blossoms. You could smell them through the open windows to either side, and hear the surf sliding along the beach beyond.

Sometimes after dinner we'd all be summoned to the living room to find Mack enthroned in the middle of an aqua-blue sofa, a stack of onionskin typing paper beside him—the product of his day's work. He'd read aloud, and we understood that even shuffling our feet loudly would bring down God's own wrath on our heads. I don't remember actually listening, just *pretending* to listen.

Though he could be gruff with us—he once provoked a huge fight, prompting my parents to drag us off in a huff to a hotel, when he declared that we kids would have to vacate the premises entirely to eliminate any possibility that we would interrupt an adults-only party— he could also be kind and entertaining.

Once, he showed us how they made floating lanterns when he was a kid in Iowa: He folded a newspaper into a box shape, turned it on one pointy end, and lit the bottom with a match. As it burned, the hot air filled the unlit end and made it rise like a balloon, the thin paper lit briefly with a flickering golden light before being entirely consumed. I always wondered how many forests had burned because of that little trick, but the lanterns' beauty, lifting into the dusk against the dark silhouettes of palm fronds, was moving. He wrote us long letters in- cluding stamps from the many exotic places he visited, and brought home spectacular gifts—like the miniature replica of a Scottish castle with a working drawbridge and metal soldiers wearing tartan kilts that I have preserved for half a century.

The year I turned fourteen, my parents moved us from the New York suburbs to a house on Siesta Key, less than a mile from my grand- father. He became a fixture in my most formative years. We'd have inevitably comical weekend dinners in which Mack, Irene, my mother, and Tim would argue with increasing passion and volume over the exact words of an alternate verse of some nineteenth-century ballad or whether they had spent the summer of '47 in upstate New York or Southern California. (My grandmother, absent the loud gene herself, always threatened to write an autobiography titled *I Learned to Shout*.) When I was in high school, Mack would let me pitch a tent on his beach, where I camped out with friends. He'd often show up as night fell, puffing on his pipe in the firelight, telling us this or that anecdote about his war experiences or his childhood adventures in the Midwest outback as we listened politely. He even pulled strings to get me a job as a copyboy with the Sarasota newspaper. When I turned it down because the job would have required working Saturday nights—date night—his disgust, so justified, was shockingly brief.

Preoccupied with my own adolescence—the football team, the girls, the parties, the endless sun-saturated days on the beach—I barely noticed his slow decline. But I did increasingly notice his reactionary politics. He was a great friend, admirer, and ghostwriter of the "autobiography" of Air Force general Curtis LeMay, who had urged John F. Kennedy to bomb the Soviet nuclear missiles in Cuba—which likely would have triggered World War III. He famously threatened to bomb North Vietnam "back into the Stone Age" and ran for vice president on a third-party ticket headed by segregationist George Wallace. We even once picnicked with LeMay and his family at a ranch east of town, which was the first and only time I shot a living thing with a rifle. As Mack and the general watched approvingly, I put the .22-caliber barrel to the head of a toothy garfish struggling at the end of a hook and blew it back to the Stone Age, from whence, no doubt, it had come.

My own political awakening was proceeding in the opposite direction, which reinforced my sense of my grandfather as a discordant relic from a bygone era. My brother and I had always viewed him with the arrogant skepticism typical of youth—especially the youth of our particular generation. We cringed at what seemed to us to be his egotism and his need to be the center of attention. At one large gathering of family and friends, he interrupted the lively party chatter in his impossible-to-ignore voice to tell a long story, glaring at anyone who didn't appear rapt. The tale went on and on. And on. Finally it reached a somewhat unsatisfying conclusion, and in the embarrassed silence, our smart-ass friend said: "Great story!" Then he pointed at me. "You remember the first half and I'll remember the second half."

That brought down the house, and Mack stormed out. I laughed with everyone else, but felt sick inside.

It wasn't just his conversational style I considered old-fashioned. I was quick to judge his writing—though I'd read little of it—as overly mannered, alternately tediously detailed and overwritten, and sometimes downright hokey. I simply didn't have the patience or the interest to give it much of a chance. Unfortunately, I represented the times well.

Mack saw this creeping disdain of a new era and raised it. He went all in, railing against modernity with a bitter intensity. My father liked to say that Mack was born in the wrong century, and Mack took that as a badge of honor. But he somehow failed to understand that the flooding cultural tide would sweep him out to sea.

Being a teenager, I never discussed this with him, of course, but through my mother and Tim, who both grew increasingly worried about their parents as the 1970s progressed, I understood that he had thought his royalties would keep rolling in forever, and that he could always get a big book advance or a movie deal. But his florid writing style and obsession with earlier centuries had gone out of fashion, and people stopped buying most of his books—followed by the publishers who'd been stung by disappointing sales on the heels of big advances.

I discovered only recently some criticism from that period that pretty much summed up what was happening. One reviewer wrote of Mack, "Your grandfather and grandmother would take him to their respective bosoms. Your present-day college son and daughter would find him strictly from 'Squaresville.'" Another called one of his novels "embarrassingly jingoistic."

At the time, I merely had a vague sense that he wasn't as famous as he seemed to think he was, and that there was tension around money. As the big paydays dried up, he kept living high. He couldn't conceive of himself as anything other than the famous author of the past. He insisted on going on a monthlong luxury cruise because he said he couldn't write at home. He picked up every check. He ran through his money and mortgaged his property. He had to rely on friends to keep from default. We eventually learned that John D. MacDonald, the perennially best-selling detective novelist who was a Siesta Key neighbor and longtime drinking buddy, had come to the rescue with an infusion of cash.

By mid-decade, Mack's life of hard drinking and his ever-darkening prospects had predictable effect and his health began to fail. In the late summer of 1977, he landed in a stark hospital room, dying of congestive heart failure and other complications of long-term alcoholism.

I was twenty-three, just embarking on a writing career of my own at my first newspaper job in Fort Myers, another beach town, to the south. I was about to become a father—my daughter was due any moment—when my mother called to say that Mack wouldn't last much longer. I begged off work and jumped in my car to drive the two hours north to Sarasota Memorial Hospital. My mother had warned me not to expect any kind of recognition: He'd descended into a near coma and hadn't spoken a word for days. As my car rolled nearer, the familiar landmarks accumulating, an urge grew inside me to turn around. What was the point, I asked myself, if he was simply lying insensate, this man who had always been so full of words now completely devoid of them? But I forced my foot down on the gas pedal as if I were holding my hand over a candle flame, ashamed of the cowardly impulse to turn away from what mortality was doing to this man whom I had always loved, if not fully appreciated.

When I arrived at the hospital, I expected to meet my mother and uncle there. I emerged from the parking lot into an empty waiting room. There were no cell phones in those days, so I had to live with the mystery of their absence, naked in my aloneness. I got the room number from the pink lady at the reception desk and took the extra-wide elevator to the floor she'd indicated. I hadn't seen him for several months, and I tried to steel myself for what I would find as I walked reluctantly down the long, oddly empty corridor past doors opening on scenes from various circles of hell. I slowed as I counted down the numbers to his room. The door was swung nearly shut. I gave it a tentative shove with my hand, and peered inside.

He lay on his side on a bed by the window, lit by the bone-colored light of an overcast afternoon. His body had shrunken horribly, his skin sallow, his breathing ragged. Tethered to a web of tubes, he looked like one of the inmates of the Andersonville prison he'd written about—tortured, starved, barely alive. I forced myself toward him, to the space between the window and his bed.

His eyelids, blue-veined, translucent, fluttered like moth wings nearing a flame. I recoiled from the scene, a panicky voice in my head again arguing that I was punishing myself for no reason, as he couldn't possibly realize my presence, much less recognize me.

One arm, the arm that had an IV needle stuck in it, was above the white sheets. I put my hand on the bare skin that had once covered a bicep. "Grandpa," I said. "It's Tom." My name caught in my constricting throat. I swallowed hard. "I love you," I said. "I'm so sorry you have to go through this."

He drew two more ragged breaths. I almost jumped when his eyes popped open. He looked straight at me.

"Grandpa?" I said. "It's me, Tom."

His eyes looked wild, his crusted lips worked as if he were trying to speak.

"What is it?" I asked. "Do you want me to get you something?"

His lips kept twisting. I leaned in closer. And then I heard a strangled croak from deep in his throat.

"Horrible," he said. *"Horrible!"*

After millions and millions of words, these were his last.

The years piled on like so many shovels full of earth on my grandfather's grave in his tiny hometown of Webster City, Iowa. He had been cremated, but his ashes weren't interred with the remains of his mother and grandparents until two years later. As family farms sold out to corporate farmers and local factories closed, the town of eight thousand souls struggled to survive, hanging on to the idea of my grandfather's fame as a slender claim to its own. The city council erected a plaque in the city park, a historical marker downtown, and a road sign bearing his name at the intersection of a cornfield and an industrial warehouse on the edge of town. Everywhere else, the passing years merely confirmed that his celebrity had been fleeting. All but a tiny handful of his books fell out of print, and even the once mighty *Andersonville* only sold at a trickle. Most college graduates would never hear his name.

Though my mother and my uncle kept trying to push the significance of their father's biography and accomplishments on us, we rolled our eyes and mostly ignored them—glanced at the old newspaper clippings without reading, thought about what we were going to do after dinner rather than listen to yet another story from the distant past. Though his many books lined a shelf in my bookcase, I never so much as cracked open a cover, save for *Andersonville*, the 350,000-word book which I attempted twice, and both times failed to penetrate beyond page 30.

For so many people, maybe even most—and it's certainly true of me and my siblings—even extreme dramas in family history beyond one generation removed become a kind of white noise, tuned out until it's too late. I can't remember the exact moment it occurred to me, but at some point a question popped into my head about my grandfather and I realized nobody alive could answer it.

Even as the details of my grandfather's life evaporated from the reservoir of human memory, my questions about him grew more numerous and insistent. I couldn't explain why it had never occurred to me that my desire to become a writer, or the fact that I had, to some extent, succeeded in that rather ludicrous ambition, might have something to do with my heritage, and specifically my grandfather. If anyone ever asked me why I wanted to write, I remembered a moment in an eighth-grade English class poetry section when the teacher chose my poem to read, and my chattering, snoozing classmates actually sat up at their desks, stopped talking, and *listened*. But suddenly, a half century tardy, I remembered that, around the time I was learning to read, I would corral a tiny portable typewriter—a functional toy (and who gave their five-year-olds typewriters as toys?)—roll in a sheet of crisp white paper, and attempt, letter by letter, to copy the text from *The Cat in the Hat*, mesmerized by the idea that by assembling words together, one typed letter at a time, one could actually create that magical thing called a book.

When I did the math in my head, I realized that this unusual childhood literary fetish would have coincided perfectly with the moment of my grandfather's maximum fame. Could I really believe it was unrelated? Had I been predisposed by nurture or nature, or simply by imitation, to tie my identity to the written word? Could so complex a skill as writing possibly be passed down in Grandpa's DNA? Could it be mere coincidence that my most fervent dreams of accomplishment were precisely those things my grandfather in fact accomplished?

I had only too late considered the possibility that I might have been formed or even influenced by the abilities, proclivities, or eccentricities of my near and distant forebears after the firsthand sources of knowledge about them had forever vanished.

Who arrives at maturity without experiencing that regret? Why, I wondered, do most of us have these dual and conflicting tendencies, resisting our genealogical past as if it were an existential threat, yet ultimately pining to connect with it, even as it vanishes before our eyes?

Suddenly, questions about the past, your past, and your family's past begin to flood in, questions that could have been so easily, or at least profitably, answered during the lifetimes of your parents or their parents, but have become literally unanswerable, lost forever behind the impenetrable veil of death.

Tracing one's lineage, a persistent psychological impulse through the ages, has also become a cultural mainstay. A 2013 *Time* magazine story called genealogy the second most popular American hobby after gardening, and the second most visited category of websites after pornography. Popular reality TV shows are filled with genealogical sleuths digging through crumbling registers and handwritten census documents. The portraits they manage to draw with great effort, even when they make lucky finds, are mere outlines providing in the end little more than ancestral stick figures.

I realized I had an advantage, a *big* advantage—if not unique, at least exceedingly rare: In the Library of Congress of the United States, which happened to stand less than twenty-five miles from my home, was a room stacked with 158 boxes filled with 50,000 items; countless pages of indexed correspondence, contracts, manuscripts, photographs, journals, tax returns, paraphernalia, and even an unpublished autobiographical novel—all of it by or about my grandfather. This vast cache—collected because a committee at the Library in the 1950s determined that my grandfather represented a "typical American writer"—was supplemented by the forty-some books that he had published, including at least two autobiographies, as well as a memoir about him written by my uncle—almost none of which I had ever read.

What secrets, what forgotten calamities and unremembered triumphs, what surprising revelations and shocking truths could be pried from those cardboard file folders, all that slowly disintegrating cellulose and black ribbon ink? Was it possible, forty years after his death, that I could get to know my grandfather, not as a teenager might remember a sometimes garrulous old man, but as a contemporary could come to know a living, breathing intimate? More than an intimate—someone whose blood ran in mine, whose most primal makeup mixed in quarters to make me who I am. In learning about my grandfather's life, what would I come to discover of my own? What would I gain from studying the minute realities of the history of a man from a now-distant era whose life and mine bore such obvious parallels? What could I learn about writing from my grandfather's mastery of words, his huge success, and his ultimate failure?

And what would that tell me about why any of us care about our ancestors? Are we blank sheets of paper, waiting to write our own stories? Or are we merely appendixes to lives already lived and largely forgotten?

But mostly I wondered if I could discover the meaning of those awful words—that *one* word, repeated—the final words my grandfather ever said to me, or to anyone. What was it that was so horrible? Was it the futility of accomplishment—the fame, success, and money that had promised so much, but in the end mattered so little? Was it the realization that ultimately his writings would not reach that high and durable orbit of the immortals, but fall ignominiously earthward to serve as footnotes in obscure histories and turn to dust in attic boxes?

Or was it simply illness and death itself—the inevitable, inescapable pain and ugliness of physical destruction that awaits us all, and, possibly, erases all good?

The answers I found were not what I expected, and far more than I bargained for. My grandfather turned out to be a deeply flawed man, in ways both anticipated and that I never would have imagined. He was also far more worthy of admiration than I could have known. I discovered a series of astonishing parallels between our lives that defied chance and made me see myself in a new light. I ran smack into stark differences that provoked insights both powerful and uncomfortable. I thought I would merely be pulling at the threads of my grandfather's life, but soon realized I was clinging to the tail of a tiger as it careened through two centuries of an outrageous American saga.

TWO

———

Just after noon on a beautiful June day in 2014, dry and breezy and not too hot, I boarded a train at the origin of the Orange Line Metro near my Northern Virginia home. I sprawled across two seats in the nearly empty car, wondering how many trips to the Library of Congress it would take to go through 158 boxes filled with the practically uncountable number of documents that comprised the MacKinlay Kantor Papers collection. I had no idea what I would find, or how relevant or revealing any of it would be in my quest to know my grandfather. As the train lurched to the east, my iPhone swooshed: a message from my thirty-something niece, who had no idea where I was or what I was doing.

"I thought you'd be interested," she began. "As you know, we've been in our house for almost five months, and we are still going through boxes. I just came across a copy of *Andersonville*. It is an autographed limited first edition with a personal note to my grandma and grandpa [i.e., my parents]. To make it even better, there are articles neatly folded inside the book, including the *New York Times* book review. Now—if I wasn't feeling guilty before (for not actually ever reading it!!) I'm really feeling guilty now!"

Perfect, I thought. Her timing was eerie, and the sentiment on point: the guilt of ignoring a notable family legacy. My guilt was ever greater, of course; one generation closer, I had known my grandfather well into my young adulthood. A great-granddaughter who was born after he died could be forgiven for having failed to read his seminal work. But here I was embarking on an intensive study of his life, and I had done no better.

In the e-mail, she included a scan of the October 1955 *New York Times* review. It took up most of the front page of the Sunday *Book Review*.

"Onto the warp of history," wrote Henry Steele Commager, one of the great American intellectuals of the mid-twentieth century, "Mr. Kantor has woven with the stuff of imagination an immense and terrible pattern, a pattern which finally emerges as a gigantic panorama of the war itself, and of the nation that tore itself to pieces in war. Out of fragmentary and incoherent records, Mr. Kantor has wrought the greatest of our Civil War novels."

I'd never seen that sixty-year-old review. I had always understood that *Andersonville* had been critically acclaimed, but this was no mere good review, it was epic. A surge of conflicting emotions surprised me. I was buoyed at the evidence that my grandfather had been, at least once upon a time, such a big deal. But there was a minor note under-lying that, a squeamish bit of discomfort, and it took me a minute to pin it down: As a writer myself (and just like every writer who ever tapped a space bar), I had dreamed of getting a review like that, by a reviewer like that, in a paper *exactly* like that. After years of downplaying my grandfather's literary significance, I suddenly found myself comparing it to my own. If he was ultimately insignificant, what was I? Until that moment, I hadn't fully realized just how personal a search this had already become.

The James Madison Memorial Building—naming it after the founding father and fourth U.S. president was the cheapskate, afterthought alternative to building a proposed separate memorial to Madison—is the largest library building in the world; 1.5 million square feet of floor space. It's big, all right. And ugly. The design, a chilly, Bauhaus interpretation of neoclassical architecture, is as derided as the original Library of Congress building, named after Thomas Jefferson, is beloved. The domed, mosaic-tiled, and mural-laden Jefferson building is a century older, all grace and beaux arts exuberance to the Madison's dour, almost Soviet utilitarianism.

I would soon discover that the Library of Congress had been a frequent home away from home for my grandfather, who spent weeks and months researching the minutiae of American history with which to fill his novels. Adored by the library's staff, even before he was designated a "typical American writer" and invited to immortalize his desk debris there, he was given special treatment, a private work space, and fawning assistance. But that would have been in the Jefferson building—the Madison was only completed in 1980, three years after my grandfather died.

My experience with the Library's manuscript division, headquartered in the Madison building, was in keeping with the Spartan surroundings. The reception at security and in the reading room itself was as chilly as the architecture. No welcomes, or even a hint of a smile—just an arm's-length, squint-eyed skepticism that made me feel like an imposition, as if they thought I might leave mustard stains on "their" materials. But I couldn't argue with the efficiency.

The Library stored my grandfather's papers "off-site," a euphemism for a warehouse in Maryland where they stuck the collections that rarely drew interest from researchers. I ordered the maximum allowed, 40 of the 158 boxes, which were transferred to the Madison's reading room within forty-eight hours. Here I could view them at one of the wooden tables arranged in neat rows and separated by aisles just wide enough to navigate a rolling cart laden with boxes. After entering the building through metal detectors, then depositing my backpack and coat in the lockers at the reading room entrance, I produced my research credentials at the front desk and took a seat in the third row. I snuck a peek at my neighbors: The woman to my right picked through boxes labeled EDNA ST. VINCENT MILLAY; the man to my left communed with the documentary leavings of the politician-diplomat W. Averell Harriman.

I learned at the desk that only four boxes could be brought to the table at a time. Since I had no idea what I was looking for, I ordered boxes numbers one through four, figuring I might as well begin at the beginning.

The rolling cart arrived within minutes. I lifted box number one from the cart and plopped it on the table. Immediately, a librarian loomed above me, tsk-tsking: You have to leave the boxes on the cart, I was scolded. Remove only a single file at a time, mark its place in the box with an oversize slab of cardboard, then examine the documents inside the file one at a time, being careful not to disturb their order.

Okay, got it.

I put the box back on the cart, opened the hinged top, and pulled out the first folder. How many of these files would I need to shuffle through before I found something of interest?

I flipped it open.

The top document, covered in plastic, was clipped to a hand-addressed envelope postmarked April 24, 1945. Inscribed in ink on the envelope was handwriting I instantly recognized after not seeing it for nearly forty years.

It said: *MacKinlay Kantor, war correspondent.*

I had remembered all those photos of bombing runs and bomber crews on his office wall—how could I forget?—but somehow it had escaped me that he was not a crew member but a "correspondent." I had never thought of him as a journalist.

I carefully removed the letter: a single piece of onionskin paper, typed roughly with a fading ribbon and crudely corrected with a black pen.

Dear Irene,

I hope you can read this. The ribbon is very faint, and some of the letters are misplaced on this queer German typewriter (made in Leipzig, not so very far from here). If anyone ever tells you again that the atrocity stories are a lot of hysterical propaganda, just tell them politely to shut their big traps. I am sitting here in some damn German family's upstairs sitting room, with oil portraits of Grossmutter and Grossvater staring stupidly from the wall: there is the smell of a good dinner being gekuchen—but I can hardly smell it—the smell of death is too persistent in my nostrils . . . the smell of the prison camp some five miles or so away—the sour-sweetish odor of rotten bodies, of pallid dead skin, of burnt bones and flesh—the perfume of burning, typhus-ridden rags and shoes, the latrines oozing with their rich concentrated filth, the old and new pools of vomit covering the ground. There are nineteen thousand prisoners still in the camp—nowhere else for them to go until a transportation path is opened through the battle lines, for many of them are Russians, Czechs, Poles and Jugo-slavs. They are being moderately well fed for the first time in months and years, but their poor wizened stomachs can't take it—they keep vomiting up the stuff they eat. And the people who come to the camp—a lot of them vomit, too.

We stood and stared at the piles of dead, scores of them, heaps, trucks with the newly dead who could not survive the shock of liberty and salvation. We poked about among great stacks of half-consumed human bones, and saw bodies still half-burnt in the none-too-efficient cremation furnaces (the good Germans ran short of fuel recently: ja, ja, they have shortages over here too). They looked like broken, shriveled black weenies that someone had forgotten and left on the grill too long.

But worst of all, to me, was the children's quarters—both in the hospital (smile when you say that, pard) and in the regular children's quarters. The dear Teutons—think how they enriched the language: they gave us the word kindergarten. A true child's garden was this. "This section for children from five to fifteen." Boys, all of them—just boys in this camp—I kept imagining Tim there. It was not too delightful, as you might say, but I imagined it. The marks of the children's last meal could be seen, if you poked around the wooden tables and filthy old comforters long enough. And good enough for them I daresay: potato peelings, all dried and curly now—gut vegetable for der kinder, ja?—and square biscuits which were part of the dog food for the Dobermans and

*shepherds of the SS guards. The kids had tried to cook those thick,
brown bone-meal crackers. And in the middle of the mess was an
eggshell. Whence came that egg? From the Easter Bunny, without a doubt.*

*I saw a lot of pulverized cities today—smashed, ruined,
pounded to extinction. I wish to God that all of Germany was
laid in such ruins.*

*I can't write more now. Good night, baby and children. Bless
you all. See you soon, I hope.*

Mack

I read the letter twice, amazed. Clearly he'd been present at the
liberation of a concentration camp—unnamed in the letter—a fact I
had never known. Though my Jewish ancestors—on my father's side,
not Mack's (I didn't know anything about his father's Jewish roots, and
his mother was anything but Jewish)—were several generations
removed from the Europe of the Holocaust, I'd always been haunted
by its miasmic shadow, by the sense that what had happened was less
the product of an aberration than an indelible stain in the human
genome. It seemed odd to me that Mack could have been present at
such a historic moment and that I would have never heard of it, either
from him directly or from my mom or my uncle Tim. And yet, a simple Google search using the reading room's Wi-Fi very quickly turned
up several references to MacKinlay Kantor being present at "the liberation of Buchenwald." In fact, some of these references said it was his
motivation for writing about the notoriously cruel prisoner-of-war
camp at Andersonville—to show that Americans were not immune
from inflicting such cruelties themselves.

"There were two smells," he said in an interview I found later,
"pine smoke and vomit, with a little bit from the dead bodies mixed

in. . . . So I thought, for all intents and purposes, I'm standing in Andersonville right now. Then I knew I was going to write it."

This origin story conflicted with what I did remember him saying: that he'd researched *Andersonville* for twenty years—which would have meant long before the war. But there was an abundance of references to his presence at the liberation of Buchenwald. And also a problem: His letter was dated April 24. The first American troops, under the command of Captain Frederic Keffer, arrived at Buchenwald on April 11, 1945, at 3:15 p.m. (now the permanent time of the clock at the entrance gate).

I reread my grandfather's letter and found that, while there was no reference to "I did this this morning" or "yesterday," it clearly referred to something that had happened recently enough so that the outrage—the smell of it—still lingered, raw and powerful. Much later I would find this quote attributed to my grandfather, which only compounded the problem: "I probably wouldn't have written *Andersonville* if I hadn't happened to set foot in Buchenwald a day and a half after we captured it."

I began to wonder if he later exaggerated his proximity to the moment of liberation. The incongruous date on the letter nagged at me like a loose thread, and I pulled at it. On a hunch, I searched for "liberation of Buchenwald" and the date of the letter, April 24, and I got this on a site called scrapbookpages.com:

After the liberation of Buchenwald on April 11, 1945, the rotting corpses were left unburied until General Dwight D. Eisenhower could arrange for a contingent of American congressmen and a group of newsmen, led by Joseph Pulitzer of The St. Louis Post-Dispatch, *to fly to Germany to view the camp on April 24, 1945.*

By then, the original naked corpses had been left out in the sun and the rain for almost two weeks. The shortage of food and

*the typhus epidemic in the camp had resulted in so many deaths
before the liberation of the camp that the crematorium ovens
could not keep up with disposing of the bodies. Since the liberation, the epidemic had not abated and more sick prisoners were
dying each day, although some were dying from eating too much
of the rich food given to them by the Americans. Their bodies
were added to the pile, so that by the time that the Congressmen
and the newsmen got there, there were many more corpses.*

There was even a photo of a scrum of journalists gathered around a
stack of naked corpses, noses buried in their flip notebooks, eyes
obscured by the brims of their ever-present hats. I examined the photo
carefully, but between the blurry image and the damn hats, there was
no way I could pick out my grandfather. So I went back to searching,
this time adding "Kantor" to "Buchenwald" and "April 24." I got just
one hit: a Louisiana State University doctoral thesis on the portrayal of
the Civil War in literature. As regards Mack's visit to Buchenwald, it
was the only Web reference that appeared to get it right:

*When MacKinlay Kantor walked through the gates of Buchen-
wald concentration camp on April 24, 1945, American soldiers
had been liberating Nazi death camps and enslavement factories
for five months.*

The PhD thesis went on to push one of those silly, overwrought
hypotheses common to English departments—that Mack had hidden
a propagandistic message in the heart of *Andersonville*, one aimed not
at the Civil War but at the Cold War. By peopling his novel with an
evil camp commandant and sadistic guards, but with noble, sympathetic civilians surrounding the prison camp, helpless to stop the

horror, he was actually trying to sell the American public on the idea that German scientists who stood by and did nothing to stop the Holocaust they were contributing to were not evil themselves. He was making this case, the thesis argued, in support of the U.S. military's project of rehabilitating German scientists to help in America's rush for postwar military superiority.

I skimmed all that nonsense. (One thing I know from ample personal experience with my grandfather is that such critical overthinking would have driven him to apoplexy. I can see him now, scrunching his nose as if smelling something rotten and raising his voice to a falsetto in a mocking, sneering imitation of whatever errant theory he'd gotten scent of.) But I kept combing through the thesis, looking for any details of use in my own quest. I didn't know exactly what I was looking for. I would have been happy with any tidbit I happened to bump into. Instead, I slammed into a boulder. It was an aside concerning Mack's association with General Curtis LeMay, noting what some LeMay biographers had said about the 1968 third-party vice presidential candidate's single most notorious comment: that the North Vietnamese had better stop their aggression, or we'd "bomb them back into the Stone Age."

This riveted my attention. In the spring of 1972, as a freshman at the University of Florida, I was still facing the possibility of being drafted. I remember lying on my narrow dorm bed in the dark, staring at the ceiling, horrified by the thought that in a matter of months I could be carrying a rifle into some Vietcong-riddled jungle in the middle of what I believed to be an unjustified intervention in a foreign civil war. I identified strongly with the antiwar movement, moved by the destruction of lives, both American and Vietnamese. I remember the feeling, like all the air being sucked out of my lungs, when on March 30, 1972, instead of ending the war, Richard Nixon vastly extended it, announcing a massive bombing campaign against North

Vietnam. As I walked around campus on a bright, beautiful North Florida spring day, everyone I encountered seemed as anguished and enraged as I was. A common idea infused the students who'd come out to protest: that our country, which had saved the world from Nazism, had morphed from hero to villain and was conducting atrocities in our name. I'm sure I must have repeated the "bomb them back into the Stone Age" quote that day to represent the epitome of the brutal, and brutally wrongheaded, mind-set of the Neanderthals forcing this war down our throats.

Before evening I would be caught in a stampede as riot-clad police charged a peaceful gathering of outraged students. Later, I choked on tear gas sprayed from an armored car at students manning impromptu barricades at the main campus intersection. Time and again, police charged and the students ran like a panicked school of fish. At one point I saw a crowd of students breaking and running in my direction. As I ran with them, my heart thumping, I felt more than saw a heavy object fly past my head, followed by a sickening thud. I glanced over my shoulder, my legs still churning. A uniformed cop dropped to the ground. I wanted to make everything go in reverse, but I just kept running.

That helpless feeling of the ground shifting beneath my feet came back strongly as I read this sentence: "LeMay's most recent biographer denies LeMay wrote the infamous and oft-quoted bluster at the end of [his autobiography] that advised the North Vietnamese to 'draw in their horns and stop their aggression, or we're going to bomb them back into the Stone Age.'"

In fact, the biographer, Thomas Coffey, wrote that LeMay maintained that his actual position had always been to use all force necessary to win, but no more, saving lives on both sides. The "Stone Age" quote, the general claimed, was "overwriting" inserted into his autobiography by his ghostwriter.

The ghostwriter wasn't named, but of course I knew it was a real ghost, *my* ghost: MacKinlay Kantor.

All these years later I had met the enemy, and he was my grandfather.

First box. First file. First document.

I assumed, of course, that such a significant find with my first cast into this paper ocean had to be a fluke—just like getting my niece's e-mail about finding the copy of *Andersonville* at the exact moment I was embarking on my first research trip. In fact, I discovered that the stunning Buchenwald letter probably shouldn't even have been in the first box, much less the first file. As I continued to flip through the documents, I realized all the rest concerned Mack's childhood and adolescence. What I knew about this period in his life was fragmentary and episodic. He had grown up with his mother, Effie McKinlay Kantor, whom he had adored, and his older sister, Virginia, in the idyllic early twentieth-century middle-American village of Webster City, Iowa, which I'd never visited but always pictured as Mayberry on *The Andy Griffith Show*. I knew his father had abandoned them. I knew he and his sister grew up poor, and that Mack worked odd jobs from very young, keeping the pennies he'd earned to buy candy—an addiction that ultimately rotted his teeth (a story he told while gleefully flipping out his upper plate to drive home the moral). And I knew that he had been an avid collector of butterflies—because he'd shown me how to net them, euthanize them in jars tainted with ether, and arrange them on collection boards.

Otherwise, his early life was pretty much a mystery to me.

One of the first things I came across was a postcard with a photograph of Webster City's main street, circa 1910. It was no rustic paradise, but an unlovely looking slice of early twentieth-century small-town America; a couple of blocks of unadorned two- and three-story buildings that, to my eye, bordered on bleak, but that Mack apparently saw as the epicenter of a mythic American boyhood.

Mack's commentary on the picture of downtown Webster City made it clear that he had studied this photo minutely, reading it as if a sacred relic. He said this: "An excellent picture of the corner of Des Moines Street and Second Street as it appeared during my boyhood. I delivered *Freeman-Tribunes* to almost every building on this street, and for years. . . . I assume we are looking south, about five o'clock on a summer Sunday morning [because] A) the shadows thrown from the east to west are very long, B) the trees at the end of the street and the vines on the hotel porch are in full life, C) only two vehicles in sight, only two or three people sitting on the hotel porch, and . . . no pedestrians. That is not a man who is standing in the deep center of the photograph behind the telephone post, that is Emil Beck's life size tailor sign."

I resolved to make a trip to Webster City at some point to see that intersection for myself and wondered how transformed it had already become by the time he had written those comments in the late 1950s. Something about the way he parsed that humble little downtown streetscape, the almost theological intensity of his analysis, ignited a powerful flash of nostalgia for my own distant past—exactly as far gone from me now as that image was for Mack when he wrote the annotation. The peculiar innocence of the 1950s suburbia of my childhood flooded into my mind's eye: the packs of roving kids playing kick the can or hide-and-seek until dark; the spinning stools at the drugstore lunch counter; the no-adults-involved, after-hours pickup ball games in the schoolyard; the big, powerful gas-guzzling cars driven without apology or guilt; the belief, never true, that we were living inside one unified and undifferentiated American culture, which anyone could define in an uncomplicated way. All of that was not just past, but nearly vanished, a world that very soon would recede beyond memory.

I stared at Mack's Webster City a long time, trying to imagine the ways in which every street corner, every storefront, would have brought forth a rich web of personal history for him. But even more revealing than the photograph itself was the discovery of these annotations. As Mack gathered and packaged his papers for shipping to the Library, he had taken the time to write several hundred pages of notes, commenting on the items enclosed. Among the first of these I ran across was this: In 1957, as he was boxing up and cataloging huge piles of old manuscripts and personal correspondence detailing his sometimes painful struggles to get a book started or finished, he wrote, "I find myself appalled at the demands of the writing business. Nonetheless, I wish I were working on a book at the moment rather than doing this."

I came up against the ingrained skepticism with which I regarded my grandfather. What instantly came to mind was: *Well, why* weren't *you working on a book then?*

His comment struck me as disingenuous. My grandfather was not big on humility. We knew, even as kids, that he gloried in the idea that his every letter would be enshrined at the Library of Congress. I suddenly remembered that when one of us kids got a letter from Grandpa— a letter we knew he had kept a carbon copy of, as he did with every letter he wrote by that time—we would only half-jokingly say that it was clear he was writing it more to the Library of Congress than to us.

But as I thought about it, I realized I was being unfairly harsh. I knew all about the powerful desire to do something, anything, other than work on the book you desperately wanted to write, but even more desperately wanted to avoid writing. When I created a writing/editing website, this is how I chose to introduce myself on the home page: "I'm sure there are writers who don't find writing to be a bone-crushing, nausea-inducing festival of self-loathing. I just don't happen to be one of them. Faced with a blank screen, I am invariably seized with the overwhelming desire to clean out my garage, give myself a root canal— do anything other than write."

Who was I to criticize a man who managed to publish more than forty books in his life—*ten times* my total.

His output should have been ample evidence that, when he said he'd rather be writing a book, he probably meant it. And who could resist the flattery of being asked to comb through all your files, everything on and in your desk and closets, to (in theory at least) immortalize even the most minute records of your existence? As a time waster, that beats the hell out of cleaning your garage. Actually, it *includes* cleaning your garage, and sending the whole shebang off to Capitol Hill.

Mack must have spent weeks or even months on those annotations. One of them that immediately caught my eye was clipped to a two-page printed menu, grandly titled:

Dinner Given by
MR. JOHN KANTOR
in Honor of the Arrival of His First Grandson

The date on the menu was 1925, twenty-one years after John had abandoned his pregnant wife, Effie, and his three-year-old daughter, Virginia, offering only sporadic and insufficient support in the following decades. Mack was twenty-one when his sister, Virginia, then twenty-five, had her first child—the grandson for whom John was allegedly throwing the lavish banquet aboard the RMS *Berengaria*, a *Titanic* clone.

The menu listed six courses, in French, each said to be prepared "à la" a family member—including *Hors D'oeuvre Parisienne Oeufs Caviar à la Uncle Mack.*

Although he hadn't been invited to the dinner—none of the family members it was supposed to be honoring had—the taste of it was still bitter on "Uncle Mack's" tongue nearly thirty-five years later.

"My father kindly sent copies of this little menu to all of us in the Middle West, evidence attesting to his affection for his dear daughter and darling first grandchild," he wrote with dripping sarcasm in his annotation. "At that time dear daughter could probably have done with a new winter coat, and dear great grandparents could have done with having their coal bin filled for the winter. . . . Anyone who examines my life and cannot understand why I hated my father with the hate of hell just hasn't really examined my life, or isn't quite bright."

I could imagine how galling this was—this "let them eat cake" shipboard dinner thrown for John's cronies when the new mother and grandson were barely scraping by in Iowa. It was almost comic-book-villain galling.

I took a closer look at the guests listed on the menu, and began to do a little research. I laughed out loud when I got this hit on the distinguished guest with top billing, a "Mr. J. Factor" in 1925 Chicago:

John Factor (October 8, 1892–January 22, 1984), born Iakov Faktorowicz, was a Prohibition-era gangster and con artist affiliated with the Chicago Outfit.

He later became a prominent businessman and Las Vegas casino proprietor, owner of the Stardust Resort and Casino. It is alleged that he ran the operation on behalf of the mob, with a lifetime take of $50–$200 million.

His friends knew him as "Jake the Barber."

THREE

———

So maybe John Kantor's villainous nature hadn't been as greatly exaggerated as I'd always assumed.

I went home and stood on a chair to get to the high bookshelf, where a dozen of my grandfather's books had stood untouched since they were placed there fifteen years earlier—a transfer from yet another bookshelf where they had long stood similarly undisturbed. They were, not surprisingly, coated in dust. I knew that he had published a book about his childhood, and that it had been titled *But Look the Morn*, but I couldn't find it until I got close enough to smell that oddly unique odor of old books gradually disintegrating. There it was. Upon close inspection, what appeared to be a blank blue spine actually had a few specks of gold ink still upon it. The letters they once delineated were unrecognizable, but beneath it I could barely make out the subtitle: *The Story of a Childhood.*

I took it down and opened it carefully—the binding was fragile, beginning to separate from the yellowed pages. On the first, blank page there was that familiar, legible, but not prissy left-slanted handwriting: *To Layne, Bill, Mike, Tommy, Susie, Charley and Buster— Love, MacKinlay Kantor.*

I smiled, remembering suddenly how it had amused us that he never signed his books *Dad* or *Grandpa* or *Mack,* but always with his full name. "Because they will be more valuable that way," my mother explained—which seemed a funny way to look at it. Layne was my mother, Mack's daughter, whom he had always called Layne-o, from the refrain to a song he used to sing to her when she was a fussing baby and he was trying to write: "Layne-o, the bane-o of my life." (It really stuck: Even to my brother and me, she was never "Mom," always Layne-o.)

Bill was my dad, a New Yorker of German Jewish descent who was in the building business with his father in New York City. Mike and Susie were my older brother and younger sister; Charley (I would have spelled it "Charlie") and Buster were my Lassie-lookalike collie and mustard-colored tabby cat. I could have dated it from the roster of pets alone. He'd signed the book in 1964, though it had been published in 1947. Maybe he thought at twelve, ten, and eight, the three of us kids were now old enough to read it. I never did.

Finally, exactly a half century later, I began to read.

It didn't take me long to find a mention of John Kantor. Ten pages in, Mack describes the circumstances of his birth. "I had a grandfather who was angrily engaged in losing the tiny fortune which it had taken him nearly forty years to accumulate. I had a grandmother adjudged to be dying of cancer. I had a father adjudged by society as a pompous and treacherous scapegrace. I had a three-year-old sister, and a mother who lay in childbed without security . . . her young life torn into ribbons. . . ."

Even so, he wrote, Effie Kantor joked during the prolonged and difficult delivery. In the political debate of the day between those who supported expansion of the nation to the limits of the continent and those who favored consolidation, Effie declared herself—huffing and puffing between contractions—a passionate adherent of the expansionist cause.

When that expansion allowed a new infant into the world, "They put me into a wicker basket and called me John," Mack wrote. "Not for long, thank heaven."

On his birth certificate it says his name is Benjamin McKinlay. The Benjamin he rejected outright—except as a joke name used with old friends. The McKinlay he altered as he entered adolescence to MacKinlay, because he thought it looked more authentically Scottish with the added *a*. (Despite the fact of my middle name—which happens to be MacKinlay—I have never thought of myself as having a Scottish origin. My guess is because my last name, and my father's heritage, was less complicated—German Jewish all around—that's how I identified. Also, I never had any definite picture of that Scottish connection until I discovered it on a "find-a-grave" website: Mack's maternal great-grandfather, my great-great-great-grandfather, had been born in Dunfermline, Fife, Scotland, in 1828. The entry, along with a photograph of his substantial tombstone, noted that William McKinlay had been a carpenter and lumber dealer, and one of the founders of the tiny Iowa town of Epworth.)

Of the non-Scottish side of his family, MacKinlay, with an *a*, wrote: "My father had 'run away.' That was what people told me, though it was not the literal truth. Rather, my mother had left him, driven by practical and economic necessity. . . . It seemed simpler, if definitely unjust to the father, to tell the child that his father had run away. I had a mental picture of him, running as I ran, a specter cloaked and featureless, scampering past the edge of the garden."

I was shocked to learn that "abandonment," the bedrock of the Bad Father story I had always been told, may not have been pure, literal truth. But Mack had no doubt that it was at least abandonment of all responsible behavior. Effie met John as a student at the nearby Drake University in Des Moines. It was a small Christian college, where John, avowing himself to be a recent convert to Christianity whose wealthy Jewish parents had disowned him as a result, must have created quite a splash. Physically imposing, well over six feet tall with a wild effusion of black hair, he would have appealed especially to a young girl like Effie, whose sharp mind and adventurous spirit would have been excited by John's exotic origins, foreign-tinged accent (he had been born in Sweden to a long line of Jewish rabbis originally from Portugal), and fluency in five-dollar words.

Effie married John in 1899, barely twenty. A photo of her in her wedding dress suggests why she might appeal to someone who could have had any number of women. Thick, dark hair braided down her back; dreamy eyes under perfectly arched eyebrows; a flawless complexion shaped by high cheekbones and punctuated with a pert nose and Cupid's-bow lips.

The wedding took place in Webster City. The humble McKinlay home had been tricked up with flowers on the mantel for a small reception. John's parents were not present. He had lied about their wealth—they were immigrants who had never even regained the modest status they'd enjoyed as merchants in Sweden.

It was only the first of an unending flood of lies he would tell.

From the moment of those wedding vows to 1904, the year of Mack's birth, "their story would not bear repeating," he wrote. "[It was] an ugly montage of lost jobs, new jobs, American Beauty roses never paid for, scrofulous hotel rooms, jail doors opening and closing and opening again, baffled tearful trips back home to Webster City, furniture dumped out on sidewalks, letters, telegrams—and always check after check written by my grandfather, checks written with a crabbed hand."

In fact, I would discover, it was immensely worse than Mack knew. Surely, if he had ever become aware of the story printed on the front page of *The Webster City Tribune* on January 3, 1902, there would have been some trace of that almost unbelievable account in the thousands of bitter comments he made about his father throughout his life. But in his lifetime, of course, that small-town newspaper was neither digitized nor searchable. Nothing he ever said or wrote in any of his autobiographical writings or in the scores of letters in the Library of Congress files that refer to John Kantor suggests that he ever knew about this:

JOHN M. KANTOR'S UNIQUE CAREER

J. M. Kantor, the young man who was arrested at St. Paul on Christmas Eve . . . on a charge of having swindled the Des Moines Life Insurance company out of several hundred dollars, has . . . enjoyed an illustrious career before landing in the Polk county jail. In fact Kantor has just come back [to Drake University, where several years ago] he wooed and won one of the most beautiful girls in the university, who is now his wife. But a few weeks [ago] Kantor is said to have deserted her and her baby daughter and started for Minnesota with a young woman of prominence. . . . Efforts to carry out this plan have been foiled, but when arrested

in St. Paul . . . Kantor is said to have been engaged to [yet another]
young woman . . . and about to marry her.

The abandoned wife—one of the most beautiful girls at Drake
University!—was my great-grandmother Effie, and the baby daughter
was Virginia.

The story, which fills half the front page, continues to sketch an
astonishing chain of events. After enrolling in Drake in 1897, "claiming to be a converted Jew," John said he wanted to enter the Christian
ministry. He took Bible and oratory classes, and impressed his teachers
as bright, but lazy. Early in John's academic career, a liveryman complained to faculty members that John had hired a horse and buggy for
the day, then abandoned it in a neighboring town without paying his
bill. When confronted by the faculty, John denied the claim and
insisted he was being persecuted because of his Jewish origin.

The faculty decided to accept his word that it was a misunderstanding fueled by prejudice.

Before his studies were complete, John applied for ordination as a
minister. He was turned down for insufficient qualifications, but managed to persuade a small-town Iowa church to hire him as a pastor
anyway. He brought Effie and Virginia there to live with him, but the
job lasted barely three months until dissension among his flock forced
him out for mysterious reasons.

The young family returned to Webster City, where John occasionally delivered sermons at the church there, which the newspaper said
were received enthusiastically as "eloquent and convincing."

He also sold insurance, but instead of giving the premiums to the
insurance company, he pocketed them, leaving those he'd sold poli-
cies unprotected. When he thought one company might be catching
on, he switched to another.

When not cheating his customers and insurance companies, he played poker—"a fiend for card playing and a most clever player," the newspaper said.

On one insurance-scamming trip out of town, the local minister was so impressed by John, he not only purchased the bogus insurance he was selling, he invited him to give a guest sermon at his church that Sunday. On Saturday night, John convened a poker game with a group of fellow traveling men. "They continued their sport until 5 o'clock in the morning, when Kantor had cleaned up the whole crowd. . . . It was then Sunday morning, and Kantor . . . stated that he guessed he would stay up and be ready for church. . . . About 10 o'clock Kantor emerged from the hotel, smooth shaven and well dressed, and walked to the Christian church, where he is said to have preached a sermon worthy of a more eminent divine."

Afterward, he claimed to have received a telegram urging him to return home immediately because Effie was ill. He told a traveling companion with family in town that he'd already sent all his money home to his wife and was in need of an emergency loan for travel expenses. His trusting companion vouched for John to his father, a well-off farmer of that town, who agreed to lend them money to pay their hotel and livery bills, with enough left over to fund a trip back to Webster City. But when the young friend awoke in the hotel the next morning, John was gone, the money was gone, the bills still unpaid.

In Webster City, the story said, John had "made many friends among some of the leading citizens, who but recently have discovered that their friendship was misplaced. For some time past residents of Webster City have been predicting that the young man would land in jail, so that the news of his arrest was not a great surprise. The McKinlay family is well known and respected in Webster City, and they have the sympathy of everyone there."

When John's misdeeds seemed at last about to catch up with him, he took off, stopping first in a town just north of Webster City, Eagle Grove, where he bought a train ticket for himself and "a young woman to whom he had been devoting himself during a stay [there]."

The girl's uncle, who happened to be a conductor on the very train John and his lady friend boarded, discovered them together and "invited her to return home with him."

John continued on to Minneapolis, where he "worked his insurance graft among the Scandinavian farmers of Minnesota so cleverly" he was not discovered until nine weeks later.

"When arrested on Christmas Eve, he was about to take part in a festival chorus in St. Paul and it is stated upon good authority that he was engaged to a St. Paul girl."

Of all these riotous facts, the most amazing of all is the dateline. These events occurred two years *before* Mack was born. Obviously, despite all the completely impossible to ignore evidence of John's spectacular perfidy as both a husband and a man, Effie took him back, at least for a time. One thing Mack never learned—and I certainly won't figure out—is why. She obviously saw and read the front page of her hometown paper—how awful must that have been?—not to mention, suffered the gossip of a very small, close-knit, conservative, church-going town. Was John's eloquence so great that he somehow managed to persuade her it was "all a big misunderstanding," just as he had persuaded Drake University officials that he was the victim of a bigoted livery owner instead of the perpetrator of petty larceny? Did her passion for this exotic, handsome, eloquent, and decidedly nonboring lover overwhelm her common sense? Was she so afraid of being left alone with a small child that even a lying, cheating, no-good husband was better than no husband?

I can only imagine it was some calculus involving all the above.

In any case, a heavy burden fell on Effie's father, who not only had to bail out his daughter's husband again and again—make good on an endless series of bad checks, provide restitution for business deals reneged on, literally bail him out of jail—but he had to put up with the inevitable small-minded, small-town whisperings. Adam McKinlay, a miller who was suffering through a downward financial spiral due to ill health and a changing world, also had to negotiate the public humili-ation. He was a difficult figure to love. I found an obituary Mack wrote for him, in which you can assume he was being as positive as possible: "A taciturn man, he did not move easily in political and busi-ness circles. The bright time of his life ended when the prairies were fenced, and telephone lines began to lace from grove to grove. Honor, integrity, silence, poverty, respect—he had these and only these."

When Effie's marital association threatened that respect, it triggered something in him. While in a drugstore, Adam overheard a man saying loudly that the McKinlay girl had "married a nigger," which clearly referred to the olive-skinned John and was meant and taken as an insult. Adam was a small man, but toughened by a lifetime of lugging heavy sacks of grain and incited by humiliation. He decked the offender with a single rage-fueled blow. According to Mack, Adam never let Effie forget her role in his sacrifice, both of reputation and money, remaining bitter and passive-aggressively accusatory the rest of his life.

John came back, long enough at least to plant the seed that became my grandfather, and then he was gone again. (On Mack's birth certif-icate, under residence of father, *Webster City* is written in ink, and crossed out. Above it is written *Chicago, Il.*) Mack didn't even know that much. Where his father was and what his father had been doing since his disappearance remained a mystery.

Effie had kept some pictures of John, but never showed them to her son.

"I didn't know what he looked like," Mack wrote in *But Look the Morn*, "but I began to hear about him. . . . He was tall; he had swarthy skin and kinky black hair."

His absent father lived only in playmates' taunts; a swirl of tense, quickly hushed comments; and his ill-informed imagination, until one night, when Mack was six, the phone rang. "Chicago is calling" is the way his grandmother put it, her hand over the mouthpiece, her eyes round with alarm.

Effie talked first, then Virginia. "I watched entranced from the sofa," Mack wrote. "The room seemed resounding with a strange presence."

After an interminable stretch of suspense, he was summoned to the phone. He had to stand on a chair to reach the handset on the wall. His mother prompted: "Say hello."

Mack squeaked out the greeting. Through the earpiece emerged a basso profundo. "Hello there, sweetheart! . . . Do you love your Daddy, sweetheart?"

Mack wrote: "Through all the years I can hear the fatuous rumble, the oily conceit of his voice. 'Daddy loves you, sweetheart. Daddy wants to send you something. What do you want your Daddy to send you?'

"I did not know what to say. This was not real, it was all an imagining and a mistake, a peculiar contrivance of nightmare. The great black voice blurting inside the sweaty receiver . . . father . . . I did not know. What should one ask of a father whom he had never seen? . . .

"'How would you like to have a bicycle? Do you want your Daddy to send you a bicycle?'

"I whispered, 'Yes.' And then as the magnitude of this proposal flashed upon me, I yelled it at the top of my lungs: 'Yes!'

"'I will send you a bicycle tomorrow.'"

This is the one part of the story I had been told many times; the single fact that, in my mind, had stood for my grandfather's childhood:

Every day for months he would wait and wait for the delivery truck carrying his bicycle, until it became a joke among the older boys.

A year later, in 1911, Mack was still wondering if one day a bike might appear when instead three train tickets arrived, one for Effie, one for Virginia, one for him—all to Chicago, courtesy of John Kantor. I would learn from my uncle Tim's book, *My Father's Voice*, that, ironically, John Kantor somehow ended up suing *Effie* for desertion after she'd given up following him on his crooked trail. He'd won a divorce, remarried, and was now separated, awaiting a divorce from his second wife. Hence the spasm of generosity in sending train tickets to his first wife and daughter, whom he'd decided he missed, and the son he'd never met. Effie, then thirty-two, must have had misgivings about the implications of those tickets, but she had been living with her parents, cleaning bedpans as a practical nurse, and working as a cashier at the Webster City grocery store—all for a pittance that was pathetically necessary to keep the economically strapped household from utter destitution. Plus, her children desperately needed a father. And, Mack would later say, in spite of everything, she was still drawn to the man.

Mack and Virginia and Effie all boarded the train for Chicago— the tickets John had sent were not for a private first-class compartment, so they all crowded into a lower bunk.

When they arrived at the ornate Chicago station, while Effie and Virginia sat waiting quietly on a bench, Mack squirmed away to stake out a spot halfway down the grand staircase leading into the station. "Presently I saw an erect man with a fleshy face. . . . He wore a tailored tan topcoat, a black derby hat, and carried a beautiful cane . . . The man saw me and began to smile. His eyes were large, tender, rather swollen. His mouth was small for such a big face. Beneath the brim of the stiff hat I could see a wealth of kinky black hair. He halted on a step below me. He said, 'Were you looking for someone?' I whispered, even while I knew that this was he, 'I'm looking for Mr. Kantor.' As I spoke, he picked me up in his arms and bore me up the rest of the stairs, laughing."

For the rest of the short visit, Mack soaked in the unfathomable grandiosity of this man who was his father.

"I was tremendously impressed by the obsequious attitude of the [taxi] driver . . . by the way in which a doorman at the theatre came speeding forward to open the taxicab door. . . . He entertained lavishly and tipped munificently. His advent in a restaurant sent waiters and captains scurrying in frenzy."

I smiled when I read this: all those grand entrances in a black limo chauffeured by liveried drivers, all those obsequious maître d's. . . . Mack's father hadn't ever given him that bicycle, but it appeared that he had given him something else: a desire to impress with the trappings of wealth.

The ability to indulge that desire would not come easily, or quickly. Remembering that first meeting with John Kantor, Mack recalled that his father took him to a magnificent theater, replete with gold drapes and sparkling chandeliers. But Mack had eyes only for the snack concession. He asked his father—intoxicated with the luxury of having a father to ask—if he might have some candy. His father made a great show of selecting the largest, most opulent-looking box of chocolate in the display, a large purple box of "sumptuous creams and oblongs of nougat."

Mack kept this quickly emptied box in a sideboard for years. Year after year, "I would open the box and push Virginia's paper dolls aside in order to sniff the perfumed comfort of the past—a comfort which I felt for one solid week in 1911, but which never came to me again until I had built it with my own hands and beneath my own feet.

"Often Virginia and I have discussed that fabulous week," Mack wrote. Effie never told them directly, but "constructing the few shreds of evidence" they'd retained in their memories, they concluded that their parents had been flirting with the idea of a marital reconciliation that quickly stalled out. Something about the tenor of John's lifestyle, so opulent and outwardly successful—Virginia watched in disbelief as her father bought Effie a black silk gown with a hundred-dollar bill—must have not rung true in Effie's ear. Something about the loud, ostentatious crowd that always surrounded him made her feel uncomfortable and shabby.

Or maybe she found she couldn't persuade herself to, once again, trust him.

On what would be the last day of the visit, Effie and Virginia went off with a lady introduced to Mack as Aunt Bessie. Mack was to stay with his father. When the ladies were gone, John smiled at him conspiratorially and said with his lingering Swedish accent, "Now I will take you to see the most lovely woman in Chicago."

Mack was sure he must mean Effie, but when John said this woman lived in a fancy hotel, the Sherman House, he grew confused. "Her name is Miss Tucker. She knows that I am bringing you, and has some lovely toys for you."

"The thought of toys put power into my feet," Mack wrote. They walked rapidly through the clamorous downtown streets, Mack's small legs pumping to keep up with his father's giant stride. As the hotel appeared, Mack flagged slightly, wondering if the disappointment of the promised bicycle would be repeated.

It would not: Miss Tucker was big and blond, wearing a dark dress covered with flashing sequins. "There was a vitality and vibrance about her." And more important, she indeed had marvelous toys for him, unique toys: a revolver in a leather holster, a papier-mâché trumpet with working keys to finger. Also, candy.

Miss Tucker turned her back on her cocktail-sucking guests and took Mack aside to assure that his plate had been filled abundantly with items from a rich buffet, including sumptuous slices of ham and bright red wedges of tomato, which she pronounced *toe-mah-toe*. She told him that she had a son, just his age, and pinched his cheek.

Lost in this whirl of improbable events, Mack had no idea how much longer they remained there. When his father finally led him away, he said, "Miss Tucker is a very lovely and accomplished woman; she is a very, very dear friend of mine."

She was twenty-four in 1911, more handsome than pretty, with a broad face, smoky eyes, flared nostrils, and a full, womanly figure (she would soon become notoriously large). She was altogether an imposing young woman who could appreciate the strapping six-foot-two John, nine years her senior. And they had something important in common: They had both abandoned their children to pursue outsize dreams of glory. That son that was just about Mack's age? He was back east, living with relatives.

Only much later did Mack discover that his father's very, very dear friend was already, when he met her that day, a star—a singer two years past a show-stealing turn in the *Ziegfeld Follies* and at the heady beginning of a nearly sixty-year career of enduring international fame performing as "The Last of the Red Hot Mamas," Sophie Tucker.

The following year, 1912, Effie traveled to Chicago, this time leaving the children with her parents, for what turned out to be a final attempt at reconciliation. She never discussed this trip, and when Mack was grown she said only that "things hadn't worked out" and that she had spent much of her time away with a friend in Wisconsin.

But when she returned to Iowa, she bore gifts from John to the children. He sent Mack a baseball uniform with a catcher's mask and mitt. Mack hated baseball, was never any good at it, or at any games involving a ball.

John also sent a children's fantasy book written in 1895 called *The Kanter Girls*. He no doubt had bought it for the coincidence of the name, and the volume's margins were filled with pompous fatherly exhortations in John's hand. On a page in which the girls discussed a ring that made them invisible, enabling them to sneak around to hear what their friends said of them in their assumed absence, John wrote: *One thing my little girl should not do.*

It is difficult to describe the impact of realizing that all these revelations, proffered so elegantly in *But Look the Morn*, had been sitting ignored on my bookshelf my entire adult life. Compared to the sketchy, scratchy details available in notations in census books, or birth, death, and marriage records available on Ancestry.com, this was like stumbling on King Tutankhamen's tomb, its abundance of gold and bejeweled artifacts glimmering in the first light of four thousand years. *But Look the Morn* was not only a moment-by-moment account of life-altering events, it was literature. Whatever I had thought of my grandfather's writing, I had not expected to be so impressed—as a professional editor. What I'd expected was to be put off by overly ornate sentences puffed up with unproductive hot air. The language was ornate, indeed, but lovely, original, precise, purposeful. Opening to any page, I encountered writing that was at least eye-catching, and sometimes breathtaking. Recounting a visit to the grain mill his grandfather managed, he described jumping into a wagon full of oats "gleaming like metal where the sun blanched over it, and showing silvery lights in the squat shade of my body. I dug my hands deep into sandy luxury; rivulets of kernels slid down through the gaps in my overalls; oats were warm and spicy, prickling my skin. . . . I lay back upon the pile and felt the kernels biting my scalp."

As I transcribed those words, my fingers pressing the keyboard in the same location and order in which my grandfather had pressed them some seventy years earlier, I almost felt as if I were following the pattern of an earlier lifetime. The sensuousness of the language, its liveliness and originality and ability to make a reader *feel* an experience rather than merely hear about it—it was all that I strived for in my own work.

And the book's impact went beyond the fine writing, resonant in the way that all good writing can seem personal to the reader. This *was* personal.

That *Kanter Girls* book? It had resided in my house, had been read to me by my mother when I was small. I loved it, despite the fact that the lead characters were girls, because of the magical nature of the world they could enter at will, to which they alone had the key. I knew only that my mother had also been read the book as a child. It never occurred to me, until I arrived at page 129 of *But Look the Morn* at the age of sixty-one, that one of my first enthralled literary experiences had come through a volume passed down from my grandfather and my mother from the actual, flesh-and-blood hand of John Kantor.

That book, and the catcher's gear, were the last contact—letters, gifts, or support of any kind—conveyed by John to his children for five years. In the spring of 1917, as America entered the First World War and prices for everything spiked, threatening to sink the McKinlay household, Effie in desperation wrote to John, asking for financial help.

This episode did not make it into *But Look the Morn*. It took him another twenty-five years to publish part two of his autobiography in a book called—cloyingly, I always felt—*I Love You, Irene*. I am looking at the book now, realizing that this is probably the first book he ever signed, individually, to me. *To Tommy—Love—MacKinlay Kantor.* Beneath that, in script surprisingly like my own right-slanted scrawl: *I love you, Tommy—Grandma Irene.*

Given the title, I'd always thought it was a book entirely about my grandparents' courtship and marriage. I'd never realized it was simply a continued narrative of his life, picking up after childhood and going through to the publication of his first novel at the age of twenty-four. I learned at the Library of Congress that he'd written much of *I Love You, Irene* years before its 1972 publication. The book had originally been titled *The Maples Were Our Gods*—a reference to his naturalistic, animistic leanings and rural upbringing—and, later, *In Russet Mantle Clad*—a continuation of the line from Hamlet, used for his first autobiography: "But look, the morn, in russet mantle clad. . . ." It was the Bard's way of invoking sunrise—in other words: the morning wearing a red cloak. In the Library of Congress papers, I would discover funny exchanges indicating that Mack's editor and agent both justifiably hated that title. Something presenting as a love story had greater appeal, they argued, than what to modern readers would be a virtually incomprehensible reference to russet mantles.

Reading the book for the first time, I learned that Effie's desperate plea to John for support in 1917 resulted in an immediate promise that both Mack and Virginia would henceforth get a twenty-five-dollar-per-month allowance—the first checks enclosed.

Mack, the magic of the Chicago visit now thoroughly tarnished and his view of his father as a fraud uppermost in his mind, protested loudly. If they needed money that urgently, he shouted, he'd quit school and get a job. At thirteen.

Instead, "our family was summoned to Chicago. . . . The suggestion was that matters could be 'talked over' and perhaps some plans prepared for the education of us children."

Mack did not wish to see his father at all. "He seemed a remote if imposing bully who had made Mother unhappy and had disgraced us flagrantly."

Nothing but vague promises, never fulfilled, would come of that journey to Chicago. But Mack got an even clearer picture of his father. By 1917, John had a job working for the Chicago headquarters of the Moose Lodge, recruiting new members. But he was clearly living beyond the means of that legitimate pursuit.

"He loved to live expensively—choice cigars, tailored suits, diamonds, suppers at luxurious restaurants. He scarcely ever drank liquor of any kind; rarely would he order a bottle of beer. I think he feared that liquor might cause him to lose the deep-voiced dignity in which he elected to be swathed.

"But he gorged himself on rare fruits, oysters, cold cuts, thick steaks. At thirty-eight he was growing fat, despite his height . . . and the excellent physique which Nature had given him. He would seldom walk a block if he could ride."

Mack later figured that his father's lifestyle could be attributed to his being somehow involved with Chicago politics and real estate. But he said he never bothered to follow his father's career in any detail. Which left a mystery: How had John Kantor escaped a small Iowa town ahead of grasping creditors, irate business associates, and the law in 1904 only to appear in Chicago in 1911 slinging $100 bills around, and becoming a literal fat cat by 1917?

It was, alas, another mystery I didn't see much hope of solving— John Kantor died sixty years ago, and the activities of a small-time hustler didn't seem likely to be recorded in any permanent record, if they had been recorded at all. But as it turned out, I was wrong about a key part of that equation: John Kantor wasn't all that small-time.

Internet search is an astonishingly powerful tool—but it's tricky. I found that simply putting "John Kantor" into search engines produced little of value—if I scanned through the many John Kantors on Facebook and the pay-to-see "white page" listings, I eventually could find, among a handful of living people by that name, a simple listing of my great-grandfather's birth and death dates, 1878–1954 (which turned out to be wrong! He died in 1956), and the names of his parents and children. And his middle name, which I hadn't known. Martin.

That was helpful.

A full-name search for "John Martin Kantor" brought up a digital copy of something called *To-morrow Magazine* from 1905, opened to a full-page ad for "The Spencer-Whitman Center Lecture Bureau," asking interested parties to send for a free circular presenting "Speakers, Subjects and Dates."

Beneath that there was the photo of a young man labeled: *John Martin Kantor, Manager.*

In the only photo I had yet seen of John Kantor he had been sixty, expensively dressed, imperious but wary, tired and jowly, with a blooming double chin. Here, he was just twenty-seven. I was looking at a face with notable similarities to my own at that age: high, prominent cheeks; long nose, slightly down-turned at the end; wide, dark eyes and a narrow mouth; all beneath his unique signature, that swelling bulge of kinked hair rising on either side of a center part like ocean waves about to break in opposite directions. He was striking at least, possibly dashing, leaning forward in a high-backed club chair, his hands casually clasped together, a hint of a smile on his slightly parted lips. He wore a suit and a shirt with an open collar—put-together, but relaxed, confident, inviting.

Somehow, just one year after he'd left—or fled—Webster City for the final time, leaving Effie to care for their toddler and bear their second child alone, he'd become the poster boy and manager for some kind of high-concept speakers bureau.

It turns out that the Spencer-Whitman Center was a short-lived experiment in semiradical thought created by the founder, publisher, and editor of *To-morrow Magazine*, a self-made philosopher named Parker Sercombe. In 1905, the periodical, subtitled *A Monthly Magazine of the Changing Order*, announced the creation of an institute for the "society of advanced thought and rational ideals, devoted to human growth and intellectual expansion," to be housed in the decaying mansion where Sercombe lived and assembled the magazine. It was a place for freethinkers to gather, a turn-of-the-century forerunner to the California hippie mecca Esalen Institute—even down to the suspicion that the institute advocated "free love." There was enough of a whiff of ferment emanating from the place that, before Sercombe and his adherents got chased out of town, it attracted visits from the likes of Carl Sandburg, H. G. Wells, and Jack London.

And there, in the middle of it all, my great-grandfather John had somehow inserted himself, not just as a lecturer, but as speakers bureau manager.

Featured in that January 1905 issue, right below the account of a lecture advocating the education of children based on the principle of "non-interference with the natural, inner development of the child," there again appears John M. Kantor, who presented, according to the author of the article, "one of the most interesting discussions we have ever heard."

The subject?

Was I hallucinating? I looked again. *Still there*:

"Graft and Grafters."

"Mr. Kantor very cleverly and entertainingly talked of grafters, political, religious, educational; a grafter, in short, being any one who sacrifices his opportunity to be steadfast in the ways of truth, and acts or pretends to think contrary to his highest conceptions for the sake of 'what there is in it.'"

This was an amazing, amusing find, but hardly the end of it.

I'd plumbed the "John Martin Kantor" search results and found nothing more.

Then I started adding other, possibly relevant terms to the John Martin Kantor search. I began with the simplest thing I could think of—dates. I put in the name and added 1906, then 1907. . . . Still nothing of significance.

Then I tried adding 1910.

Up came an inside page from *The Rock Island* (Illinois) *Argus* from August 29, 1910:

NEW HEAD OF GRAND LODGE

Today's session opened this morning at 10 o'clock. . . . The business of the meeting was the election of officers of the grand lodge. . . . The contest for office was warmly fought by the various delegations present, and much time was occupied in the balloting. S. Willner of St. Louis was elected first supreme vice commander and John Martin Kantor of Chicago was elected second supreme vice commander.

God. "Supreme vice commander." Mack would have hooted about that.

The lodge in question was the Order of Knights of Joseph, a supposedly nonprofit organization of the early twentieth century whose goal was to sell insurance, and cemetery plots, to immigrants.

All three of these items—insurance and cemetery plots and "warmly fought" elections—would appear as a recurring theme in John's crooked career. Insurance, I already knew about. The other items would soon snap into place like pieces in a jigsaw puzzle.

First of all, politics. The lodge election was a warm-up, a light workout.

By 1915, John was making appearances in far more consequential political news. I found a reference to him in a 1930 book on Chicago Mayor Big Bill Thompson—perhaps the most corrupt mayor of any city in American history—recounting the election of 1915, when Thompson first grabbed the city's top job by bringing down his opponent Robert Sweitzer. The book's author, John Bright, describes how Thompson drummed up support with the help of rabble-rousing ward heelers, who would say whatever was necessary to scare up votes—*scare* being the key word.

"Among these the most sedulous was John Kantor," Bright wrote, "a man possessing the fetching and imposing appearance of the popular orator, and plenty of enthusiasm for Bill's cause. Announcing theatrically (in the proper locality) that he was of the Jewish faith and hence stood for racial equality, he would assail Sweitzer for his injection of the religious element into the campaign. Bearded Hebrews, grubbing for a living in the Maxwell Street markets, with the Cossack's lash still stinging upon their backs, were not difficult to persuade to vote for William Hale Thompson, Zionist and Friend of the Jew."

Even as he was pandering to his fellow Jews' fear of discrimination,

John was fanning racial hatred in other venues. News accounts reported that John turned heads and votes when he charged that, as county clerk, Sweitzer had granted a marriage license to the African American boxing champ Jack Johnson and his white fiancée, a deed that John cast in the most manipulative possible terms. Sweitzer, he charged, "permitted the black man to marry the white woman, and tore to pieces the heart of [the fiancée's] little mother."

"Kantor labored so zealously and effectively," Bright wrote, "that he was rewarded both politically and socially by Thompson, becoming a close friend of Bill and his wife for the years following."

One news story described John as "the tall, curly-headed" personal associate of the mayor who made more pro-Thompson speeches "than any other spellbinder in the organization."

In those years, Thompson became open allies with Al Capone— who made huge cash contributions to the campaign—Bugs Moran, and other gangsters as they executed a virtual mob takeover of the city. Two portraits had places of honor on Thompson's office wall: Abe Lincoln and Al Capone. Thompson maintained that the FBI G-men were a bigger threat to Chicago than the gangsters. During elections, explosions had a way of going off outside precincts favorable to his opponents. In his final campaign in 1928, sixty-two bombings took place leading up to the primaries and at least two politicians were killed.

Late in my research, looking through my mother's papers, I came across a remarkable photograph—a tintype actually, with an image imposed ghostlike on the mirrored surface. I found it in a manila envelope along with a sixty-year-old letter addressed to my grandfather, care of *The Saturday Evening Post*. It was from the office of the State of Illinois Auditors of Public Accounts, signed by a man named Leslie P. Volz, who had read a story Mack had written for the magazine. "Someone told me," he wrote, "that you are the son of an old friend of mine,

John M. Kantor, who was one of the top orators in the successful campaign of William Hale Thompson for Mayor in 1915. He contributed greatly to Thompson's election by the force of his arguments. . . ."

The photograph, he said, was taken at a ceremony celebrating the collection of more than one hundred thousand signatures from voters pledging to vote for Big Bill. Dead in the center of a crowd of maybe a hundred people on a flag-draped grandstand is Big Bill himself, standing tall, belly bulging against his white vest and coat, a small American flag flying from a stick in his right hand. The scene behind him on the crowded platform—police wearing those old-fashioned Keystone Kops–like star badges, women in flowered hats, potted ferns, and flowery wreaths—looks astonishingly similar to the famous cover of the Beatles' *Sgt. Pepper's Lonely Hearts Club Band* album. Just to Big Bill's right, one man stands out, second only to the mayor. He's wearing a bespoke suit and holding a white hat to his heart, his large heavy-lidded eyes fastened intently on something just offstage, the amazing profusion of wavy, center-parted hair tumbling over his forehead, and a big cigar clamped in mid-sneer in the left side of his mouth. John Kantor.

His reward for services rendered went beyond lavish dinners and hunting trips with the mayor—he began to show up in news stories as a city "real estate expert." Less than five months after the election, *The Chicago Tribune* ran a story accusing him of offering to bribe the Board of Education to pay a vastly inflated price for a piece of property in exchange for a cut of the profit. The story quoted a board member speaking about John Kantor:

"He has a beautiful voice. He could gather a group of pedestrians around him at the corner of the city hall, and after using up a few minutes in oratory he would have those fellows shelling out for the first installment of payments on the 'hall.'"

Apparently, John weathered the bribe allegation, and he wouldn't have to work so hard for his commissions in the future. *The Chicago Tribune* would eventually expose the long-term scam in which Thompson and his cohorts cheated Chicago out of $2.25 million—more than $50 million in 2015 dollars—by charging fake expert fees on city real estate projects.

In early 1917, just months before John would send train tickets to Effie and the children, a *Chicago Tribune* story began: "It became known in the city hall yesterday that John Kantor, a 'real estate expert' . . . politician, and a close follower of Mayor Thompson, will provide the windup for the . . . graft inquiry before the grand jury. To his astonishment and that of his friends, Kantor was served with a grand jury subpoena to appear. . . . He will be the last witness before the state asks the Jury to vote approximately fifteen indictments late today."

In a 1954 memoir, Colonel Robert McCormick, publisher of *The Chicago Tribune*, said that phony real estate expert cronies of Thompson got $1,500 a day for work that had always paid no more than $50 a day. One of Thompson's "close personal friends" netted $600,000—the 2015 equivalent of $14 million—over two years' time. Much of that money was kicked back to the Thompson organization, but there would be plenty left for the personal enrichment of "close friends."

McCormick didn't say that particular friend was named John Kantor, but it may well have been.

Mack never knew about the ongoing real estate expert graft scandal—which exploded just months before his visit and would linger for years, ending without any convictions—but now that he was thirteen, he could make his own judgments about his father.

This visit, he was less impressed and more wary, especially since John seemed intent on treating Mack more like another bauble to show off than a loved son.

It was a particularly vulnerable time for him to begin with. Not long before they'd left Webster City, Mack had found himself living a nightmare. Among the group of paperboys delivering the morning news around Webster City, the most socially awkward was an innocent, lonely child named Charley Morean—Mack and the others called him "Chink" for the odd slant to his eyes. They all sneered when Charley put a naive classified ad in the paper that said: "WANTED. Boys to join a boys' club. Inquire of Charles Morean."

The next time Mack ran into him, he said scornfully, "Well, how's the wonderful boys' club doing?"

Charley got a hurt, bewildered look on his face, missing the sarcasm. "They didn't come," he said. "I waited and waited, but nobody came at all. I had the wienies all bought, and everything."

"If a stone cornice had fallen from the roof of the building above," Mack wrote in *I Love You, Irene*, "I could not have felt more crushed."

To make up for his thoughtless cruelty to Charley, Mack began insisting that he be included in his group of friends. They did in fact become close friends, and were in the Boy Scouts together. On a July morning in 1917, Mack and another friend bicycled out to Charley's farm to fetch him, then they all went into the nearby woods to hunt butterfly specimens ("an enormous black butterfly drifted above horsemint weeds like a runaway handkerchief of velvet"). They ate lunch on the bank of a river, then went swimming in a quiet stretch of water.

The three sunned on rocks in the middle of the river, then began to swim back: "When my hands began to touch bottom I stood up in shallow water. . . . Chink was still out in the middle of the river, and he was making dreadful sounds. He skirmished and flapped, his hands were splashing aimlessly, his mouth seemed pulled half below the surface . . . [and he was making] a croaking and gobbling noise, as if he cried in a foreign language."

Mack thought "any boy ought to know better than to pretend that he was having trouble. . . . I heard my own short laughter rise and die, and Herbert's laugh did the same. Suddenly we knew that this was truth."

Mack was closer and got there first. He tried to approach Charley from behind, as instructed by the Boy Scout handbook, "but he whirled around as I reached him, and his eyes were nearly shut, and his face looked like the face of an utter stranger. . . . A great claw seized me above the left knee. It clamped as the arm of an octopus must clamp. . . . Under we went, and down, and down, deep, deep. Silver lights came bursting inside my skull."

He kicked free from his friend's panicked grip and lunged for a floating piece of wood to use as a life preserver, but Charley sank and disappeared.

The boys ran for help. They had to run a long way. When they finally roused some adults to search the river, all they could hope for was to discover a boy's dead body.

Mack couldn't look away when they found him. "I never saw anyone look so thoroughly soaked. It was as if that long-ribbed body could hold nothing but water within it . . . like a little girl's doll lost in a garden pool."

It was barely two weeks later that Mack found himself in Chicago, following his father's towering stride (his father loomed a full foot above him, a five-foot-two late bloomer at thirteen). Once again it was to a hotel, but this time to luncheon with a table full of his father's cronies.

They had barely settled at the table when John said, "Son, tell these gentlemen about the drowning of Charley Morean."

"Again silver lights would burst in my brain, and my tongue would seal against the roof of my mouth. Dully I'd gasp, 'I . . . just don't . . . want to . . .'

"Dad flashed a look of contempt from his handsome brown eyes. Then settling himself in his chair, he turned to the others, beginning the tale to suit himself. 'Boys my son had a very, very dear friend, out in the rustic village where he lives. Charley Morean was his dearest friend. . . .

"'One day a few weeks ago, the children went swimming in the old swimming hole. . . . My son attempted to go to the aid of his chum, but Mack had not been properly instructed. . . .

"'Son, show these gentlemen the lesson which I have taught you. Show them what you will do the next time you encounter a drowning person.'"

Quaking with suppressed rage, humiliated beyond comprehension, Mack forced himself to demonstrate what his father had pedantically insisted was the proper response to a panicked swimmer: a firm punch in the face. He clenched his fingers, lifted his fist. . . .

In that moment, Mack wrote, he thought his father the cruelest man who ever lived.

Effie, Mack, and Virginia returned to Webster City with nothing to show for their visit but the memory of too-rich meals crowded with John's loud companions, and for Mack, the still-searing humiliation. But it wasn't over. The next summer, a telegram arrived from John to Virginia:

"You and Mack are to take the noon train to Chicago on next Monday and Daddy will meet you. I am very lonely for my darlings and shall take this opportunity to express the great affection for my children and try to make up for unhappy years which have passed. Give your mother my love. Tell her my sins have been sins of omission and not sins of commission. Kiss your wonderful grandmother for me. . . . All my love to my dearest daughter and son."

Mack had learned not to trust his father's promises—of affection or support—but John's proposition was difficult to turn down. John offered to put all three of them—Effie, now an underemployed thirty-nine-year-old single mother; Mack, fourteen; and Virginia, seventeen—in a one-bedroom apartment on Sheridan Road, near the lake. This time it wasn't an effort at marital reconciliation. John was married again, but separated and living with yet another "very dear friend." Effie and Virginia shared the bedroom and Mack slept in a converted sunroom. John provided Effie with a small allowance and paid the rent on the apartment from the proceeds of what appeared to be a legit job, and an impressive one at that: chief fiscal agent for the Consumers Packing Company—a food processing and shipping concern. Mack enrolled in a large-city high school, a severe culture shock, but having a father, one who was around and not the subject of snide remarks and gossip, served as compensation. Despite his bitter experience, Mack allowed himself to believe.

For the first few months, John visited often, though not to spend the night. He chatted, played games, told elaborate ghost stories in his magnificent bass voice. He talked about his hunting trips with Mayor Thompson and other influential friends. Effie kept his favorite snack, boiled potatoes and sour cream, ready in the small icebox for when he'd stop by. Effie later said of those visits that John seemed like the boy she first knew in college, the charming young man she thought she had married.

Then the ferocious Chicago winter descended. The sunroom turned dark and gloomy. John's visits dried up, the potatoes turned rancid, and the rent checks disappeared.

When Effie prodded John, he'd curse the incompetence of the postal service, his office staff, the landlord, swear he'd dispatched the check and would get to the bottom of the delay.

The landlord remained remarkably patient—deferential perhaps to Mr. Kantor and his political connections—but when the weeks built one upon another and still no check appeared, he became insistent. Mack was dispatched to the Loop on the El train, to the Otis Building and the grand offices of the Consumers Packing Company.

He'd made the trip before to discover his father behind a big desk, puffing cigar smoke and assurances. This time would be different.

As Mack told the story in the unpublished manuscript pages of *In Russet Mantle Clad*, when he arrived at the offices a riot was in progress: cameras flashed and newsmen pressed toward the uniformed police guarding the inner sanctum of his father's office. Mack pushed through until he got to the open door. A strange man with a badge, wearing a cheap suit John Kantor wouldn't be caught red-handed in, sat in his father's chair.

Mack said who he was looking for, and the man said, "Well, kid, you came to the wrong place," and directed him to the U.S. Marshal's office in the federal building.

"No need to hurry," the man smirked. "I guess he's going to be there quite a while. He's been arrested for fraud."

The Consumers Packing Company scandal is an obscure piece of twentieth-century history now recorded only in the scratchy microfilm images of newspaper pages. But in 1917 and 1918, it was huge news, a shocking revelation that fraudulent stock sales could destroy the lives and savings of ordinary people literally sold a bill of goods by grifters disguised as corporate suits.

By recruiting janitors and office clerks and other ordinary folks to peddle shares of Consumers Packing Company stock to their friends and neighbors in a kind of pyramid scheme, in less than a year the company had managed to sell more than $800,000 (equivalent to $13 million today) worth of stock, which was actually worthless. The photographs of full warehouses, loaded trucks, rolling train cars, and impressive ledger sheets shown to prospective buyers were fictional. One front-page story featured a waitress who lost her life savings of $631 by investing it in the fraudulent shares, persuaded by photographs of facilities actually owned by other companies and false assurances that the stock was backed by the government.

At the center of it all, the man identified in the news stories as the stock sales manager was John M. Kantor. He was the one who had recruited the little people to do his bidding, guaranteeing them that the shares would produce dividends of 16 percent a year, lies they passed along to the marks, who handed over their Liberty Bonds and the paltry contents of their bank accounts.

After he was arrested that day when Mack went to look for the missing rent check, John Kantor was held in the county lockup on $30,000 bond, which was eventually paid by three men identified in the newspaper as "saloon keepers."

The case was tried by Federal Judge Kenesaw Mountain Landis, the man who two years later would be recruited to restore the tarnished image of professional baseball after the Chicago "Black Sox" scandal. Eventually, some of the officers of the fake company were sentenced to seven years in Leavenworth, and others were fined from $1,000 to $10,000.

John got off with a $5,000 fine, with the stipulation that he remain in jail until it was paid.

Mack was later told that, when he had managed to raise the money and make the payment, John's first move was to take the judge to lunch.

By then, Mack, his mother, and his sister were all back in Iowa. They didn't hear from John again for years.

FOUR

———

I became a journalist not out of love but desperation.

I was nineteen years old. What I wanted to be was a fiction writer, a novelist. It would never have occurred to me to add the words "like my grandfather" to that thought. It would not be accurate to say I believed my literary ambition had no connection with my grandfather. That would indicate I thought about a possible connection to him, the Pulitzer Prize–winning novelist, and rejected it. In fact, I never considered the possibility at all. As far as my ruminations about motivation were concerned, he might as well have been a plumber.

If I had been forced to specify an aspirational role model, I would have said Harry Crews.

Harry Crews died in 2012 at the age of seventy-six, dissipated by a lifetime of hard living, too many drugs, oceans of alcohol, and an uncounted number of fists to the face. I couldn't recognize the hairless, bloated, toneless seventy-something man in the *New York Times* obituary picture, the man described as a "little-known" but larger-than-life novelist with an enthusiastic cult following, a writer of "dark fiction" filled with southern grotesques and wild violence. The Harry Crews I remembered was fixed in a thin slice of space-time, a stretch of six months or so in Gainesville, Florida, forty years ago. He was in his short-lived "speed freak phase." He'd given up drinking—very temporarily, as it turned out—but he was definitely on something that turned up the wattage. He'd become a serious runner possessing almost zero body fat and a Mr. Clean gleam, both on his shaved skull and in his eye. He had recently published a novel about a man who eats an entire car, piece by piece. Just because.

In the fall of 1972, I managed to get into one of his University of Florida creative writing seminars as an undergraduate, a sophomore no less. I don't remember if I had to produce a writing sample, though I must have. I can't imagine what it would have been, aside from a few embarrassing fragments of adolescent attempts at poetry. For someone who longed to write fiction, I can't recall that I had actually written any. But whatever thin wisps of prose I possessed, I offered up.

Crews was a writing god in 1972 Gainesville. "Little-known" he may have been in terms of a *New York Times* obit, but then and there he was the most famous man in town, a swashbuckling Hemingway-esque figure who made flesh the cliché of living legend—at least to an eighteen-year-old with dreams of literary fame and fortune. I do remember being summoned to a one-on-one interview in which Crews studied me the way a hawk must study a chipmunk. He accepted maybe a dozen students into his seminar that semester, a three-hour marathon one night a week that was less of a class than a performance. I have no idea why I was among the chosen ones, but I have been forever grateful for that fluke of luck.

Crews spoke in great roiling torrents, extolling us like a tent revivalist doing his unlevel best to save a particularly sorry bunch of sinners. His gospel was the nakedness of truth, the necessity for a writer to peel away all egotistical posturing, to abandon caution and conceit, and care only for revealing his inner world in all its sick and twisted glory. That we were all sick, twisted, and glorious was the basic tenet of his faith.

He made it quite clear he had no use for convention in life or literature, and appeared to us as the embodiment of Bob Dylan's creed "To live outside the law, you must be honest."

There were periods in his pedagogic career when he was not the most attentive teacher. He'd show up late and half-baked to stumble and mumble around. Or, fully baked, not show up at all. Twenty years on, when I was editor of *The Miami Herald*'s Sunday magazine, I assigned a talented young woman to go up to Gainesville and profile him. He showed up for the interview wobbling drunk and propositioned her within the first ten minutes. Before she could even react to the lewd suggestion, he peed his pants and vomited expansively on the upholstery of her car. So: not always the model of professorial rectitude. But in the brief moment of time in which I sat at an old-fashioned wooden writing desk in an antiquated second-floor classroom, the syrupy scent of jasmine drifting in the open windows, he was an exemplar. Sometimes he'd begin by reading us something he'd been working on—it would eventually become a novel called A *Feast of Snakes*—raw passages ripped from his typewriter only hours earlier. This was thrilling, terrifying, and disconcertingly intimate. He read with such fierce energy and conviction, we were all swept up and carried away in the flood of prose, each and every one of us forever embedded with the desire to write as if we were dancing around a ring, trying to deliver a knockout punch.

That was the downside of his charisma. We weren't so much students as disciples, and to this day his manic rhythms throb in some recess of my brain whenever I sit at a keyboard.

Here's the upside: One night he walked into class with a twenty-page manuscript in his hands and announced that he was going to read a student piece. He set to it with the same drama and passion he'd delivered for his own work. His reading was so riveting, it wasn't until several sentences in that I realized that it was my story he was reading, the story I'd suffered and strained over, finishing only shortly before dawn on the day it was due, having grown to detest each and every word.

I think now it wasn't all that bad. I'm certain it wasn't all that good, either. But as Crews read it, pacing manically before us, flailing his free arm and belting out my words as if they were fists of fury, I could see my classmates leaning forward in their seats, rapt. And for the first time, I truly believed I could become a writer.

I went off to Europe the following summer, just turned nineteen, for a year abroad. I brought a blue spiral notebook in my scant luggage, imagining that I would fill it with prose sketches and short stories inspired by my ensuing adventures, which indeed turned out to be abundant. But the great bulk of pages in that notebook remained stubbornly blank. I tried sometimes, even managing to scratch out a few (pretentious) sentences or (derivative) paragraphs with a groaning effort completely unjustified by the result.

Over the Christmas holiday, two friends and I paid $75 each to nearly freeze to death in the back of an unheated, unlicensed truck from Amsterdam to Barcelona (we hid behind mattresses at the Spanish frontier while the driver bribed the border guards). From there, we hopped on a ferry to the island of Ibiza—still semirural in 1972 and not yet fully transformed into an Iberian Miami Beach. Landing at the docks of the one large town, we purchased a plastic tarp, a loaf of black bread, garbanzo beans, and wine sacks filled with cheap red wine, then set out to make the three-day walk from one end of the island to the other. We arrived at the opposite coast on Christmas Eve, improbably discovering the ruins of what had once been a substantial beach house set on high ground above a small cove surrounded by mounds of wave-thrashed volcanic rock. On the walls of what had once been a living room someone had writ large in red paint, *Dommage petit oiseau, tu va mourir.* I had enough French to translate: "Too bad, little bird, you are going to die." The Charles Manson–ish vibe, just three years after the satanic drifter and his disciples had butchered the very pregnant actress Sharon Tate, was disturbing enough on its own, and made rather worse when we lifted a bucket from an abandoned water well in the courtyard to discover it contained the moldering corpse of a cat.

Nonetheless, we spent Nochebuena, the Good Night of Christmas Eve, in this decidedly *no bueno* shelter, dragging seaweed up from the beach to soften the concrete floor beneath our plastic tarp. All night, the tarp rustled alarmingly every time one of us tossed or turned, which was continuously. In the morning, nauseated from lack of sleep, we discovered an additional cause for our nocturnal misery—the seaweed beneath the tarp had been infested with stinging sand fleas, which had left painful red welts liberally distributed across our unwashed bodies.

Merry Christmas to us all.

Understandably, we'd each grown grumpy and more than a little weary of constant companionship. We walked into a small town not far from the house and found some blissfully dark, powerful coffee. Fortified, I left my friends sitting on a wrought-iron bench in a date-palm-lined square and followed the small road out of town, where it almost instantly became a dirt path winding steeply uphill past terraced gardens and tiny mud-walled homes, the fragrant scents of people's breakfast wafting from sun-baked brick ovens.

As I climbed, the terraced fields gave way to woods and a few clearings with larger, more prosperous homes. At the extreme limit of habitation, as I made a hairpin turn on the steep switchback path, I heard a child's voice crying, improbably in English, "It stands!" I pivoted and saw three children of stair-step heights standing back to admire a small Christmas tree they had erected in a clearing. I had a powerful sensation that I was not looking across a few feet of space, but through years of time, back into my own childhood. I stood, hidden by the tall pines of the forest, staring as the children romped excitedly about the tree, laughing and placing decorations. I remembered with astonishing clarity a Christmas morning at my grandfather's house fourteen years earlier. My brother, three years my senior, woke me in the dark and led me into the living room, where the tree rose, bristling with colored glass balls and tinsel that shone dimly in the light of a tropical moon. But even that dazzlement could not wrest my attention from the object rearing up before the tree, a red ribbon perched like a cherry atop the handlebars: a pristine red and white Schwinn bike, with an old-fashioned bulb horn and training wheels. I felt lifted on a billowy cloud of joy, no less awestruck than I might have been at nineteen if I awoke to find a ribbon-bedecked Ferrari roadster parked outside my front door.

I did not know then—would not know for years yet—about the cruelty of my great-grandfather and the promised bicycle that never materialized. There is a photograph taken later that morning—I couldn't go back to sleep, no surprise—when my grandfather took pity on me while my parents slept interminably. He brought me out to the crushed-shell driveway to take my first tentative spin on my new bike. In my uncle Tim's photo, my apple-cheeked face is alight, gleaming with the prospect of a life filled with ecstatic surprise. My grandfather stands well back, pipe clenched in his jaw, fists propped proprietarily on his hips. He gazes at me intently. A touch of pride is unmistakable, but there is something else, something deeper and unreadable.

Knowing what I know now, I'm sure he *had* to be thinking of it, how could he not be? The bicycle he never got must have once gleamed as brightly in his little-boy imagination as mine did in reality. Perhaps no small portion of the pride, the satisfaction so visible on his face, arose from knowing that he could make possible for me what had not been so for him.

That day in Ibiza I wasn't thinking of my grandfather's past but my own. That sudden, unexpected transport to my childhood had a powerful effect on me. Like Proust, rung like a gong by the redolent taste of a tea-dunked cake, "I had ceased now to feel mediocre, accidental, mortal."

Suddenly everything connected, became meaningful. I had an overwhelming need to convey this sensation, to make of my own past, so puny yet so vivid, a story worthy of the emotion bursting inside of me. I kept climbing, wheels spinning round and round in my head.

The path petered out and I found myself scrambling up or around a series of large boulders, clinging to roots and slender trunks to make my way higher.

The day was cool, and cooler still, as I gained altitude, but now I had begun to sweat with steady exertion, which shut down the whirring in my head. I can't say how long I had been thrashing forward, my heart pounding and breath sawing in and out, when I broke from the trees and realized that I was looking downhill. I spun around. Through the trees in the far distance, a shocking blue. I'd been climbing so long, so deep in my own head, I had forgotten I was on an island. The entire southwest coast of Ibiza stretched before me, sheer rock cliffs plunging like daggers into the seething sea, white-foam breakers icing at their base, so distant they seemed frozen, unchanging.

I found a flat-topped boulder and sat, feeling a million miles away from the house of horrors below, just as far from my friends waiting in the town, and even farther from the life I had led to this point. I thought: *Not one person in the world knows I am sitting here on this hilltop gazing out over the waves that bore Greeks and Romans on their way to world conquest.* I took out the blue notebook from my rucksack and opened it, reading the few pathetic entries that seemed nothing more than empty posturing, and mourning all the empty pages beyond. I picked up a pen to try to scratch onto the page what I was feeling, but every word I chose seemed labored. I felt that grinding void I often felt when trying to write, a combination of nausea and terror. I shut the notebook as if I were twisting away from physical pain.

Then a voice sounded in my head; I heard more than thought the words "You want to be a writer, but you don't *write.*"

The image of Harry Crews proclaiming my story like a sermon popped into my mind. Not a great story, but it had at least been a finished one, something I'd conceived and brought to fruition. Why had I been able to do that and no more?

Another word materialized: *deadlines.*

I knew where I could find deadlines, and plenty of them. The college newspaper. I cringed. I had always imagined journalists to be as they were portrayed in old movies, crude buffoons who ran roughshod over subtlety and sneered at sensitivity. The thought of becoming one myself made me slightly ill. But I knew then, with no doubt in my mind, that when I returned to Gainesville that summer, I would join the paper.

———

E arly on in my forays through the documents in the file folders at the Library of Congress, still in the single-digit box numbers labeled FAMILY AND BIOGRAPHICAL FILE, I came across a letter from Mack that surprised me. It was dated 1922, when he was just eighteen, under the letterhead WEBSTER CITY DAILY NEWS, addressed to his mother and sister.

"Apparently this is the first time I was left in sole charge of the *Daily News,*" he wrote in his annotations.

I had been vaguely aware that, early in his career, Mack had contributed short pieces to a *Chicago Tribune* column called "A Line O' Type or Two," but I never realized he had started out as a newspaper reporter. Another surprise: Atop the very stationery on which Mack wrote the letter, the *"Daily News* literary editor" was listed as E. M. Kantor.

Effie.

As I began to look around for context on these surprising facts, I stumbled on yet another vein of gold, a book fully digitized on the Internet that my grandfather wrote in 1944 after he'd already had several best-selling novels—enough success anyway so that a publisher thought there would be a market for *Author's Choice,* a collection of forty lesser-known pieces of short fiction he'd written for magazines. But once again the gold in this mine, for me, was not so much the pieces themselves but the explanations he'd appended to each story, or as he put it in the subtitle: *With copious Notes, Explanations, Digressions, and Elucidations; the Author telling frankly why he selected these Stories, why they were written, how much Money he received for them, and of his thrilling Adventures with wild Editors in their native Haunts.*

A "digression" following the reprint of the first story he ever published explained his tenure at *The Webster City Daily News* like this:

On June 20th, 1921, my mother [then forty-two] took up the editorship of The Webster City Daily News *and I was at her side from the start.*

Mr. Fred Hahne, who owned and published The Daily News, *had asked my mother to be his editor a couple of months before, and she had told me previously that she would consider the proposition only if I promised to go back with her to Webster City, our native town, and help her with the paper. She didn't like some of the people I was running around with in Des Moines, and wanted to lure me into what she considered the comparative sobriety of a county seat town before I got into any more trouble than I had already gotten into, which was plenty.*

I found a richer view of that moment in the pages of Mack's unpublished autobiography.

He resisted at first. "I felt that I was a man, there was no reason for me to be tied to my mother's apron strings."

But Effie insisted. "I won't leave you in Des Moines."

Mack protested that he knew nothing about covering news. Then he recounted a long speech from Effie, which he clearly couldn't have remembered word for word, but it was a sentiment that he later repeated dozens of times as his own view of the matter: "You want to write fiction—that's the thing you want to do in life. It seems to me that in order to be any kind of writer at all, you're going to have to write lots of words. Words, words, more words! Social notes, news notes, things that happen in local courts; people, people all over the place, doing trivial things, doing big things. People trying to live . . ."

They were back in Webster City within the week, Effie ensconced at the editor's desk squarely in front of a wide storefront window.

Which left me wondering. I had learned early in my research about Effie's somewhat desperate stints emptying bedpans and manning cash registers. How had she suddenly become the editor of a daily newspaper?

I found the answer in *But Look the Morn*. Effie's lively mind could not be fully occupied with her menial tasks or exhausted by the life of a single mother. She was a passionate amateur local historian. Mack remembered the "days she spent driving along country roads, searching out some decrepit millwright who had a story to tell."

Possibly her interest was fired by her own lineage, of which I had known very little. Her mother, born Evalyn Bone, was the daughter of Joseph Bone, an Iowa pioneer, veteran of the 7th Iowa Cavalry and the Indian Wars and owner of one of the first grain mills in Hamilton County. Adam McKinlay, Mack's grandfather, came to Webster City as a teenager, apprenticed in various mills, eventually managing Joseph Bone's mill until, at twenty-six, he married the boss's sixteen-year-old daughter and became a part owner.

When a local printer decided to publish a two-volume *History of Hamilton County, Iowa*, Effie, who literally had the county's history in her blood, was tapped to provide an eleven-page chapter about the key development necessary for a town to arise: Hamilton County mills.

"Her eyes were alive with the zeal of research," Mack wrote of his mother's scramble to make good on the assignment. "We lived only for the day when the volume would actually be printed and we could hold a copy in our hands." Then, one night, Effie arrived home bearing the thick volumes.

"With tender fingers I touched the page which bore Mother's

name, and regarded her with a wonder not as yet mingled with any hope or desire for emulation."

I found a passage from Effie's first published work on the early mills, expecting something tedious, archaic, clearly the work of an amateur. In fact, it had style, literary fire, sensuality, and astonishing deftness for an unpracticed writer—even by contemporary standards. Effie wrote: "Often a warm night in early March broke up the ice and the swelling, menacing roar aroused the family. Great cakes of ice weighing many tons, carried by the swollen flood, piled up in the bend of the river, wedged against the bridge piers, against the mill foundation, hurling themselves upon the corner of the mill which stood upstream, leaving nothing but destruction in their wake. . . . Fire could be combated with water, but water and ice knew no defeat; they carried everything before them."

The words piled up and hurled themselves at the reader, just as the ice was hurled by the flood. *Water and ice knew no defeat.* . . . Poetry, pure and simple.

No doubt, though only a small handful of volumes were published, after her hardship and the scandal her marriage had caused, Effie must have been profoundly gratified to find she'd managed to improve her status in her own eyes and that of her neighbors. Effie McKinlay Kantor was a lot of things, but she was now also that remarkable creature: a published author.

After the history was distributed in 1913, the managing editor of one of three local papers—even a town of nine thousand had three newspapers in 1913—asked Effie, then thirty-five, to try her hand at being a reporter, a position that, as Mack wrote, "had a dignity that approached eminence" as well as paying more than her previous menial jobs.

Effie attacked her reporting with energy and passion, bringing the sensibilities of a small-town crusader to the paper's pages. She campaigned for parks and other civic improvements while earning several promotions with accompanying pay increases, just as her father's career and finances were sputtering to extinction. Joseph Bone had sold the mill and invested in properties in Washington State. Adam McKinlay had become unable to perform the necessary tasks of millwork due to asthma contracted over years of breathing in flour dust and was forced into a succession of lesser jobs. When the western investments didn't work out for Joseph Bone, Adam found himself depleting his own meager savings to provide his father-in-law with loans that were never repaid. Finally, he could find no job at all, and the family struggled to survive on Effie's salary and proceeds from the sale of the undeveloped portion of their small homestead property.

So for a few years Effie had status, and earned enough to keep her family afloat. Then, in 1917, *The Freeman-Tribune* failed. It was following this disaster that Effie wrote her desperate appeal to John Kantor and John put her and his children up in a Chicago apartment until he got caught up in the real estate expert scandal.

When John's rent checks disappeared, the family moved back in with Effie's parents in the ever-shrinking house in Webster City. Her father's prospects remained moribund, and it seemed that every job Effie could have aspired to had already been claimed by a returning World War I veteran. Just when total financial collapse seemed inevitable, Effie discovered she had friends in Webster City, friends who had been impressed by her energy and zeal as a newspaper reporter and who had attained political power in the Iowa capital of Des Moines, just an hour or so drive away. Those friends called in favors until they found Effie a clerical spot that paid enough, barely, to move Mack and Virginia to the capital city and still send money home to her parents.

I could find no mention of this time in Des Moines in any of my grandfather's published autobiographies, and it was mentioned only in passing in the files of correspondence. Then, months into my commuting to Capitol South and the Madison building, all the way into box 139 of the Kantor Papers, I found it: a carbon of the original typed manuscript of what my grandfather had intended to be the sequel to *But Look the Morn* but never published. As I read through the pages, I quickly realized that the time in Des Moines, just two years, was more than a brief digression in my grandfather's life: It was seminal.

Moving seventy miles away from Webster City had a fringe benefit for Mack: obtaining a safe remove from a town where his last name had been featured frequently on the front page of the local newspapers in connection with the ongoing scandal in distant Chicago. Free from the constraints of his hometown, where his life history was not only known but discussed and clucked over, Mack must have felt free to reinvent himself—and not just free, but driven.

Mack found himself at the high school hangout, the drugstore lunch counter, mingling uncomfortably with his new high school classmates but drawn to another group only a few years older, "who bore the unmistakable stamp of those who had gone far and seen much, no matter how young they were."

These were youthful veterans of the war "over there" in Europe, now belatedly resuming their high school careers.

"I felt that I too had gone far and seen much," Mack wrote. "I imagined that I was more at ease among these ex-soldiers than with boys my own age. It was not without design that I wore a khaki shirt and overseas cap when first I sipped soda water in that drug store."

Just looking the part wasn't enough. Mack began to casually drop references to "my regiment" in conversation, and refer to battles that of course he had only read about. Soon the subtle hints turned into bald lies about the action he had seen, always based on accounts of battles he had read about in fervid secret sessions in the public library and presented in what he imagined to be self-deprecatory fashion. "Oh, I didn't have it so bad. Sure there was a lot of lead flying, but the boys up in the hedge rows had it far worse!" He showed off a scar on his calf he casually said was torn by a German bayonet when in fact it had been impressed by a German shepherd. He even bought service ribbons in a secondhand store and pinned them to his flannel shirt. At first he felt the thrill of his purloined identity. "The girls of 1919 were more impressed by a veteran of school age than by a football hero."

But soon, of course, the lie grew legs and careened around town, forcing him awake to the horrible shame of what he had done and to live with the constant threat of exposure. He lay sleepless at night, searching for a way out, fantasizing about calling a school-wide assembly and confessing all.

The true veterans didn't take long to detect contradictions and false notes in his increasingly elaborate tales, and word spread. His former friends snubbed him, or had places to be when he came around. "The worst thing about it was that I despised myself even more than other people could despise me," he wrote. He was left to struggle with the terrible possibility that maybe he was his father's son after all, compelled to lie for personal gain or glory by some blood poison stowed away in John Kantor's seed. The stain of his shame sank into the fabric of existence. "It is impossible to exaggerate the remembered drabness and bleakness and chill and ugliness which lay over my life at this time. . . ."

But I knew. I knew exactly how it felt. It may seem ridiculous to compare—he was fifteen, and I was only six, but the nature of my lie, the motivations behind it, the yearning for recognition I was too young to attain and didn't deserve, were freakishly similar right down to the lust for the badge of a service uniform. The depth of the shame, too, cut across age differences—even as an adult I have hesitated to speak, or even think, about this episode. But when I came across those unpublished pages, sitting at the wood desk in the Library of Congress manuscript reading room, cringe-inducing memory flooded in:

At some point in first grade, I became profoundly impressed by, and envious of, the slightly older kids who got to walk around school wearing those buckle-on white belts slanting across the shoulder like a beauty contestant's sash. These were members of the safety patrol and the belts were the badge of honor that marked them as the Chosen Ones. I lusted after those white belts, made of shiny plastic, smooth and cool to the touch.

Safety patrollers were selected by an election, certifying the admiration of their classmates, which may have been the real distinction I yearned for. Their role—standing prominently in front of the school at the first and last of the day, encouraging their fellow students to walk, not run, to and from cars and buses—seemed to me a dazzling spotlight, drawing me like a moth to flame.

First-graders were too young to be designated as patrollers, and elections wouldn't even be held until the second grade began.

But my mother didn't know that.

I think I must have daydreamed about it for days, if not weeks, until one afternoon I blurted, "Guess what happened in school today? I was elected to the safety patrol!"

I don't know what kind of response I expected. I don't think I even cared. I just wanted to hear myself say it, to create an alternate universe in which I was the popular kid, the one whom his classmates respected and the adults deemed worthy of Special Responsibilities.

I still remember the shock when my mother raced right past—"How wonderful, dear"—and bustled about, excitedly planning early breakfasts to accommodate my new pre-school duties. I was taken aback by her enthusiasm, and a thousand calculations whirred in my brain. Well, okay, I hadn't considered that my mother would actually do anything other than praise me. It was disconcerting that she seemed so action-oriented, but I was pretty sure I could still deal with this. When she asked me where my patrol belt was, my mind whirred some more and I said, "Only second-graders get those. We're going to make ones out of paper and leave them at school."

I would think that would have tipped her off, but she kept coming, like a monster in a nightmare. Now she was calling my father at work. Now she was dialing up the other mothers in our carpool to let them know I'd need to be picked up ten minutes early. I knew then I was doomed.

Here came the shame, the self-loathing, the soul-searing, world-crushing knowledge that I had gone too far and there was no way back.

Oddly, I don't remember my mother confronting me when my absurdly clumsy lie collapsed of its own ridiculous weight. I recall no lecture about honesty. What I remember is every day thereafter walking into school like a condemned man awaiting execution. And each day that no ax fell became a hellish eternity, making me yearn for the flash of the blade and the blow that would put a final end to the misery, along with all else.

Finally, what seemed like weeks later but was in reality probably a couple of days at most, after suffering through another endless stretch of watching the clock until the bell rang my release, I was shuffling guiltily toward the door when my teacher said, "Tom, can you stay for a minute?"

The blow I had feared, and hoped for. I froze, light-headed, weak-kneed.

She walked to where I stood and cocked her head. "Tom, did you tell your mother you were elected to the safety patrol?"

I flushed, my heart thumped thirty-second notes in my chest, my entire body throbbed with alarm. Something sprouted in my six-year-old brain and bloomed from my lungs. "There must be some kind of misunderstanding!" I shouted, and sprinted from the room. Fortunately, none of my classmates ever discovered the nature of that "misunderstanding."

For Mack, a teenager exposed for all to see, the consequences of his lie were simply unbearable. He quit school and found a job testing gravel, sand, and cement for the Iowa State Highway Commission. Dropping out was easy enough to explain by saying his family needed the additional income. It was also true.

The commission was charged with the transformation of hundreds of miles of muck roads into modern highways, for which a bottomless source of pavement would be required. Mack's job involved digging samples from gravel pits, then running rote tests in labs leased from the university. At night he hung around the neighborhood pool halls, mingling with drinkers, gamblers, and in some cases, thieves.

One day, a pool hall buddy showed up at Mack's lab while he was alone, running tests. He was in the neighborhood, the buddy said. Mack was glad for the company, but slightly uncomfortable with the companion, whom he knew to possess a set of tools with which he boosted headlights from parked cars to sell to shady garages. The two chatted for a while, pleasantly enough, until his buddy noticed a stack of factory automobile tires piled in the corner, and a transom window above the door that swung open and had no lock to secure it.

Now he boxed Mack in a corner, speaking under his breath, proposing they meet back there that night. Mack could help him up to the transom. He'd do the rest—wriggle through the slot, drop to the floor, and unlock the door. Then he'd need Mack only to help roll the tires down an alley to his car.

Mack mumbled something noncommittal. But when his "friend" left and his boss returned, Mack pointed out the lack of a lock on the transom, and urged him to have one installed immediately.

Then, when Mack was alone again, a chain of thoughts began grinding in his head.

"I suddenly saw the pool halls for what they were—dull, spiritless abodes of the idle and the disappointed and the incompetent. . . . If someone wanted tires, why not go to work and earn money to buy them?" Then he thought of his father, always trying to find ways to grab money that he hadn't earned.

"God, I said to myself, I want to work. I want to work hard. But at what? I didn't want to be a laboratory assistant all my life."

He tried to think about what he was passionate about. Butterflies, the woods . . . Perhaps he could be a naturalist. But as soon as the thought occurred, he dismissed it. "I realized that what I loved about moths and butterflies was the romance of their pursuit and capture, the unbelievable color and delicacy of the creatures themselves. . . . Mine was merely a poetic fascination, a grand worship of Nature. I was not cut out to be a scientist."

Still, those moments he spent in the woods had moved him. He could still see them so vividly, even in the industrial confines of a cement lab. The more beautiful they had been, it seemed, the more fragile and fleeting. How could he hold on to them? How could he make the world see what he saw?

And then he knew. "I thought: If you imagined it clearly enough you could make it come true for yourself. And if you wrote it down, you could make it come true for everybody. You could write the good and bad things, reconstruct all existence."

He had always been a reader, enamored of tales of adventure and daring. Now "I saw for the first time what books were really for. They were a means of cementing the past, which otherwise would have perished, a way of holding beauty and legend, unfading, shared and dreaded and loved far down the centuries."

Mack raced home that evening, his transformation shining from within. He was no longer disappointed, aimless, bitter about what life had dealt him. He had a goal, a great ambition.

"I lay across the bed and began to write. My mother came in and asked what in the world I was doing. I told her, 'I'm going to be a writer,' and she came over and kissed me on the back of my head, and I went on writing."

Perhaps of all single mothers in dire need of practical moneymaking support within a thousand miles of Des Moines, Iowa, only one, Effie M. Kantor, would have uncomplicatedly, unambivalently rejoiced at such a declaration.

Her need for practical solutions would soon increase dramatically. A farm belt depression hit hard at Iowa's state budget. First, Mack lost his job in the lab, followed quickly by Effie, who lost her clerical job in a steep reduction of state office staff. Only Virginia, who was going to college, managed to hold on to her part-time job. They put off the landlord and lived on bread and beans and made thin soup by boiling bones donated by a sympathetic butcher. Effie made a pittance in change by playing piano for dance classes and church socials.

And then, within months, the miracle occurred. Hahne—a job printer specializing in livestock catalogs who thought printing his own newspaper might launch his political career—offered Effie the editorship. Despite her current destitution, and what must have seemed like an astronomical salary offer of $40 a week (the equivalent of $535 a week in 2015), she didn't agree right away. She told Hahne she had one condition: that Mack could come on as an unpaid apprentice.

Despite his reservations, Mack soon felt at home in Hahne's small newspaper office in a red-brick storefront on the edge of Webster City's small downtown.

"The two of us put out the paper, a four-page tabloid," Mack wrote in his unpublished account.

We didn't carry any wire stuff. Everything was local news and had to be written by one or the other of us. Sometimes we had a lucky windfall in the form of a report from the State Park Commission, or copious verbatim extracts from church bulletins which the local clergy wanted us to print. Generally speaking, we wrote every column that went into the paper, with my mother doing the lion's share.

It was hard work but it was fun. I doubt if ever a mother and her son enjoyed a professional association more heartily than did we two, in those years of the early 1920s.

Each week I had perforce to write thousands of words: obituaries, sports, civic happenings, social activities, everything that went on around the town which my mother thought I might be capable of covering. On the whole I think that Mr. Hahne was pretty long-suffering, and so was Webster City. Of course some folks thought it highly indelicate—practically obscene in fact— for a seventeen-year-old youth to come baying after their news. Occasionally I editorialized, too, but neither the townfolks nor Mr. Hahne knew that. They thought it was Mother. She took considerable blame for mistakes which I made, but was serenely confident that her firm shoulders could carry the load.

When I was sixteen, Mack published a series of essays and stories about small-town America for a book called *Hamilton County*—there are ten counties in America by that name, some distinctly rural, some containing large cities, but all essentially middle-American, and that was the point. The text was accompanied by photographs taken by my uncle Tim, who at that point had become a professional photographer with some national magazine credits. Some of the photographs featured teenagers, and Mack wanted to imagine authentic-sounding dialogue to go with them—but didn't believe he was in touch enough with my generation to produce it. So he asked me to write some up. I did—three separate pieces of dialogue suggested by the photos. I am afraid to read them now, but as I handed him the few typed pages, I felt that, after a somewhat disconcerting struggle with the empty page, I had actually come through and produced something that more or less worked. I remember watching his face as he read, holding the pages with his right hand and his pipe with his left. I could see his eyes switching right, then left, as they moved down the page. His focus on the words seemed complete, but I couldn't tell what he was thinking. Then he looked at me and smiled. He said nothing, but he transferred the pipe to his mouth, reached his free hand into his back pocket, and pulled out his well-worn billfold. Now he needed two hands. He put the pages down, reached into the wallet, and handed me three crisp $20 bills. This was long before the era of ATMs on every corner, and crisp bills were a novelty. The feel of the cash in my hands, conveyed for words I had somehow conjured from nothing, then put on paper, had a "Jack and the Beanstalk" magic to it. The bills weren't the seeds, but the words were. From something that had seemed so tiny and inconsequential had grown something miraculous.

Months later, I received a copy of the book in the mail. I remember opening it to the title page where it said that "three generations" had been involved in the making of the book, and there was my name.

There is an odd, hard-to-explain, and impossible-to-duplicate thrill that comes from seeing your own name in a print byline. However slender a slice of prose it is attached to, however likely it will be seen only by the tiniest fragment of the larger world, it is still your name, preserved to some degree, creating some infinitesimal but real possibility of the immortality shared by the likes of William Shakespeare, Charles Dickens, Ernest Hemingway.

At least, it is license to dream.

For me, those dreams never included working for a newspaper.

A few months after *Hamilton County* came out, in the fall of my junior year of high school, Mack played his celebrity-writer card to persuade the local newspaper to offer me a job as a weekend copyboy. I was willing, reluctantly, until I discovered the hours included Saturday nights. Giving up date night was not a sacrifice I was prepared to make, so I turned it down. Mack, of course, was embarrassed and disapproving. I cringed at his back-of-the-throat grumbling. I felt guilty for letting him down. But all of that was nothing beside the prospect of losing my Saturday evenings with that cute blonde.

Only as I read the letter from the teenage Mack on *Webster City Daily News* letterhead did I grasp the true significance of my grandfather's gesture. In arranging that newspaper job, he wasn't just doing a favor for his grandson, he was seeing himself in me; was, in his own way, trying to share one of his fondest, most formative memories—by finagling me a job in a newsroom, just as his beloved mother had done for him.

I felt guilty all over again, decades after the fact, for turning down that Saturday night job, and was rather amazed that he hadn't been even more upset than he was—the incident was almost immediately forgotten.

It wasn't long before I came across something else he wrote—an explanation for his tolerance of my venality, and a reprieve for my guilt. In one of his annotations for the Library of Congress, he wrote about a high school job he had clerking in a downtown shop where he was supposed to work until ten every Saturday night: "Never once did I work all of a Saturday evening." When his boss saw how antsy he grew as date night neared, "he would kindly let me go. I would jabber a word of thanks and get out of the store as fast as possible without knocking down any old ladies."

That letter he had written from *The Webster City Daily News* in 1922 was a joy to read. He was all of eighteen when he wrote it, working at a local paper in a rural state in a time that is long gone. Yet the attitude of the amused observer, already cynical and aloof like a jaded pro journalist laughing at the multiple ironies of his situation, is so familiar to me. He mentions, sardonically, that Fred Hahne, the paper's publisher, who is listed at the top of the letterhead, above Effie, had placed both of *his* stories—stories that Mack clearly felt may not have completely deserved it—on the front page. "Of course! Why not?" he snarked.

I had faced just such humiliations and frustrations as a beginning reporter, not much older than Mack was when he wrote the letter. I worked for a bureau chief who had been making a reverse career commute—from *The Washington Post* to *The Miami Herald* to progressively less impressive papers until he wound up chain-smoking foul-smelling low-tar cigarettes and sucking his dentures loudly in the tiny strip-mall office of the Cape Coral bureau of the Fort Myers *News-Press*. Every day he'd wander next door to the bar sometime before noon, and I would be left alone to generate the required three news stories and three briefs a day on such earthshaking events as city sewer and swale commission meetings. Once the boss decamped, my only company was a middle-aged southern lady who handled the society news. Underneath a patina of syrupy sweetness, she had the disposition of a barracuda and the ethics of a hyena. To survive the triviality, I developed the same sort of appreciation for the absurd I saw in Mack's letter, in which he tells his mother, "No great difficulty came up, except when I called that bird—John Young—who [here he handwrote an *m* to make it *whom*—a distinction that troubles me still] you told me to call about someone having their tomatoes stolen. I said—'We were told you could give us some information about some tomatoes which were stolen.' I guess he thought I was insinuating that he had stolen them. He got pretty mad. But I couldn't get anything out of him."

Around the borders of the stationery, he had sketched ink drawings illustrating various points in his letter; a man with a burglar mask carrying a bag overflowing with tomatoes, for instance. The style of the primitive but somewhat charming little sketches leapt out at me like some hand reaching from the void. This was the selfsame style of cartoon drawing with which, some forty years later, my grandfather would decorate the hand-inked birthday cards or kiln-fired painted ceramic cups and bowls he distributed to us grandchildren on our birthdays, some of which I have preserved in dusty frames or kept propped on shelves in the back of a closet. As I thought of these corny, sweet gifts, wondering if I could find any of them, an image popped into my head: a cartoon figure he drew of me on my fourteenth birthday. In the identical style of that ninety-three-year-old letter, he portrayed me seated at a desk wearing long hair and blue jeans, a pen in my hand and a roll of parchment before me. The caption he wrote was: *O God, we fear he will be a writer.*

FIVE

In the summer of 1974, I returned to Gainesville from Europe, grimly determined to carry out my pledge of joining the college newspaper. *The Independent Florida Alligator* was a feisty student newspaper that had been kicked off campus by the university administration the previous year after the student editor engaged in an act of civil disobedience, defying Florida's antiabortion laws by publishing a list of abortion clinics. The charter separating the newspaper from the university was punitive—administrators had cynically designed it to force financial failure, with the ultimate goal of entirely eliminating the irritating voice of a student press while maintaining deniability in its demise.

Inadequately capitalized as it was, the only office space the *Alligator* could afford was the unrenovated kitchen of a defunct fast-food restaurant just across University Avenue from the oldest part of campus. The "front door" opened off an alley usually populated by homeless men sleeping off drunks, empty bottles of Mogen David 20/20 scattered about. On a sweltering, suffocating day in late June, I walked through that door for the first time. The space was long and narrow, big enough to fit a one-lane bowling alley, with a glass office at the end where the bowling pins would be. Along one wall was a continuous counter supporting a row of manual typewriters that hovered suggestively above aluminum folding chairs. It was early afternoon, the slow part of the day for a morning newspaper. One or two reporters sat at typewriters, pressing the keys without any particular urgency. On the other side of the room, beneath an industrial-size stove hood still caked with years of blackened, crusted burger grease, a student about my age sat behind a massive desk. The desk was scarred and dented—an obvious castoff from one of the classroom buildings across the way—ornamented only by a long-legged girl in tight, tiny blue-jean shorts perched on the front edge, sucking languorously on a chocolate-coated frozen banana.

The guy sitting behind the desk watched me react to this unlikely tableau with an amused smile. He wore a faded T-shirt and blue jeans. His brown hair fell to his shoulders, framing a droopy mustache. I might have been looking in the mirror.

"Can I help you?" he asked.

"I want to write," I said.

"Do you have any experience writing for a newspaper?"

"No."

"That doesn't matter."

I may have done a visible double take.

When the silence stretched to a breaking point I asked, "What *does* matter, then?"

"Just show up," he said.

Beginning the very next afternoon, that's what I did.

I was expecting to have to hold my nose and dive in to an uncomfortable and unwelcoming environment, but the opposite was true. From the minute I walked through that door, I knew I was home. These were my people.

It was a heady time for journalism. Bob Woodward and Carl Bernstein at *The Washington Post* had taken down a corrupt president. Writers like Tom Wolfe, Gay Talese, and Hunter S. Thompson were injecting the excitement of narrative technique into nonfiction reportage, making their accounts of everything from politics to cultural turmoil read like novels, rippling with memorable characters, action, and psychological depth. Many of my new colleagues at the *Alligator* shared my reverence for making the world comprehensible through the telling of stories, and they shared my irreverence and suspicion of authority, as well as my sense of humor. I had always been a bit of an ugly duckling in those creative writing classes. Except for that one electric moment when Harry Crews performed my story for the class, I felt like a fraud among frauds. My fellow students struck me as effete and pretentious. After one student read a dark, self-involved, self-consciously literary piece that was all too typical of the group, I was called on to comment. I'm afraid I made no friends with my assessment. "What it lacks in clarity," I said, "it makes up for in obscurity."

I knew that critique was cruel and, worse, hypocritical: My own work was equally full of hot air. The painful truth was, I never felt I really *knew* enough to write a convincing piece of fiction. What did characters feel inside? What motivated them? Unless they were all stand-ins for me, how could I know?

In Philip Roth's novel *The Ghost Writer*, the protagonist, an aspiring writer and obvious Roth stand-in, is invited to stay at the home of his idol, a literary lion of the first order. The idol has a pretty secretary a generation his junior, and the aspiring writer begins to suspect theirs is more than a business relationship. Staying in the downstairs guest room, he hears raised voices in the master bedroom above him. Compelled to eavesdrop, he decides to push a glass to the ceiling to amplify the sounds. He looks around for something to place atop the bed as a stepladder, and all he can come up with are the thick, collected works of the man he is spying on. As he stands on the books of his idol—literally elevating himself atop the master's lifework, his ear pressed against a glass pressed against the ceiling—an astonishing secret is revealed. He sees himself as if from the distance, and realizes exactly why he will always be a second-rate novelist.

"If only I could invent as presumptuously as real life!" he cries. When I read that line, I felt an electric shock of recognition.

Now, as a journalist, I could search out the facts that real life outrageously invents. Instead of trying to spin a story from the closed-loop redundancy of my own mind, I could dig it from reality, fact by fact, observation by observation. I would no longer stare, defenseless, at the blank page in the typewriter. I would have notebooks filled with material with which to build. My aim was still to tell a tale—I couldn't really bring myself to care about simply delivering information—but now, instead of inventing a story, I could *discover* it.

I have been happy and fulfilled as a journalist my entire adult life, but have never completely dismissed my regret that I failed my early ambition of writing a novel of the type that has supplied me with my own most memorable reading experiences, the type of fiction that manages to attain a reality somehow truer than actual events. At one point early in my journalism career, my narrative news pieces won an award that paid what at the time seemed like quite a bit of money—the equivalent of almost six months of the tiny salary I was then making. I decided to use the windfall to attempt to write the novel I still

dreamed of. I was living in a soon-to-be-demolished relic of Old Florida, a cottage on the banks of a river shaded by groves of mangoes,
coconuts, oranges, and grapefruit. I set my typewriter up on a card
table on the back porch and sat on the increasingly sticky vinyl couch
as the heat rose through the day, stripping to my shorts as sweat began
to drip from my forehead and splash on the keys. Frequent breaks to
eat frozen condensed orange juice out of the can with a spoon did little to cool things off, or jump-start my novel. I did type, painfully,
slowly, filling a few pages of blank paper, but once again I felt that old
fraudulence, that frustrating inability to break through to an imagined
truth. I could feel my arms, and heart, grow ever heavier, until I simply
ground to a halt. The six months disappeared, leaving nothing to show
for the time but a handful of pages I couldn't even bear to read through.

That basic failure of imagination would not prove to be a problem
for my grandfather, who would go on from his first newspaper job to
write hundreds of short stories, novellas, screenplays, stage plays, and
even songs—not to mention the novels that made him, for a time at
least, an American celebrity—many of them from the broad cloth of
his own invention. When I first read through the simple list of titles of
his published work in the Library of Congress index, a list that went on
and on and on, my stomach clenched with envy and self-criticism.
From the time he was a teenager, his career thrived by the fertile use
of just that facility I seemed to lack.

The letter he wrote from *The Webster City Daily News* was dated
1922, the same year a short story he wrote called "Purple" won a contest sponsored by *The Des Moines Register*, earning him a few inches
of newsprint and a check for $50.

I discovered Mack's account of that momentous achievement in
his *Author's Choice* annotations. The first summer that he worked with
Effie at the Webster City daily, he wrote:

Mother kept after me to enter the Register *short story contest. I had quite an inferiority complex despite her encouragement and her faith in me, and I protested a lot before submitting my work. I said that I didn't think the* Register *contest amounted to very much; probably I was only afraid that I couldn't make a decent showing. But eventually my ambition overcame my reluctance and I did write two new stories. I remember doing part of the typing on 'Purple' while sitting under a wild grape arbor in our backyard, with a portable typewriter on an old wash bench . . . smoky Iowa dusk coming down to deaden the page before my eyes: the long dusk of late summer, with children calling at their games in distant yards and cars buzzing in off the prairie.*

He submitted the story under the required pseudonym, Sheridan Rhodes, after the street address of the apartment his father had rented for them in Chicago.

In *Author's Choice*, he describes what happened next:

For a while I dashed eagerly to our post office box each morning, expecting to find a check for the $50 First Prize.

Months went by, but still no fifty dollars—no blue ribbon, no anything. Maybe my manuscripts had gone astray; I wrote to the Des Moines Register *to make sure that they hadn't. No reply. Maybe the* Register *had decided to call off the contest. Maybe— After Christmas, I began actually to forget about that contest for days and weeks at a time.*

On February 25th, 1922, we stopped at the post office as usual, got our morning Register *and a few letters out of the box and went to the office. We worked hard through most of that day and lunched at the Greeks'. After the paper had gone to press about four o'clock, I enjoyed my weekly leisure and wandered our populous main street through the slush and trample of a winter Saturday. Just before dusk ... I drifted back into the office. Mother was at her typewriter doing three things at once, as she could do so well: writing up a Farm Bureau meeting; laughing over her shoulder with Miss Ella Stickney, the bookkeeper; and talking politics with Charley Hoffman, the boss printer. That morning's* Register *was hanging across a chair by her desk.*

Idly, as I listened, I examined the front page of the Des Moines paper—the bottom half, which I hadn't paid much attention to that morning. The thing that gained my curiosity was a box about five inches square at the bottom of the page, and I had to hold my head on one side in order to read it.

I spoke in a shivering trance, reading the words aloud:

Purple

By Sheridan Rhodes

First Prize Winner in the Register's Annual Short Story Contest

I had set out wanting to get some insight into the beginning of my grandfather's writing career, and I'd expected to piece it together from fragments plucked here and there from correspondence and clippings. Instead, I had this lyrical, second-by-second account by a fine writer:

We went haywire around there for a while. In memory I can see Mother's face before me now, gray eyes bulging, mouth laughing, brown hair flying wild. ...

Mother didn't do any more work on Monday's paper then. [We] took a walk through the melting snow clear down to the

Second Street bridge. We stood and watched a pink glow in the western sky and saw cakes of ice drifting silently on the black waters of the Boone beneath us. By that time I couldn't talk at all, which was and is unusual for me.

Once, nearly twenty years later, when I was feeling disgruntled and blue and annoyed at the supposed financial failure of a book of mine, a man with a slip of paper in his hand caught up with me in the Pennsylvania Station in New York, and pulled me off a train bound for Florida. The voice of Hollywood had spoken, and I was richer by a small fortune.

Still, the news he brought didn't seem as important then or even now as the news which I read off that upside-down paper hanging over the chair in Mother's office, half-hidden by her shabby old sealskin coat.

That combination, seeing your words in print beneath your name *and* getting paid for it, is an explosively addictive combination. I knew the indelible thrill of it, from the moment Mack himself handed me those three $20 bills for my contribution to *Hamilton County*, a figure curiously similar to his own initial payoff for "Purple."

Now I had yet another irony, a synchronistic connection to the story of "Purple" itself, to consider. The more I thought of it, the more astounding it seemed.

For a short story concocted by a teenager in 1921, "Purple" was remarkably assured writing. It had compression, rhythm, point of view, descriptive prowess. It showed the single most salient characteristic of a natural writer, the one strategy with which I begin every writing class I've ever taught—it showed rather than told, demonstrated with detail instead of begging for belief with generalities and summary.

"Purple"—a story about a farm couple who splurge to buy an art photo of an idyllic countryside scene, never realizing the photo was of their own farm—begins:

It was a foreign looking motor car to appear in an Iowa lane, but it purred steadily along, as if accustomed to such surroundings. It was piloted by a chauffeur who seemed rather soiled by the heavy dust that hung over the highway they had just left behind them. The auto's only occupant besides the driver was a lithe, dark man who glanced from side to side as if hunting something. Fields stretched away on every hand—corn with stalks beginning to grow crisp and tough, oats piled in golden stacks as far as the eye could see; the early morning sun glistened on freshly clipped stubble, and a tiny warbler in the grasses at the roadside invited the world to come and share his store of seeds.

In 2008, eighty-six years after Mack won his first literary prize, a moment he deemed among the most significant in his career, I had a very significant moment in my own career.

It came about through a story I assigned and edited for *The Washington Post Magazine* that began with a passage oddly parallel to the opening paragraph of "Purple":

He emerged from the Metro at the L'Enfant Plaza station and positioned himself against a wall beside a trash basket. By most measures, he was nondescript: a youngish white man in jeans, a long-sleeved T-shirt and a Washington Nationals baseball cap. From a small case, he removed a violin. Placing the open case at his feet, he shrewdly threw in a few dollars and pocket change as seed money, swiveled it to face pedestrian traffic, and began to play.

The anonymous figure in both first paragraphs was a famous artist appearing out of his usual element—a photographer in rural Iowa in "Purple," and a musician in a gritty subway station in the *Post Magazine* article. My friend and colleague Gene Weingarten and I had prevailed upon world-renowned violinist Joshua Bell to play his heart out on a $3 million Stradivarius outside a Washington Metro stop, unannounced. When Bell had performed in a heavily promoted concert in DC just weeks earlier, people had lined up to buy tickets at a couple hundred dollars a pop.

But when he played anonymously in the Metro during the morning rush, without the official sanction of a concert hall and a famous name to announce his virtuosity, it was a very different story. During the forty-five-minute concert—some of the greatest music ever written, played by one of the world's foremost musicians on one of the finest instruments ever made—hundreds passed within feet of him without so much as a sideways glance or a hitch in their stride. A scant handful idly tossed him a quarter.

We called this story "Pearls Before Breakfast," and it instantly struck a global nerve, going viral on the Internet and passed link by link to millions around the world. Months after publication, it was awarded the 2008 Pulitzer Prize for feature writing.

This was a story about how people become so lost in the grind of life that they are unable to see great beauty right under their noses. That exact description applies equally to "Purple."

The nature of archival research most often requires sifting through heaps of irrelevant or otherwise unhelpful material, trying to stay alert (and awake) long enough to notice the glint of the proverbial needle, all but imperceptible in the bale of hay. This is what I had prepared myself for in attacking the thousands of folders and tens of thousands of document pages at the Library of Congress. What I hadn't prepared for was finding almost every paper I touched to bear something of interest and intrigue:

A baby journal written by Effie, which recorded not only Mack's hefty birth weight—ten and a half pounds, "fat and round," she wrote— but the fact that she initially intended to name him John, yet another reminder of this otherwise strong woman's baffling continued commitment to such an obvious reprobate. A child's crayon drawing of Civil War soldiers that Mack had done for a school presentation; ironic, considering. A 1911 elementary school report card for my grandfather from Webster City public schools in which "Busy Work" was listed as one of the subjects. (He got an "E"—for "excellent"?) A handwritten spoof of a high school newspaper that Mack and his friends had created (slogan: "Published whenever we get a notion—get me?"), which was astoundingly similar to a spoof paper my friends and I had come up with, *The Monthly Moppage*, which almost got me suspended from school because the principal thought the *MOP* in *Moppage* meant "Make-Out Party."

After less than a week I had snapped hundreds of page images with my iPhone camera, and after a month, thousands.

Many were more than interesting. They propelled the story forward, like pieces of a jigsaw puzzle that had a key color or shape I'd been searching for to complete a partially constructed portion of the ultimate image. Or a completely unfamiliar shape, announcing an entirely new section of the puzzle. Sometimes both.

One of those was a 1925 letter from Effie to close friends.

"You will be surprised," Effie wrote, "to learn that the *Daily News* ceased publication January 5th. Mr. Hahne's financial condition would not allow him to continue the expense of the little paper, so the town is getting along without it. Of course it is needless to say I miss the active work—the pleasure of it—and in another way, I am glad to be released from the strain of producing so much each day, regardless of whether there was news or not."

Effie was putting on a brave face. In fact, Hahne had lost an election for mayor and no longer needed a newspaper to promote an aborted political career. This development meant, of course, that both Effie and Mack were once again out of work. Mack, who had finished up high school while working at the paper, found odd jobs when he could. But apparently, at the moment Effie wrote the letter, he could not.

Three weeks after the paper closed, she wrote, "Mack sustained the second operation upon his leg, by which the steel plate, with its six screws, was removed from the bone. He was confined to bed and his room for three weeks. . . ."

As I read, an image emerged from the obscurity of half a century, of my grandfather, wearing a wicked grin, joyfully rolling up his baggy trouser leg to horrify us grandkids with the sight of the nastiest scar we had ever seen—a jagged maw, crisscrossed by keloid tissue that looked like fat white worms crawling one atop the other, down into the sagging, puckered cavity where thigh flesh should have been. And then I remembered—there was something about a car accident. A bad one that nearly killed him. And despite his injuries, he pulled someone out of the destroyed and burning car, a hero.

I now remembered my mom emphasizing this last point, surprised that I could have nearly forgotten such a dramatic tale.

Desperately, I searched through the files of family correspondence for more mentions of the accident. I came across a tantalizing reference in Mack's annotations to "my mother's account of my accident," but I couldn't find it anywhere.

Just when I was about to despair, I discovered it, misfiled, in a folder dealing with much later years—and once again my expectations were exceeded. Effie, writing within days of the event, recounted it in moving detail.

I get up in the morning, eat breakfast and go at once to the hospital. . . . After the paper is out and I get something up for the following day, I eat downtown and go straight to the hospital.

The left thigh is fractured, the middle third. It was a compound fracture, the splintered ends of the bone having just the covering of skin to keep the bone from penetrating. He also has a rib or two that are fractured. He is skinned from top to bottom, both elbows, his forehead, by his eye, his shoulder, his chest, his hips, his knees and a badly sprained right hand. His glasses were broken all to pieces and one eyeball badly bruised. He is living only by a miracle, and that miracle was an elm tree about eight inches thick and thirty-five feet high.

Nineteen-year-old Mack had been on a picnic with seven of his friends, five of them in the car he was in, a Chalmers touring car that had just been in the shop.

"The brakes worked well," Effie wrote, an observation Mack corrected in his annotations: "The hell they did. I was with Charlie that morning about ten o'clock, before the accident, when he attempted to park downtown in Webster City. He banked almost up over the curb, because the car wouldn't stop. Nevertheless, we went, knowingly, into a region of steep hills. . . . How half-witted can young people get? The answer is: very half-witted."

After the parking mishap, they'd driven more than an hour outside of town to property owned by the family of one of the party. On the way back, they began to ascend one of the steepest hills in that part of Iowa.

"The hill is one mile long and has a turn near the top of the hill," Effie wrote. "The grade is toward a forty-five-foot precipice with only a board fence.

They had been driving about thirty-five mph but slowed to fifteen as they started down the steep incline. Charles (who was driving) says the brakes held-slipped-held-slipped, and Mack, seeing that the car seemed to be gaining momentum, called "throw her in reverse." Charles then tried the emergency brake, but it would not hold. By the time the car reached the curve it was almost beyond his control; he made the turn all right but in a few rods further down the very steep hill, the left front wheel struck a rock, tore off the tire and rim and that sent the car straight over to the right where it shot thru the fence and over two tree tops, landing right in the top of the third, an elm, which slowly settled under the weight which uprooted it, and the car and the tree went over together. The tree trunk is peeled as with a knife of bark, limbs and leaves. The machine turned over at the bottom as it struck the ground. There were several eyewitnesses. It was seven p.m. When they got there, all were unconscious except Mack and Charles. Charles had presence of mind enough to drag out two girls and turn off the gas and run with dirt to put out the flames which were rising from the car. Mack was trying to climb out thru the shattered top but seeing his twisted leg behind him remarked that "it looked like his—the trousers matched!" And then he fainted. That was when the bones came through the flesh. By that time there were dozens on the scene and they thought Mack was dying. Blood was coming out of his ears, nose and mouth and because of his injured chest they thought his ribs were penetrating his right lung and he thought so too, for he could not get his breath.

At first they couldn't find the doctor and were panicking. When he did arrive, he also thought Mack was dying.

The operator got me at 7:20 p.m. . . . We had just finished dinner when that phone rang. The operator said, "Mack Kantor badly hurt in auto accident near Lehigh. Can't find a doctor. Bring one at once and come."

One never knows how they will feel. I neither felt like crying or screaming and so didn't do either. I just went.

Of course we did not know where to go. But as we started down that awful hill and turned the corner, there was the crowd and cars and lights. We stopped and asked where the children were. They said folks had carried them all over into town. Then one woman detached herself from the crowd and said, "All but that boy that was hurt so bad. They took him in an ambulance to Ft. Dodge. His leg was broken, his chest all crushed in and his head hurt. His first name was Mack!"

But the ambulance hadn't left yet. As Effie approached, she saw Mack through the open back doors, lying on a stretcher, "laughing and joking with the crowd. I'll venture there were twenty-five young fellows outside the window giving him oranges or water or wanting to do something for him. They still thought he was dying, and he did look ghastly, but on feeling of his chest, I was sure he was all right. He could talk with short gasps, and kept winking at me. I may have been proud of Mack through his writing, but I have never been so proud of him as I have been through this. He never yelled, or cried, or swore, although he fainted once."

I didn't have to guess how Effie felt; I would find out all too soon—within weeks of reading that account. On a March afternoon bearing the first promise of spring after a brutal winter, my phone rang with a number and area code I'd never seen.

"This is Martin, Sam's boss, in Costa Rica," he said. "Sam's been in an accident."

Sam is my son, twenty-four at the time. While he had been briefing a group of clients about to go on a guided paddleboard tour at a high-end sports adventure shop on one of the most beautiful beaches in the world, a freak gust of wind picked up a fifty-pound board lying on the sand and sent it flying end over end into the side of Sam's face. It knocked him unconscious for at least twenty seconds. Blood streamed from his nose and mouth. I learned later that, just as with Mack, witnesses thought he was dead or dying. His boss had driven him for an hour over rutted dirt roads to the nearest hospital, by which time Sam was conscious but couldn't remember his address or even his age. The ER doctors flew him to the best hospital in the country, forty-five minutes by medevac helicopter, for reconstruction of his fractured jaw and further tests to determine if he'd suffered traumatic brain injury.

The surgery would be in the middle of the night, and there was nobody to call us with the result. When I boarded a plane at six the next morning, I had no idea if he'd suffered permanent brain damage or come through the jaw reconstruction without complication.

Just like Effie, I couldn't think. I just *went*.

Twelve hours later, I walked into his hospital room. He was sitting up, looking like someone had stuffed a football in his cheek, and, just as with Mack, now sporting a steel plate with multiple screws piecing him together. When he saw me, his smile, even though he had only half a face to smile with, lit the dingy room with the irresistible light of a rising sun. Through all the slow, miserable, liquid-diet days that followed, he never once complained or bemoaned his bad fortune.

Sam has Mack's light coloring and his long, strong-jawed handsome face. Maybe he's got something else from him as well.

As I thought more of Effie's account of the car accident, something stuck out like a compound fracture: Mack hadn't been the hero, as my family's oral history had always emphasized; his friend Charles had been the one who pulled a girl from the flaming car.

I went back and found Mack's annotation. Sure enough, he addressed the discrepancy:

> *I seem to come off very well as quite a hero, but I discover now that Mother didn't yet know that it was I, and not Charles Jones, who pulled Dorothea Western out of the burning car. I didn't know it myself, because I couldn't remember. Some of those Lehigh coal miners came to the hospital later and told me, because they had witnessed it from across a nearby creek.*

Okay, so who are we to believe here: a professional journalist (also his mother!), who came on the scene minutes after the accident and talked directly to the victims, or hearsay from a bunch of coal miners who had watched from across a creek and probably couldn't tell one teenage townie from another? And how could someone with a compound fracture who kept fainting pull an inert body out of a crashed car?

Also consider that Mack was no more than a few years past masquerading as a returning war vet, desperate for the glory and manhood attributed to those who perform under physical threat.

I found it intriguing that even into his fifties, writing those annotations, Mack still clung to the clearly absurd conclusion that he was the hero of the story.

Mack's mythmaking didn't do any harm this time, and in fact, it merged into a productive response to his prolonged disability. Effie noted in her letter that, during his layup in the hospital, he kept dismissing any concern that he might end up permanently hobbled by his injuries. He kept telling anyone who inquired, "Writing is my game; just think, it was only my leg. Isn't that great?"

And to prove it, he didn't just sit around and mope. He wrote.

SIX

Early in 1925, a thirty-eight-year-old Kentucky spelunker named Floyd Collins entered an unexplored cave entrance, hoping to find a magnificent cavern that would become a tourist attraction. When his lantern began to sputter, he hurried back toward the surface, but got hung up in one of the narrow passages he'd barely been able to squeeze through on the way in. As he struggled, his lamp fell and guttered out, and the cave ceiling collapsed above him. Now he was in total darkness. A boulder pinned his foot against a rock wall, and mud and gravel from the cave-in buried him up to his hips. Friends found him the next day just 150 feet from the entrance, but they couldn't get through the tight passage to dig him out. They handed him crackers and gave him water and promised to bring help. As rescuers began to dig a rescue shaft above him, even more rubble fell. A rookie reporter making $25 a week was sent down from the Louisville *Courier-Journal* to see what he could, ahem, dig up on the story. William Burke Miller had two valuable assets—a great byline, thanks to his nickname, Skeets, and a slight stature. At only five foot five and 117 pounds, Skeets, lowered by the heels into the eighty-foot-deep cave entrance, was able, with great difficulty, to crawl and snake his way through the cold, wet, increasingly obstructed passages until he was face-to-face with the pinned explorer.

"My flashlight revealed a face on which is written suffering of many long hours, because Collins has been in agony every conscious moment since he was trapped," Skeets wrote in his first dispatch. Miller continued to visit, talk to, and feed Collins over the next few days. Even as Collins weakened, he refused to give up hope. Miller's dispatches from the cave became a national sensation. Crowds began to form outside the cave entrance and grew to the tens of thousands. Radio broadcasters did live reports from the site and vendors set up shop, hawking food and souvenirs. It was the original media circus, foreshadowing the Lindbergh baby kidnapping seven years later in the macabre hold it had on Americans' imaginations from coast to coast. Miller would come out of this with a Pulitzer Prize, but attempts to dig a rescue shaft continued to cause cave-ins, so soon even Miller couldn't get to Collins. Without food and water, the situation became hopeless. When a rescue shaft finally reached him seventeen days after he'd been trapped, Collins was dead, his leg still pinned to the wall. His father had to be asked for permission to sever the trapped limb so that the body could be removed.

Collins died in his natural tomb as Mack was still recovering from his own crushed leg. It had been three years since Mack had won $50 in the fiction contest for "Purple," which he would later say set him to writing for all he was worth, churning out stories as if he'd discovered a press that spit out greenbacks.

I thought with quivering satisfaction that I had now arrived. I was a writer in a big way. If anyone had told me that nearly six years would pass before I ever got any money out of a story again, I simply would not have believed him. . . . In school and out, I wrote stories and sent them confidently to the big magazines in the East, but the manuscripts bounced back like tennis balls. These successive failures continued, to my rage and astonishment, until I decided that I might be a poet instead of a writer of prose.

"The news about Floyd Collins, known previously only as a bumpkin who liked his moonshine, reached us on Tuesday, February 17th, 1925," Mack wrote. "I was thirteen days past my twenty-first birthday, and still lame . . . from another profitless operation the previous month. I shut myself off in the living room, turned on a storied green-shaded lamp, and appointed myself poet laureate of Sand Cave."

Mack had already been in the habit of writing poems and sending them out, hopeful. He even had some encouragement. One letter I found from 1924 was addressed to Mack from the publisher of a small magazine, with both encouraging and discouraging news: "I have never paid for verse . . . but yours are so good I am enclosing merely enough to assure you that I appreciate your kindness, namely $1.50."

Still hoping for a bigger payoff, the budding poet wrote a ballad in faux dialect called "Floyd Collins' Cave" and sent it off to the mighty *Chicago Tribune*. He was thrilled when it was printed in the paper's popular, Talk of the Townish, "Line O' Type or Two" column.

FLOYD COLLINS' CAVE
(Written as the ancient song-ballads of Kentucky were written.)

Oh, they say he is buried as deep as can be,
And the shovels thud down on the oily clay
Oh, Floyd Collins slid to a hole in the hill
And he's buried thar fur from the gold of the day.

And thar's moaning & moaning
Back in the cave,
Floyd Collins' cavern is Floyd Collins' grave!

Floyd ruther crawl to the gateway of hell
Than work with his Pa who loved him so well
Down in the earth thar was fairies and elves
And they tole him secrets that he wouldn't tell . . .
What's jest beyond, in the turn of the slide
Thar in the damp whar the cave crickets hide?
Less' go and see, Floyd, less' go and see
And they left him to sleep in the tomb whar he died.

And thar's moaning a moaning
Back in the cave,
Floyd Collins' palace is Floyd Collins' grave!

Yay! And he found it a silver lit hall
Further than Egypt and under a wall;
Big di'mond boulders that dripped with gold,
Fox-fire torches and that wasn't all . . .

Nobody ever saw Floyd's cave afore,
Nobody crawls in the hole anymore;
Floyd in his deep palace rules thar alone
Floyd in his last sleep guards the one door.

And thar's angels a-singing
Fur in the cave
Floyd Collins' heaven is Floyd Collins' grave!

Today it may be difficult to see much appeal in this rustic bit of verse. But in the midst of a 1925 media feeding frenzy, Mack's poetic telling of "Floyd Collins' Cave" hit, and hit big.

Mack felt the first tremors when the then legendary Richard Henry Little—a former war correspondent who edited the Line O' Type column—placed a long-distance call. "I remember his deep rumble and the ardent words," Mack wrote. "'Well, well, well, you're raising Ned all over the country!'"

"Raising Ned." Now there's an expression you don't hear much anymore. Still, I got the drift: The New York *Daily News* ran the poem as the editorial of the day. Papers across the country all jumped on the bandwagon, either printing the poem or making it the subject of weighty editorials on life and death. This, Mack wrote, was "the first great alteration brought about by my writing."

Little invited Mack to read the poem on the *Trib*'s powerful WGN radio—told him he'd put him up at a hotel, but that Mack needed to come up with the train fare, which he couldn't do. Plucky Webster City was behind him: A clerk at a bank where the family was in arrears on several loans handed him a cash-stuffed envelope for the ticket, and off he went to the big city.

I found a letter in one of the family correspondence folders—from Effie to her son—describing how, in March of 1925, all of Webster City frantically tuned in to WGN to catch the great moment:

"My dearest son," Effie began . . .

> Words fail to describe my feelings of today or last night when I heard you. The whole town listened in, or tried to. And while it is one of the most difficult stations for this locality to get, many were successful. . . . Mr. King had Mr. Parkhurst working with his wireless for a while, then Mr. P ran home to see if he could get it with his while Mr. K worked with all his might. Wilbur, Dorothy and I were over at the King's, and when presently Mr. P called over to tell us to come over at once, he had WGN, we jumped into the electric and went right over. There was quite a little gathering there, and though there was a lot of static, we heard everything fine. Kathryn almost had a paralytic stroke. She called grandpa and was shouting so he is laughing yet. She was never so excited in her life. The whole town was listening, all but poor Bill Corisis, whose candy pot caught on fire, and called out the department at 7:55 p.m.

After the reading, Little encouraged Mack to stay on in the city: "He thought that the *Tribune* would want me," Mack wrote. "That settled it for me. I was off to Chicago."

SEVEN

In 1925, Richard Henry Little was fifty-six years old—closer to John Kantor's age than Mack's, and an instant mentor and even a father figure to a young man who sorely needed one. He was storied and colorful enough to capture any aspiring writer's attention—and he lived in the fast lane, a mode of living Mack found increasingly attractive. An "eccentric round-shouldered giant . . . never truly sober," Mack called him. When Little died in 1946 his old paper wrote of him, "He was an Abraham Lincoln type in appearance, tall, gangling, and stoop-shouldered; a homely humorist whose vein was characteristic of his native prairies. Ben Hecht, who knew him well, once wrote: 'He might have become another Mark Twain.'"

Before settling into the folksy sinecure of the Line O' Type column, Little had covered the Spanish-American War, the uprising against American rule in the Philippines, the war between Russia and Japan, the Russian Revolution, and World War I. He was known for calmly remaining at the front lines when the shooting started and every other correspondent was sprinting for cover.

Not surprisingly, that nonchalance led to injuries: He was seriously wounded by shrapnel when embedded with a White Russian army unit battling the Bolsheviks.

"Life will have few charms for him until hell breaks loose again," his hometown paper observed admiringly in 1920. But by that point Little was fifty-one, and still troubled by his injuries, so he became a theater critic, then took over the Line column—gathering around him a group of talented contributors who, given his preference for hell breaking loose, also became companions for wild, boozy nights of hard partying.

In short, he had all the qualities that would move Mack to veneration.

Except one: His prediction that the *Trib* would find a place for Mack widely missed the mark.

"My virtues as a possible sensation were unappreciated by the powers there," Mack would later write. "I found myself twenty-one years old, with no great skill at verse, and a newly completed and perfectly frightful novel. I worked at one job after another, and wrote endless dirges and ballads for RHL's Line-O-Type column in the *Chicago Tribune*."

Yes, Little allowed him into his circle, and continued publishing small bits of his verse, but that wouldn't buy a hot dog on Michigan Avenue. Mack found lodging in a slum apartment and nursed his wounds, both emotional and physical. He'd discovered to his horror that no publication in Chicago was overly impressed with his career as a cub reporter in Webster City and his radio appearance as a poet. The short stories he sent out with such hope all came limping home without so much as an encouraging note. And his leg hurt as much as his pride. After several operations, the thigh injury from the auto accident had never properly healed, the shattered bone had developed a chronic infection called osteomyelitis, draining pus steadily through a wound that wouldn't close into bandages he had to change several times a day. He needed a cane to get around.

In one of the folders filled with clippings, I found a newspaper column in *The Sarasota Herald-Tribune* describing those early jobless days in Chicago. "The day came when young Kantor sat alone in his tiny, dingy room fearing immediate eviction, without money for food, with all job prospects exhausted . . . bandaging his ulcerating legs, trying to ignore his empty stomach and fearing the footsteps of the landlord. His only hope, at the moment, was that the mailman might bring some small check from a publisher. Finally, the mailman came and he did bring a letter [from his grandmother in Webster City]. Times were hard . . . , she wrote, and she was faced with imminent loss of her home . . . unless delinquent taxes in the sum of about $40 were paid. . . . 'I believe this was the darkest day in my life,' Kantor recalls now. 'I believe it was the only time I ever thought seriously of destroying myself.'"

Possibly drawing a lesson from his father about the power of making friends in Chicago's political structure, Mack wrote a letter to Anton Cermak, the president of the Cook County Board who would follow Big Bill into Chicago's mayor's office in 1931, only to be assassinated two years into his term at a political rally in Miami by an unemployed Italian bricklayer who was trying to shoot FDR instead. No copy of Mack's letter to Cermak was in the files, so I don't know if he used his father's name to make an impression. But why else would Cermak have pulled strings to find a job for a twenty-one-year-old unemployed writer from an Iowa farm town?

The job wasn't much—a surveyor's helper at $35 a week—but it brought him back from the brink.

Tromping around the county holding a surveying pole was not the best job for someone with pus oozing from the open wound in his thigh. In the annotations, Mack said he actually enjoyed having a job that took him out into the open air, but ultimately the physical requirements simply proved too much, given his condition. Plus, he found alternative employment that would at least make nominal use of his writing talent: creating ad copy for American Flyer, the toy-train company then based in Chicago.

Employment of any kind, though he was still barely getting by, produced enough optimism for him to try to connect to life in the city. Looking to meet people his own age, he responded to an ad in the *Tribune*: "Wanted. Talented people to join drama group. Write Apartment O, 541 North Michigan Avenue."

And by people his own age, I mean women.

Of his ensuing theatrical career, Mack said, "I pursued one babe after another."

Based on what I'd seen, this was more than believable. In his letters to friends as a teenager he was frequently gushing over his latest crush, one after the other. A typical passage: "You sure ought to see her. Blue eyes and a wonderful complexion. Exquisite brown hair. I never knew her until the beginning of second semester, but the moment I walked into history class, I *knew*."

I had to read the letter several times before I noticed the most telling point. The "brown" in "exquisite brown hair" was overstruck on his typewriter. Looking closely, I saw quite clearly that he had originally written "exquisite blonde hair" before he'd revisited his indelible impressions. Obviously, this great love wasn't destined to last. In fact, in the annotations, Mack noted that when he left for Chicago in 1924, "I was in love again" with a different girl back in Webster City. Clearly, young Mack had an enthusiastic eye for ladies in the aggregate. Not an uncommon trait, but one that I shared and sometimes, when I found myself appreciating a passing feminine form fervidly to the point of rudeness, wished I shared to a lesser degree.

I had my first crush, and girlfriend, in kindergarten: Karen Harvey. We made a clubhouse in a storage room in my basement, collected rocks, climbed up on the roof of the shed, and pretended we were flying to the moon. There was nothing physical between us, but my attachment to her was passionate, unlike any friendship I had with a boy. When her family announced they were moving out of town, heartbroken, I went into my toy closet and collected some of my favorite plastic cowboy and Indian figures to hand to her as she left. After that came Eileen, then Erica, then Sherri, the physical impulse becoming more prominent as childhood bled into adolescence. I'd often assumed there was a spectrum of sexual drive and that I was on the high side, at times to my shame. In Mack's unbridled enthusiasm for women, I realized I might be seeing my own, literally, as in a particular chain of twisting chromosomes passed through my mother that, in some unfathomably complex way, through the production or repression of proteins, resulted in that particular flame burning hot. I did some searching and discovered that, in 2006, Israeli researchers provided some scientific support for that idea: Test subjects who scored high on sexual interest questionnaires were more likely to have a particular gene sequence than those who did not. And this was just one of the hundreds (thousands?) of gene sequences that determine the brain chemistry involved in sexual desire. So clearly it would be possible to inherit an array of such genes, all tending in the same direction.

In any case, there's no avoiding the fact that the male brain is the product of two million years of evolving the ability to recognize, and respond to, the visual clues of female fertility. One hopes it's also evolved to recognize that women are far more than the sum of their parts. I've always admired men who never let a voluptuous figure make them forget that essential reality for even the briefest moment—if there are any such men.

Anyway, Mack wasn't one of them.

By Friday, April 2, 1926, Mack had become a member of the cozy theater group—named the Graeme Players for their grande dame and director, Sigrid Graeme, who Mack described as middle-aged even though she was only thirty. Producing plays was the least of what went on in Apartment O. On most nights, it was more like a social club than an acting studio, and this particular Friday was no different. After a modest communal dinner of bologna, macaroni, and cabbage salad, the stalwarts were helping Miss Graeme paint her bathroom when the buzzer rang.

She said, "Somebody please go down and tell the visitors to *go away!*"

"I'll get rid of 'em," Mack said.

Predictably, some of the other boys said not to get rid of any good-looking girls. Mack needed no instruction on that point. He descended the five flights of stairs and opened the door:

"She was a trifle over five feet tall, dainty on her high heels, and she wore a maroon winter coat with gray squirrel trimmings, and a little aqua hat. Her face seemed made mostly of eyes . . . great gray-green ones."

Much later, Mack would learn that Irene recorded her own impression of that first encounter in a diary she had been keeping for years.

It read: "Went to the Graeme Players, an amateur drama group, for the first time tonight. Met MacKinlay Kantor who writes for the Line O' Type column. I had already cut out 'Floyd Collins' Cave' and 'Leather Gods.' But he ran down to answer my ring wearing an old khaki flannel shirt and a black vest. Ugh."

Apparently, I also inherited my grandfather's fashion sense. Fortunately, his literary qualifications seemed to compensate in Irene's estimation. I also noticed something else, something telling. According to Mack, "She neglected to write in [her diary] any more, soon after we met."

But on that evening, Mack was unaware of either his own attire or the effect he would have on Irene's future literary output. Getting rid of her was the last thing on his mind. He invited her in, warned her of the long climb, then gestured for her to precede him up the first flight "so I could have a chance to see if I liked her legs."

He did. And at that moment, Mack trailing behind her, appreciatively, up the stairs, I became a distinct possibility.

Irene Layne was a commercial artist who had been laid off from her job and now was "temporarily" painting lampshades in a kind of assembly line of kitsch. She wanted to be a real artist. She came from a large middle-class Chicago family touched heavily by tragedy. Her mother had birthed seven children, one of whom died in infancy. When Irene was seven, despite warnings from the doctor, her mother got pregnant again. She died a week after giving birth, and the new baby girl died weeks after that.

I learned all of this from Mack's account of their first date. Irene unaccountably felt she could tell him everything, even though she'd never talked about it with anyone before. Mack was struck by her openness and warmth. He fell hard.

He was twenty-two, and Irene was lovely, and had good legs, and it could have been that simple. But maybe there was something else, something deeper and more forceful even than a well-turned ankle that powered Mack's need.

Deep into my research I came across a letter from him to his sister from that same time period that stunned me. He wrote of "a very startling July morning when a brusque German doctor told me that mother would do a very remarkable and unlooked for thing if she recovered."

At first I didn't know what he could be referring to. I had grown up knowing very little about my great-grandmother's life, and less about her death. I eventually figured out that she had suffered permanent heart damage from childhood rheumatic fever, and had a near fatal cardiac episode more than five years before she died—just three months after Mack and Irene met.

"That knocked me cold," he wrote to Virginia of getting news of the heart attack. "I was weak, yet stony, not knowing if the future held anything or not. Mother dead . . . No, I couldn't go through it alone. Mother lay there in bed with her heart pounding away, fretfully yet energetically discussing plans for the future 'as soon as I am up.' You with your baby four hundred miles away. Grandpa and Grandma old and dependent. . . . No one to tell or talk to, but Irene."

Irene, too, suffered—and something far worse than a scare. In early May, just a month after meeting, Mack and Irene returned from a date to discover Irene's father, Charles, hurrying out the front door with Kenny, her fifteen-year-old brother—the youngest of her siblings and her favorite—bent over in his father's arms, his face white and his big brown eyes wide.

They got to the hospital too late. The boy's appendix burst, and he died.

Mack—who had already become a regular in the family home on Wilson Avenue and no doubt saw it as an omen that he, too, had grown up on a *Willson* Avenue (with two *l*'s) in Webster City—became a source of solace not just for Irene but for the whole Layne family. His warmth and humor had been welcome from the start. On his first visit, he sat for a more or less formal vetting by Charles, who worked on the Chicago Mercantile Exchange as a farm products broker. When Charles asked Mack what he was interested in, Mack answered, "Poetry, for one thing."

Charles jumped out of his chair with excitement about their shared interest, exclaiming, "Poultry!"

They all laughed long and hard about that, and the memory of humor lingered even when Kenny's loss extinguished all ability for joy, giving some hope of a world that offered feelings other than pain to anticipate.

So Irene had Mack to tell, and talk to, just as Mack had Irene.

By Friday, July 2, 1926, Mack had been carrying a wedding license around in his pocket for three weeks. Then, either the morning before or that very morning—"a very startling July morning," the letter had said—he got the bad news from the German doctor.

He never said it directly, but the dates left little doubt: Hearing that his mother might be dying spurred him immediately to action. His recounting of that second day of July in a letter he wrote to his sister almost three months later made it even clearer:

"I was so worried about mother and feeling so blue, wondering if it was a wise step or not, and assailed by a thousand doubts."

This letter was dated September, yet he was telling his beloved sister of his marriage for the first time, begging her forgiveness, and trying to explain why he had kept it a secret for so long: he had creditors who would look askance . . . Effie was in no condition . . . and other excuses that were equally unconvincing. I think the real reasons must have been that he was so young and unsure and frightened about making his private reality an actual reality. Frightened, mainly, of telling his mother, because he knew what she would say—thinking of his future, not wanting him to be so burdened so young. When he finally did tell her, her response was the temperature of a corpse stretched rigid in a morgue freezer. "I don't know what to say. What is there I can say? You've told me that you are married. I suppose that's it."

The letter to Virginia was two pages long, age-darkened, stapled with a rusty bit of metal and torn around the edges. The typewriter used to type it had clearly been old in 1926, leaving letters smudged and unevenly struck, bleeding line to line on the close, single-space margins. As I read further, grasping what this letter was, I instinctively caressed the page with my fingertips and felt a chill run through me. It was just a letter, yet I felt transported through time, paradoxically present, in a sense, at my own creation.

It said:

> I called Irene at noon and told her I would meet her when she came from work that night. . . . We walked east on Madison street, and stopped in a doorway between Michigan and Wabash. Everyone was rushing by from work—I remember seeing an acquaintance pass with some friends. It was a smoky warm evening with the sun bravely shining through a fog over the western buildings. We discussed whether we really ought to get married then. Irene was a bit doubtful, while I became more and more convinced—quite blindly—that it would be a good thing. We went over and ate at the Polly tea room. It is a very prosey

inexpensive place with groups of chattering shop girls smoking all over the room. We ate on the balcony and I don't think we ate a lot. There was cake for dessert, and I put a tiny piece of each of our cakes in a Melachrino cigarette box. We still have it, and you may like a crumb some day. It is probably turned to stone by now.

Then we walked up Michigan Avenue and took a bus at the library, riding north to Chestnut street, where we walked east to the big gray Fourth Presbyterian Church on the Drive. We went into the church office and told the young man at the switchboard that we wanted to be married, and went to wash up in the toilet rooms. When we came back, he informed me that one of the ministers would probably be around in about an hour. We couldn't have waited an hour if the bishop himself was to have married us, and very nervously told the young man that it was all right—oh quite all right—but that would he mind if we were married elsewhere? He glared in a very un-Christian manner, but we fled. I shall not detail the extent of our wanderings over the lower North side on that eventful evening. We never knew how really rare ministers are. Like policemen, when you find one you don't need him—and when you want one you can't find him. At least in Chicago. We visited Methodist and Evangelical book stores in hope of finding a stray parson or two. We consulted the Red phone book and checked off those at nearby addresses. One was in a gloomy tenement. "I wouldn't be married by anyone living there!" declared Irene. One was a woman minister. "I wouldn't feel we were legally married by a woman minister." And so Irene banned that, too. We waited half an hour in St. James Episcopal church—the holy of holies for Chicago's rich—while an obliging janitor hunted in the study, bathroom and coal bin for the rector, who he assured us, would be back "pooty soon." Well pooty soon came and he wasn't back. The old rectum didn't look so good after and we decamped.

I went into a Masonic Hall where a meeting was in progress, but the chaplain belonged to some other profession—plumbing I think—and was positive that he couldn't do the trick in a sacred manner. A lot of the addresses proved to be those of Catholic priests, who weren't eligible. Finally, we followed up a tip from some worthy and sought the Moody Bible Institute at Chicago Ave. and La Salle. The library was full of studious young people of all sexes and sizes. They hunted a fat, genial Mr. Lundquist out of his office. He was an ordained minister from Indiana, and hadn't married anyone for ten years or so, but was certain he could do it. Our patience was at an end and our feet tired. Thus we were married by a wet Baptist. The witnesses were future missionaries to the cannibal islands. . . . Irene said "I will" at one vague, musty place where she should have said I do, so I'm sure we're living together illegally. Then everyone shook hands, the witnesses signed, and I gave the minister an American Flyer envelope with three dollars in it—all I had—while we ran before he could open it and kick us where it would do the most good. . . . We ran over [to] the Graeme Players for an hour, and then home, and Irene had to give me car and bus fare. . . .

No persons were married—ever—under less auspicious circumstances, and none will ever be happier, I am sure.

On the last Sunday in June of 2014, three days short of the eighty-eighth anniversary of my grandparents' impromptu wedding, my wife, Lisa, and I set out from our hotel in Chicago with the vague intent of finding the Moody Bible Institute, if it still existed. We had been married for more than a quarter of a century ourselves at that point, and I had seen enough in the Library of Congress files to suspect that we were indeed a couple that disproved my grandfather's prophecy by being happier than he and Irene had been—but that's getting ahead of the story. In any case, I'd been pondering the impulsive Friday night proposal in 1926, considering it a bristling example of youthful folly. Then I did the math. At exactly the same age, exactly half a century later, I committed my own impulsive union. That marriage, though it produced a beautiful child, struggled along for nine years before it ended. She had beauty, charm, and intelligence. We managed some good moments, tried ineptly, or impossibly, to make it work for the sake of the daughter we both adored, but I suspected from the start—from before the ceremony—that it just wasn't right. I wasn't ready to marry anyone.

During the most difficult moments, I often had cause to think about the nature of the twenty-two-year-old male brain, doomed to a false belief in its own maturity. When I tried to remember my state of mind, recall what I had been thinking, exactly, when I recited the marriage vows I had written myself, I had to confess that I hadn't thought about it in any coherent way at all. I had simply lunged, trusting that if I didn't look down, the lack of solid ground beneath me would somehow not be a problem.

Twenty-two.

But youth can't explain why, ten years later, I proposed to Lisa only three months after we'd met, the same mad schedule by which Mack had proposed to Irene. We had been swinging in a hammock in my backyard, and it suddenly seemed absurd to me to behave as if she were anything other than the woman with whom I wanted to spend the rest of my life. I would argue that this time it was a vision, not an impulse, that compelled me. But maybe it was some genetic predisposition after all. The discovery of these parallels between my life and my grandfather's were beginning to get a little eerie.

In any case, when I blurted my proposal there in the hammock, Lisa, then thirty-one, had the good sense to say, "Ask me again later."

After a barely respectable interlude, I did. One year following our meeting we were married, not by a random wet Baptist, but by the mayor of Miami Beach, which was random in its own way. Now, twenty-seven years later, we were in Chicago on a warm, humid summer morning, hunting for coffee. Neither of us knew the town well, so we just walked down Michigan Avenue until we passed Millennium Park. The waterfront, with its sculptures and fountains and gardens, was in full bloom. I discovered later that, in 1926, it would have been an unsightly tangle of train tracks and parking lots. We turned right on Madison Street. Just a block in, we noticed the back entrance to a patisserie. Good coffee, good pastries, long line. When we finally got a table, I pulled out my phone and googled Moody Bible Institute. It was still there, I discovered, and not too far to the north, almost a straight shot up Michigan back the way we had come, on the other side of the river, barely a mile and a half distant. We decided to walk. As we made our way north, the warm air grew hot and sticky, and the streetscape stark, uninviting. I tried to picture my grandparents, giddy, scared, filled with joy and anticipation, walking toward the same destination, and the rest of their lives. For them it was a summer evening, not midmorning, so the hot sun wouldn't have been a bother, as it was for us, and the world would have been set aglow in any case by the terrifying, exciting romantic adventure they were lost in.

Perhaps this slice of north-side Chicago we walked through would have been livelier, more fascinating, in 1926; or perhaps it would only have been so in my grandparents' glittering eyes. As we approached a Gothic-arched side door of the Bible Institute, the place seemed deserted, but the door was unlocked. It opened into a small alcove with steps leading up to a locked glass door on which a sign read FIRE-ARMS PROHIBITED.

No wet Baptists in sight.

I couldn't guess which door Mack and Irene had entered, or where they stood when their improvised ceremony united them. I tried to feel some connection to this place, these bricks that were undoubtedly the same, this very mortar somehow tied to my own existence. I tried, and failed, to see anything more than a not-very-interesting building.

Back home in Virginia, I reread the letter describing the elope-ment and began to plot on a map the route my grandfather had described in such detail, starting at the point where Mack pressed his proposal. "We walked east on Madison street, and stopped in a door-way between Michigan and Wabash."

I had a funny sensation, and thought, *It couldn't be.* I searched for Toni Patisserie, where Lisa and I had begun the morning with a long wait for good coffee. I clicked on MAP and it materialized on my screen: the back entrance where Lisa and I exited our breakfast to embark for the Moody Institute that morning was a doorway, between Michigan and Wabash, on Madison Street.

If it was not the exact spot where my grandfather had proposed to my grandmother, it was within ten feet.

EIGHT

—

I got a very nitty-gritty view of my grandparents' early marriage from a 1927 letter Mack wrote to Effie. After living apart for several months following the wedding—ostensibly to keep their marriage a secret (from creditors and from family)—they finally dropped the charade and found themselves in a tiny walk-up apartment with two windows, one of which was painted shut, looking out on a dreary air shaft between buildings. At the end of the hall was the single bathroom shared by all the residents of that floor.

Last night I did some necessary work here at the typewriter. Irene sits ironing while I pound the keyboard. This letter is being written at ten in the evening; when finished I shall get into bed while we read Under the Lilacs *and eat our usual late evening*

*lunch of popcorn and milk out of Japanese bowls I bought for ten
cents each. . . .*

*The French girls still tramp up and down the hall with towels
and soap and more towels and soap, but have found their usual
regime sorely shattered since I became publicly married, for Irene
and I work the bathroom in shifts as they used to do, and they
come tapping at the door, muttering in heathenish jargon and
departing in disgust. . . . I sing the "Marseillaise" or "Mademoi-
selle from Armentières" most of the time as I wash in the morning
for their especial benefit.*

This bare-bones ménage might seem a little grim, but for the newlyweds it was a heavenly improvement. One day at work, Irene, bursting with love, snuck into a stockroom to write Mack a letter that
couldn't wait:

*You are part of me—the sweetest most thoughtful lover and
husband a girl could ever have. What does it matter that we're a
bit poverty stricken now? Some day we'll look back at now and
laugh and be happy over it all—and never think that I shall slave
and save for you and be unable to keep up with you when the time
comes—Ah, no, Adorable! You are saddled with me for life! . . .*

Mack appreciated their new arrangement from a more practical
vantage point: "At a conservative estimate I spent more than 180 hours
during the more than five months from the time I met Irene until we
announced our marriage in riding back and forth from her home on
the street car. More than a week of twenty-four-hour days! At that rate,
I actually lost three weeks of sleep. . . . So you can imagine the benefi-
cial change our new circumstance has made. . . ."

In October, he wrote Effie a letter for her forty-seventh birthday, "still trying to sell Mother on the idea that my marriage was all for the good, and that she was still very important in my life," he noted in his annotations.

His plea began "Since Irene and I were married, I've begun to realize how many things you taught me which have made my married life happier by far than it ever could otherwise have been. I mean your efforts—so many times grievously unrewarded!—to instill a bit of patience, foresight and steadiness in the breast of a kicking mule.

"Just because I cannot write long letters often, is no reason for you to believe that I no longer love you as I did. . . . I think of you always."

The reason he had so little time was that, when he wasn't working, he was pounding away on the typewriter on a seemingly endless series of stories, all of which got him nowhere. Mack noted that, between 1923 and 1926, he'd submitted hundreds of manuscripts for publication with next to nothing to show for it. "Most of these were misguided, inept and unsuccessful for I had little to offer as yet, except a scorching ambition."

It was the inevitable chain of disappointment that tests any writer's will. In one letter he lamented: "The damndest luck! I submitted a story to the *DeMolay Councillor* and yesterday got the manuscript back with a letter saying they had planned to buy it but that the *Councillor* was going to be suspended this month. Isn't that hell?"

Still, both he and Irene had slightly improved their employment situations. Mack had quit American Flyer to work in the claims department of Mandel Bros. department store, writing letters to people whose merchandise had been lost or broken in shipping. He'd gotten a raise to $30 a week with the additional benefit that Mandel's was in the Loop, just across the street from Irene's new place of employment— she'd traded her hated chore of window-shade painting for a job advising customers in the art framing department of Carson's department store on State Street.

They luxuriated in the ability to meet for lunch during the workday, and on weekends socialized with fellow Graeme Players or Dick Little's crowd. Mostly they enjoyed each other's company. One weekend they went to Lincoln Park Zoo and Mack howled at the wolves until they started howling back and the keepers chased them off.

But Mack suffered in his work: "I was finding affirmation of a hideous truth. Most people didn't like the jobs which life compelled them to hold. . . . Far cry from the small town newspaper effort of an earlier epoch. Mother and I worked day and night and . . . truly loved every minute of it."

Trying to spin their situation positively, Mack wrote home, "We are well and fine and have no children or prospects! We are awaiting all breaks of luck. . . ."

And soon a lucky break would come, in the form of an unassuming "While you were out" message left on Mack's desk in the claims department at Mandel Bros., waiting for him when he returned from lunch one day.

I came across that note, sitting by itself, in one of the Library of Congress files. Written in pen, in a feminine cursive hand, it said, *Kantor / Call Mr. Farquhar / R 540 Great Northern Hotel.*

I recognized the note immediately, because Mack had mentioned it in his autobiography sequel:

"The key landed in the dungeon cell with a clang, sooner than had seemed possible. On my desk appeared a note concerning the publisher of the *Cedar Rapids Republican.*"

The notepaper was in remarkable condition, and the ink appeared as dark and unsmudged as the day it was written.

I was impressed that this humble slip of paper had survived the chaos of all the life that followed it, and ended up here in the Madison building. It had been just one year shy of ninety years since some secretary or switchboard operator had neatly inscribed that cryptic, but oh so portentous message.

I understood why he had kept it. I had such messages in my life, deceptively mundane but life-changing messages that had reared up on this or that desk or sideboard, radiating alarm or promise, instantaneously altering the look of whatever place it lay—the very light surrounding it—with a rush of blood to the brain. Some of the portents were not good ones: for instance, the torn scrap of notebook paper left on my desk at *The Cincinnati Enquirer* by a colleague in the middle of the day, greeting me as I returned from an interview, which said, "Call your brother." It wasn't that I didn't frequently talk to my brother on the phone, I did, but in this pre-cell-phone era he had never, not once, called me at work.

The expression "My heart is in my throat" stops being a cliché in moments like that. As I dialed, I knew I didn't want to know. I found out anyway: My father, a heavy smoker for forty years, had coughed up a significant amount of blood. Within fifteen months, he was gone, and in my mind, it always began with that slip of a note lurking malignantly on my desk.

But mostly I thought of the good messages, and one especially, exactly parallel to what Mack found waiting for him at Mandel's that day ninety years ago, a note that said, "Call Joe Workman, Fort Myers *News-Press*," which led me to that claustrophobic suburban bureau with the hard-drinking bureau chief and the nasty society lady, which led to other such messages, and other jobs, and a career in newspapers that stretched through thirty-three years to one final, unexpected note waiting on my desk, announcing that I was eligible for, and encouraged to take, a buyout from *The Washington Post*.

———

James S. Farquhar published a medium-size city paper in Cedar Rapids, Iowa—1926 population, 55,000—130 miles from Webster City. The father of Dick Whiteman, the one Webster City friend Mack would remain close to his entire life, was a prominent businessman with many contacts—including Farquhar. The elder Whiteman had put in a good word for Mack with the publisher, who looked up some of Mack's work for *The Webster City Daily News* and the *Tribune*, and now he was sitting across the dinner table from him at a Chicago hotel.

Farquhar talked about the job. He liked what he had seen of Mack's work, as the stories he'd done on old pioneers and ancient Civil War vets and quaint local customs were exactly the kind of thing the publisher was looking for. It all seemed to Mack too good to be real. And then Farquhar asked him how much money he would need. He heard himself, as from a great distance, say, "Could you manage $50 a week?" The figure—more than what Mack and Irene now made jointly—seemed preposterous, and when Farquhar countered with $40, Mack was almost relieved. It was a 33 percent increase in pay for Mack, and it would go as far in Cedar Rapids as the full $50 would have taken him in Chicago.

In Cedar Rapids, he and Irene could live on his salary alone. Later that night when he gave Irene the news, the two of them held hands and danced in circles in their crummy little apartment, imagining a much richer life in Cedar Rapids.

That Sunday, they continued their celebration with a dinner at Irene's folks' house. Mack lost himself in the fragrant casserole dish filled with fresh lima beans baked overnight with onion, Worcestershire sauce, brown sugar, and a dash of mustard, and didn't even notice when Irene was summoned from the table. He did notice when she didn't come back. He found her out on the porch, staring into the night, gripping a folded sheet of paper until it warped and twisted in her hands. When he looked at her questioningly, she extended it to him.

Mack opened the folded sheet to the letterhead of an advertising art agency. This was the company Irene had applied to before she and Mack had met, the job she coveted but thought she had no chance of getting. The letter explained that the agency had no openings when she'd applied, but they had noted the quality of her portfolio and filed it. Now they wanted to offer her a position as a staff artist.

Mack wrote that he felt like tentacles had wrapped around his chest, squeezing so he could barely breathe. Forcing out the words, he said he guessed maybe he could stand the claims department a little longer, until he could start selling his short stories, anyway, and that with the salary Irene could get as an advertising artist, plus what he made pursuing broken lamps and scratched furniture, they could get a decent apartment. . . .

Irene stopped him. "I will write to them and tell them I can't possibly consider it," she said.

The tentacles released their grip.

"You won't be angry, jealous, resentful?" he asked.

Of course not, she said. "I'll just take pride in the fact that these people did want me after all."

"Those years of struggle to attend classes at the Chicago Academy of Fine Arts and the Art Institute had borne only this small and suddenly sweetly bitter fruit," Mack wrote. "That night I would awaken to find her crying."

Any regrets about the impact on Irene of their move to Cedar Rapids quickly dissipated in Mack's mind. At twenty-three, he had obtained his dream.

"I was subsisting by the typewriter itself—by activity of fingers, memory, and whatever perceptivity I had acquired . . . and, above all, whatever skills one might burnish in the management of words. . . . Here was a typewriter on its scant desk in the newsroom, and my name and title on a card fastened against glass up above . . . *Special Assignment Reporter.*"

I knew just how he felt. My first professional reporting job, exactly a half century later, was for a paper of precisely the same relative size and stature (allowing for a near doubling of the U.S. population) as *The Cedar Rapids Republican.* In those days, even a midsize paper loomed large in its own domain. I'll never forget the swell of power, the frisson that came with picking up the phone and appending the name of your newspaper to your own. You sensed the people on the other end of the line growing instantly alert—whether through alarm, curiosity, or delight. Being a reporter throughout most of the twentieth century had sex appeal, dash, *significance.* People made movies about reporters, wrote books about them—we were *players.*

It's become a more complicated calculus in recent years—given the decline of newspapers and the rise of chaotic and ubiquitous communication on the Web, where amateur bloggers, "citizen journalists," and Twitter feeds have diluted and confused the cachet of being a working reporter. Reading Mack's description made me realize that my career in newspapers—beginning in 1976 and stretching into the first decade of the twenty-first century—had been as similar to his experience at *The Cedar Rapids Republican* as it was alien to that of a twenty-something hired by *The Washington Post* today as a "mobile innovations optimizer" or "viral meme checker," or whatever incomprehensible job title they come up with to mask the stark fact that professional news organizations are groping blindly toward a problematic future.

And though, in the 1970s, I would not have seen Cedar Rapids,

Iowa, as a destination for someone with literary or media ambitions, in the 1920s, the American Midwest emerged as a cultural hot spot. Writers and newspapermen like Ernest Hemingway, F. Scott Fitzgerald, Sherwood Anderson, and Sinclair Lewis all drew heavily on their Midwestern backgrounds for inspiration. All those fertile plains and that pioneer can-do spirit fed a uniquely American aesthetic and reflected the dynamism of a continental power rising to world preeminence. This somehow translated into surging creativity in the letters and arts.

So it was somewhat more than a freakish coincidence that, when Mack and Irene rented a room in a former mansion, the two large south-facing windows overlooked a rooftop apartment in the renovated barn of a funeral home that was the home and studio of Grant Wood— not yet, but soon to become, one of the most iconic American artists of the twentieth century. Wood would live in that apartment—in which he had famously adapted a glass coffin lid for use as a front door—for many years. But when Mack and Irene became over-the-back-fence neighbors in 1926, Wood was still early in residence there, and in his career. Soon he would become a pillar of the growing "regionalist" movement in art, or as he put it, "an American way of looking at things, and a utilization of the materials of our own American scene."

Whether Mack articulated it or not, his profound affection for his Webster City upbringing and the broad-shouldered grime of Chicago, his reverence for the rugged pioneers of the generations preceding him and pride in the growth of American power—and even the fact that his education had been rustic, at best, innocent of the European focus of an elite university—made Wood, thirteen years his senior, a natural role model and inspiration.

"His standards were exacting, determined," Mack wrote of him. "Requisitely he painted with sublimity in the face of popular opinion, popular belief and acceptance. . . . I had been of the same inclination from the start of my writing days at sixteen, but sometimes feared that I was mistaken in this course."

His association with Wood confirmed for him that, as he put it, "my way was right and another man's way—the wrong way."

That certainty is astounding considering that, when Mack arrived in Cedar Rapids in 1926, he'd yet to publish anything of significance, beyond a short story and a few poems. Yet here he was, assuming common ground with Grant Wood! The fact that Wood had just established a community theater, much like the Graeme Players, the previous year—even staging the group's first production in his loft studio—made his mind-meld with the young couple next door complete.

They quickly became close friends.

I had no idea. None. Like everyone else, I'd seen *American Gothic*—the gaunt, elderly rubes rigidly facing the viewer, propped up by a pitchfork—in various incarnations and representations, about ten million times. As an editor, like a million editors before me, I'd commissioned parodies of Wood's most famous painting at least twice—and probably more, I am not proud to admit.

And yet I remember not a single mention, from my grandfather, grandmother, mother, or anyone else about this close association with the man on every list of America's greatest painters.

Like other intriguing pieces of my grandfather's life, the full picture didn't emerge in a single passage in a book, Google hit, or yellowing piece of typing paper. It was, rather, like an archaeological dig, the shovel chunking on a tusk, or thighbone, followed by the careful scraping away of the surrounding sediment to reveal other fragments in particular relationship, each changing the initial idea of the find until an overall pattern emerged. And the pattern of his friendship with Grant Wood would alter surprisingly as I dug deeper.

When I first searched for joint mentions of my grandfather and the painter, I came up with something that indicated quite other than reverence in Mack's attitude toward Wood. In R. Tripp Evans's 2010 biography, *Grant Wood: A Life,* a book that critics said "blew the cover off Grant Wood's homosexuality," my grandfather was granted a surprising role in the artist's evolution.

Evans cited a gossip item that Mack had published about Wood. Speaking of him as a "confirmed bachelor," the gossip piece continued: "Pink of face and plump of figure, he was most nearly in character one night when he appeared at a costume party dressed as an angel—wings, pink flannel nightie, pink toes, and even a halo, supported by a stick thrusting up his back."

As one reviewer of the book pointed out: "Not only did Kantor link Wood's costume to common stereotypes of the 'fairy,' but after comparing Wood to Snow White, who lay imprisoned in a glass coffin awaiting her prince's kiss, Kantor wrote: 'The front door of his apartment is made of glass, but it's a coffin lid. OOOOOOoooooh!' Kantor then exhorted the 'boys' among his readers to 'look [Wood] over.' The meaning of all this is quite evident, unless one doesn't want to see."

Not only did Evans suggest that Mack, Wood's supposed friend, was outing him as a homosexual against his will, but that this had the effect of forcing Wood to abandon his frequent use of a beret in favor of the decidedly unfeminine overalls he took to wearing to bolster a "farmer-painter" pose, and—more significantly—to turn away from his earlier painting style of impressionism, fearing it might appear effeminate, in favor of the stern Gothic realism that led directly to *American Gothic,* which, when it was exhibited in 1930, made him an instant international celebrity.

I had to laugh at my grandfather's apparent Forrest Gump–like ability to pop up in the background of these historical tableaus. First "bomb Vietnam back into the Stone Age," and now shaming Grant Wood into *American Gothic*?

I found nothing to indicate that Mack had ever been accused of outing Wood during his lifetime—which by any calculus would have been a dishonorable move, even if it did push Wood to create his masterwork (which I doubt). Instead, I found this passage Mack wrote about Wood in the 1970s:

"People . . . whispered he was a homosexual. He was nothing of the kind. He was simply asexual—withdrawn by inclination, habit and choice. . . ."

As I dug deeper into ever-higher-numbered boxes at the Library of Congress, more pieces of the puzzle emerged. It certainly became clear that Grant Wood bore Mack no ill will. On the contrary, through the years he sent hand-lettered Christmas cards with breathtaking original lithographs he'd made of rural scenes accompanied by affectionate personal notes. (I found myself greedily wishing that my grandfather had passed these particular documents along to me, rather than to the Library.) In 1935, after one of my grandfather's novels—about foxhunting with hounds in Missouri—was reviewed harshly in *The New York Times*, Wood wrote a long, passionate letter of defense to the book section editor.

Because the novel afforded me a great deal of delight and because a parallel case might be found in the criticism of painting, I could not resist writing with regard to it. Mr. Kantor has dared an extremely difficult form of art and in addition has chosen a phase of American life, which, while perfectly authentic, is almost unknown and thus extremely complicating the problem of a novelist. Yet he has emerged with a novel which is a work of art.

But I also found a bitterly angry 1974 letter from Wood's sister, Nan Wood Graham, the very woman who posed for the indelible character in *American Gothic* (and, judging from that face in the painting, not the individual you want pissed at you). The letter, ironically, was not referring to the 1920s gossip item, but to what Mack thought of as his defense of Wood as being asexual, not homosexual—which had just been published in his memoir.

"I am very hurt and bewildered at what you have done to a fine man's memory," she wrote. "Grant considered you a friend and confided in you but you certainly haven't turned out to be such. Even his very worst enemies did not suggest that he was neuter."

She went on at length, suggesting that Mack "jumped to conclusions" because her brother had "high morals" and refused to consort with "immoral women" as well as possessing a "great fear of syphilis." That he was a "perfectly normal, decent man.

"The night you claim you sat up all night drinking, no doubt *you* did plenty of talking too. But Grant was too much of a gentleman to betray your confiding in him, let alone bray it to the world. . . ."

In conclusion she wrote, "It is a shame he ever met such a cheap person as you . . . his pretend friend."

Evans's biography closed the case for many by insisting that Wood was in fact obviously and conspicuously gay. But *New York Times* art critic Deborah Solomon was not convinced:

> *A man who stifles his desires to the point of near extinction cannot accurately be called gay, and by the end of the book the reader has no idea whether Wood was ever intimate with a man. Affairs are hinted at, but the author is unable to document them; Wood himself claimed to be innocent of carnal satisfactions. One of his friends is quoted in the book recalling a night when Wood*

seems to have confessed to being chastely asexual, which is not implausible.

Knowing what I now know, it is clear that friend was my grandfather. And maybe he was right.

But that was not the most intriguing thing I discovered about their relationship. In early January 1941, Wood's friend and PR person wrote Mack to say,

> *You are about to lose a dear friend. Grant Wood has been ill for several months with what we first thought was a gall bladder ailment. Recently an operation was performed. The doctors found cancer of the liver. Of course, there is no hope. . . .*
>
> *I know that Grant would like a letter from you. Just a casual note, mentioning perhaps that you read of his operation in the paper and hope that he is feeling better. He speaks of you frequently: wonders how your work is coming and how you and your family are. I'm sorry to write you this stunning news. But I knew you would want to know.*

Mack responded—how could he not?—though no copy of the letter is in the file. But two weeks later, on January 23, Grant wrote what must have been one of the last letters of his life.

> *Your note was waiting for me when I got back to Iowa City. . . . I intended to get in touch with you (when we were both in New York) but I came down with a bad case of the flu. . . . I'm back home taking it easy for a while. Florida sounds fine and I'd love to see you and Irene. But I'm afraid that's out of the question just now. . . .*

Along with the letter he sent another stunning woodblock: three horses standing in the snow behind a barbed-wire fence, staring—eyelessly—at the viewer beneath a threatening sky. The fact that the horses number three could not be a coincidence. The image is stunningly apocalyptic. The creatures are so black only the outline of their bulk is visible, except for the wisps of manes and tails blowing in a cold wind—a stunning, frightening void. Even so, there is something about their pose, the slant of neck and head perhaps, that suggests expectancy, as if they are waiting for something, possibly warmth, or comfort.

Though the letter is dated January, the piece is titled *February*.

Eighteen days later, on February 13, Mack got a telegram: "Grant Wood died peacefully Thursday night."

It's interesting to speculate what would have happened to Mack if, like me, his first newspaper job had led to a slightly better job or a slightly bigger newspaper, which led to a mediocre larger city newspaper, which led to an excellent big-city newspaper, which led to one of the great newspapers in the world.

But it didn't.

In early 1927, not yet a year after Mack took the job, the *Republican* was bought out, and the entire staff canned.

"After publishing for 56 years, it was sold overnight to the Cedar Rapids *Gazette*, our hated rival," he explained in his Library of Congress annotations. "Ninety-odd men were out of work with less than two hours official notice, without one cent of severance pay. Farquhar announced his intention of starting a paper in California on his own. . . . He said that of all the people on the *Repub*, he wanted to keep me with him."

But Farquhar's prospects were far from certain. He hadn't owned the *Republican* and didn't profit from its sale. The new paper was still pure speculation. He said he couldn't afford to pay Mack and Irene's travel expenses to the Pacific, in any case, and they simply didn't have the money to go on their own. Mack had the idea that he would work some odd jobs, sell some stories if he were lucky, and save up a small grubstake, permitting him and Irene to hitch their way west. He even got as far as soliciting recommendation letters from various worthies to ward off local authorities who might otherwise arrest the couple as vagrants.

He would never get around to using those letters, but he kept them, and thirty years later sent them along to the Library of Congress, where, eventually, I would get a kick out of reading them.

From the editor of *College Humor* magazine: "Very quick to follow our suggested ideas. . . . Enjoyed popularity in Chicago for quite some time."

From the Iowa Railroad commissioner, who apparently wanted authorities to know they had the right vagrant: "Height 6'1", eyes greygreen, weight 130–135 pounds; left leg badly scarred."

From his Cedar Rapids publisher, J. S. Farquhar: "I commend the splendid genius of MacKinlay Kantor. . . . The time will come when his name will be known all over America."

But the plucky plans of this tall, painfully skinny young man to migrate masked the depression he must have been feeling. After a promise of liberation from a life of jobs he couldn't stand, a brief sampling of the excitement and fulfillment of daily publication—excitement and fulfillment that paid a living wage—it was a cruel blow to have it all collapse in the time it took for his boss to say, "Mack, come in and close the door. There's something I have to tell you."

For the time being, he and Irene went to ground, back to the family home on tree-lined Willson Avenue in Webster City, where he had grown up. If Mack didn't hear the whispers directly—about how the big-shot town poet who'd won that contest and read his work over the radio had been forced back to town with his tail between his legs—he heard them distinctly in his inflamed, humiliated imagination. Decades later he would still resent it.

Effie was home to greet them, but she'd been staying thirty miles up the road in the slightly larger town of Boone, where she had been invited to start up a small community magazine charmingly named *Community*. There would be no salary, but the pressman would provide paper, printing, postage, and supplies for a split of any revenue. Effie would write every word, sell the advertising—even write the advertisements herself. The first issue had a distribution of six thousand— just about half the town's entire population. After they split the proceeds and paid incidental expenses, there might just be a little left over to pay the taxes on the Willson Avenue home and buy bread and winter coal for her sickly and unemployed parents. But Effie, who had refused to buckle under the doctor's dire prognosis the previous year, seemed as energetic as a healthy woman half her age.

"In this moment she was ardent in adventure," Mack wrote. "No one ever sparkled more flashingly than she in such condition. The valvular heart trouble which had plagued her . . . ? A bagatelle!—she never thought of it. She aspired to be the recording angel of her adopted Boone."

There are several issues of the all-Effie Boone monthly *Community* magazine in those Library of Congress boxes. The issues are fairly thick, glossy, professional-looking. In a place of honor in each is an "editorial" about the month of publication, Effie's confident, straightforward signature at the bottom. Her prose has something, I thought as I read it. It is clear-eyed, faintly poetic:

"The yellow leaf, the fading flower, the gentle rain falling on the carpet of dead leaves . . . for a short time, in October, everything is warmly, vividly alive . . . then, a few frosts. . . ."

Reading those "month" essays provoked a faint memory. Could it be? I briefly rooted around online, and there it was: a 1986 special issue of *The Miami Herald's Tropic* magazine, containing a year's worth of calendar pages, each month's page paired with an essay about that month. Sure enough, I had written one of those essays, about the almost unbearable South Florida August:

"The heat is like an injury you keep reinjuring. You begin to worry that all that pain has got to add up to something bad. It bakes your paint job and cracks your vinyl dash. It melts the asphalt and lingers spitefully at night. . . ."

More hard-boiled than poetic, I guess. But still.

I had not set out to recapitulate the life and career of Effie Kantor. At the start, I didn't even know she had *had* a career. Now, once more, I'd stumbled onto this odd parallel.

B ack in 1927, as Effie commuted from Webster City to Boone and back, Mack began to prepare for his trip out west by doing odd jobs, but making so little at them that they seemed pointless. Irene began to urge him to use his time instead to write the novel they'd been talking about since Chicago.

There had been two moments during their courtship and early marriage when, had it not been for Irene, Mack might have been sucked into the same fog of Chicago corruption and cronyism in which his father had dwelled. While at Mandel's in the claims department, he found a way to pick up an extra $20 whenever the city went to the polls by being a poll watcher for one of the political organizations. On one such assignment, Mack watched as his precinct captain stole the opposition's voter list, then covered for him when cops came asking about it. As a reward, the precinct captain offered to make Mack a precinct captain himself, on the condition that he and Irene were willing to move to another precinct.

All Mack would have to do, the boss said, was keep in touch with the voters in that precinct they knew they could count on and make sure that on election day they all got to the polling place and voted the right way. For that, he would get $200 a month—enough so that he could do nothing but write when he wasn't doing his political work. Mack was elated until Irene nixed the idea. In Chicago in 1926, it wasn't unheard of for a precinct captain to be summarily dismissed via tommy gun. It was in the course of the coming election, after all, that those sixty-two bombs blew near polling places, killing two politicians and an unknown number of more or less innocent bystanders.

Another sweet opportunity presented itself when an acquaintance from the Line O' Type gang showed him a stash of bootleg wine and suggested he could act as neighborhood distributor, making a cut of every sale. Again, Irene exercised her veto: Wasn't their neighborhood already the territory of a big-time gangster, who might not look kindly on amateurs elbowing into the picture?

She was unconvinced by Mack's contention that the wine sales would be too small-time to upset anyone.

"You won't let me do anything!" Mack exploded in frustration.

"Oh, write a book about it," Irene said.

Now that he had time on his hands and a desperate need to jump-start his writing career, she repeated her exhortation. This time Mack took her seriously.

As he began to think about a novel involving Chicago gangsters, he remembered a time in February 1926, just before he met Irene, when he found himself in a poker game with waiters, bartenders, and several shady characters on the edge of organized crime. By dinner, his pockets were stuffed with large bills. He knew he wouldn't be allowed to simply walk away from the ongoing game so far ahead. So he returned after dinner. Sure enough, he lost all his winnings, and then some, going into debt by hundreds of dollars he didn't possess. Under terrible pressure, he managed to walk away from the table by handing over a gold cigarette case his father had given him "with ornate ceremony in the presence of business associates." Aside from its melt value, that case meant nothing to Mack, and he was not unhappy to part with it, but there was still a large debt to pay, and he was unemployed. The gangster types made their impatience, and the consequences of delay, pretty clear. Mack wrote to the only person he believed might help him out, a Webster City banker whose bank was in bad shape, but nonetheless sent $50. His creditors grabbed that, too, but still weren't satisfied. Mack took to carrying around a .38 revolver until the worst of his creditors had been chased out of town by cops or competing gangs.

As he sat down to write, that near-miss experience was money in the bank.

His novel would be about a young reporter, leaving his job in a small town very much like Webster City, hoping to break into newspapers in Chicago. Not only does he fail to find a job on any of the papers, he fails to find any job at all—until a gangster, hiding out from hit men in the would-be reporter's dingy apartment house, offers to pay the young man to run errands so he can stay safely off the streets. As part of the reward for his service, the mobster pulls strings to get him a patronage job in city government. In other words, Mack was imagining what might have happened if Irene hadn't stopped his slide into the ethical, legal morass of Chicago's corruption.

Mack didn't waste his precious time as I did in 1980 on my Florida back porch. He knew he was onto something. He pounded the typewriter furiously in his two-fingered hunt-and-peck style, and after a couple of days had amassed twelve thousand words, enough to build a small stack of paper in the basket to the side of the table he'd set up as a writing desk.

"The manuscript!" he wrote. "I was dying to hold it in my hands— dying to read aloud, to feel that renewal of strength which powers a writer, and engages the machinery of his intellect and emotions, of his whole body, in each heartbeat as he reads."

Effie had come down from Boone for the weekend, and Virginia and her new husband, Jim Sours, a small-town minister, were there, too, providing a ready audience. So, as Mack's heart pulsed, he read, and when he was done his audience cooed adoringly, insisting he couldn't possibly give up working on so promising a project. Effie said, "I've been making notes as I sat here. I couldn't help beginning while you were still reading, because it was so much in my mind. Children, I have been reworking my own budget. I have found a way whereby I can send you four dollars each week."

Virginia and Jim offered to contribute the $5 and $10 tips Jim received each time he presided over a wedding.

I thought of all those times I'd been summoned to stand around on the hard black slate floor of my grandparents' living room while Mack chanted his latest work aloud, my eyes rolling back in my head from boredom. Clearly, I owed my brief discomfort at Mack's command performance to that seminal moment in 1927 when his family rallied around to support and validate him.

How I wish that I had actually listened.

Even taken together, the financial tokens from his family were barely enough money to sustain two souls. Considering his alternatives—paying his own way out to California and an iffy newspaper startup, or to Kansas where some old man wanted to pay Mack a pittance to ghostwrite his memoir (no matter how hard up he got, he'd never be a ghostwriter, he vowed)—Mack's choice was clear, and universally endorsed by this enthusiastic family focus group.

He accepted the money and went back to work, hunting and pecking on the typewriter so furiously his index fingers became bruised, then broken, splitting along the nail, oozing blood and pus into bandages for the duration as he typed.

When he finished the book—which he called *Diversey*, after the street where the semifictional boardinghouse resided—he hitched a ride in the caboose of a stock train carrying hogs to Chicago and, still smelling slightly of livestock, presented the four-hundred-page manuscript to his sometime editor at *College Humor* who had been buying scraps of verse from Mack for a few dollars apiece. Somehow Mack got the not very realistic idea that the magazine could run his novel as a serial. The editor was not quite as supportive as Mack's immediate family. He was fond of Mack, but not above having a little fun at his expense. He balanced the paper-stuffed envelope on his palm, then tossed it in the air and caught it. "It seems about the right weight!" he cried. "But I'm still not sure you can write a novel."

When the editor stopped laughing, he promised to read the manuscript and let Mack know his decision, but Mack already knew. So it wasn't a surprise, but still a crushing blow, when the envelope returned to Webster City and the book remained unpurchased. Rattled now, Mack sent the pages off to an agent in New York whom he'd had some dealings with, all ultimately unsuccessful, in the past.

Today, a writer seeking publication of a semiautobiographical first novel would have about the same chance of success as someone buying a lottery ticket at a convenience store. I doubt the odds were much better in 1927.

Weeks passed. He heard nothing back. To make matters worse, Mack was once again dealing with a painful flare-up of his osteomyelitis.

As I pieced all the above together from various sources, I realized that this had been the background for a revealing letter from Effie dated August of 1927.

My dearest son,

Your little note this morning makes me sorry that you were blue so I am writing just a line of type or two to tell you to cheer up. You know that we cannot put hard honest work into things without a return sometime. It may be slow in arriving, but it WILL arrive, so do not forget it. It is harder to wait, than just to work hard. . . . Just keep up a brave heart and your ship will come sailing in. It may be only a little boat at first—those things have a way of never giving warning, but again, it may be a big sailing vessel or even an ocean liner.

The hardest part of life is waiting . . . don't I know? . . . waiting for letters that never come, for money that never comes. . . . But women have most of that sort of thing to do. Men, even when they wait long, never have the waiting part as hard as women. . . . Darling boy cheer up. . . . When once you can get well again, things will look brighter to you. . . . I seem always to see you lying in bed, pale and wan, but trying to smile—the finest and bravest boy I ever knew. . . . That from a mother who knows you well and who cannot think of the years when we became so very well acquainted without a few tears of my own unworthiness and complete failure to be the exalted being you should have for a mother. . . . But I believe in you as I believe in a supreme being, and trust you also, as I do Him. . . .

At the time Effie wrote this, Irene, who is never mentioned in the letter, was three months pregnant.

NINE

———

On the night of their engagement, Mack told Irene flatly that he didn't want babies, and Irene agreed—though she later told him she hadn't really meant it and figured she'd eventually change his mind. Together they snickered at the annoying antics of other people's children. Commenting on Virginia's baby son, Mack wrote, "I loathed small children."

They'd been using some primitive form of birth control involving little brown cones purchased at the pharmacy for insertion. Irene realized she was late for her period as Mack was working on *Diversey*. Before he had finished, she was sure.

Though Effie had made no mention of it, the prospect of soon being responsible not only for Irene but also a child, with no job and only the most unlikely hopes of selling a novel, obviously contributed to the mood addressed in her letter.

Her optimism about Mack's ship (or at least "little boat") coming in, proved prescient. Within days, a letter arrived from a big-name magazine, *McClure's*, which was trying to relaunch itself and was soliciting short stories from a select group of writers. Mack had already sold some verse to *McClure's*, but his "repeated failures" to sell short stories had knocked the confidence out of him: "I thought the *Register* contest . . . had been a fluke, and believed I was never cut out for a short story writer. I seemed to have no proper plots, and didn't know how to set about getting them. Still, it was flattering to think that an editor who had actually bought verse from me was now soliciting my stories, and something had to be done about it."

He rummaged around desperately for a story, consciously trying to tap into the creative engine that had pumped out *Diversey*. One thing Mack had always been fascinated by was the Civil War. As a child he remembered a door-to-door book salesman leaving a sample of a book with lithographs depicting battle scenes that had mesmerized him. He always had a keen interest in and curiosity about the elderly veterans of that war who marched down Webster City's main street on Decoration Day. As he thought about the veterans he had known, he remembered an itinerant handyman he'd interviewed for the Cedar Falls paper. The man claimed to be a Civil War vet himself, and told so many presumptively tall tales about his adventures in the war and out West that he'd become a joke among the locals, who referred to him as the Biggest Liar in Cedar Falls. Mack wrote a four-page story about "a spotted relic in his faded coat and soiled hat" who was mocked by all until the Wild West Show rolled into town and, in front of all his detractors, his tales were certified by the star of the show, Buffalo Bill Cody.

Mack sent off "The Biggest Liar in Eagle Falls" (he changed the name of the town to protect the guilty) to *McClure's* and waited.

He didn't have to wait long.

"Irene was down at Mrs. Atkinson's with a lot of the other girls in the town, arranging a style show for Old Settlers Day at the county fair [when] the postman brought a white envelope from *McClure's* magazine. I tore open the envelope and then staggered to the phone and called Irene. . . . We talked it over and we finally concluded that we might receive twenty to twenty-five dollars for the story. The check was for one hundred dollars [the equivalent of $1,400 in 2015]. I began to think that maybe there was something to this writing business, after all. We went to the movies that night and saw Clara Bow, and stopped at Pete Pappas's place for ice cream afterward, and generally had a hell of a time."

Now they felt they had enough money to rent a tiny apartment of their own, and they lived there happily, if nervously, as Irene grew larger with the fetus they took to calling Calliope, a self-consciously literary reference to the mythical muse for epic poetry and consort to the gods. Irene cooked, and Mack typed, writing forty short stories in a matter of months. He had hoped and believed that his sale to *McClure's* had broken things open, but that wasn't the case. Of the forty stories, only one sold, and for a fraction of the amount he got for "Biggest Liar."

On a cold morning in December, Mack's landlord summoned him to the phone. Long distance. Mack's heart quickened at the thought that it might be news about his novel, but the unforgettable bass on the other end of the phone popped that dream like a bubble.

"Oh, hello, Dad," Mack said.

Mack had not known where John Kantor had gotten to after the stock scandal in Chicago a decade earlier. But Effie had stayed in touch with some of her ex- in-laws, and possibly John himself.

As I now understood, this was the ultimate mystery about my

great-grandmother, this smart, strong, talented, straightforward, self-made woman, ahead of her time in so many ways; in fact, a feminist forerunner, seizing the initiative in the nearly all-male world of publishing. And yet . . . Well, let Mack say it: "I thought of John Kantor, upholstered with fakery. Ponderous, pompous, deep-spoken, Sephardic— She had always been fascinated by him, and had gone back to him cheerfully time and again after he'd deserted her. She left him only because of an obligation to her children: she could not keep coming home, and finding furniture out in the street and her husband gone. Gone where?— with warrants for his arrest snapping behind him. Still she loved him with passion to the day of her death."

Was she so blinded by that passion she didn't see what a fraud he was? Did her compassion not extend to all those cheated by his schemes? Did she simply ignore the harm his manipulations had done her beloved children?

"Probably peddling some phony stock," Mack started to say about his father's new "legitimate" enterprise, but the pain on his mother's face made him swallow the words. Grudgingly, he had complied, sending off a copy of the magazine, and now the deep voice on the phone was saying, "My son, I am offering you a job."

Not only a job, but a writing job. Somehow John Kantor had managed to leave the headline-making scandal of the Consumers Packing Company—where he'd presided over the sale of phony stock as "chief fiscal agent"—behind him to turn up working for something called the Gold-Copper Trove in Montreal. His new title? "Chief fiscal agent."

As a principal in the mining company, he said, he wanted to "instill a certain amount of humanity and appeal in publicity."

Having read the *McClure's* story, and other of Mack's articles he said he'd obtained "never mind how," John said he had been persuaded that Mack could accomplish that goal.

Mack told his father he was married now, and that his wife was seven months pregnant, and a move to Montreal would be too difficult and expensive.

"I'm prepared to meet all necessary expenses," his father said—including paying for an obstetrician and the hospital delivery.

Mack still distrusted the man, but held on to a faint hope that he would finally come through for him. Given his and Irene's (and Calliope's) circumstances, the offer was too generous to turn down—even if it might be too good to be true.

As a hedge against the latter possibility, he told his father that they could come only if they had not only travel expenses there, but an open ticket back home, in case things didn't work out.

Mack claimed to remember his father's response verbatim. That's hard to believe, but I do think he probably caught the essence of John Kantor's unique cadence: "Very well, my son. If that is requisite to your peace of mind, all I can say is, 'It shall be done.' I shall send you the necessary funds immediately. Give my love to your beautiful mother. . . ."

The necessary funds—including the open return ticket—arrived in short order, much to Mack's astonishment.

In Montreal, the next surprise arrived in the form of John Kantor's wife—what number wife, Mack wasn't sure. Either way, he hadn't known his father had not only a new wife, but a daughter, Thelma. Thelma was a comely girl on the cusp of adulthood and about to be engaged—old enough, clearly, to have been an adolescent when Mack had visited his father in Chicago in 1918—and yet, he had never known of her existence.

Mack and Irene were put up in the Mount Royal Hotel, one of the most luxurious in the city, and the address for John Kantor's business office. They had barely unpacked when the room phone rang. It was a woman identifying herself as John Kantor's secretary, saying she needed Mack to bring her the return ticket so that she could enter all the information needed for the expense report. Mack was having none of it. He carefully copied every number that appeared anywhere on the ticket and took that piece of paper to the secretary. The ticket he taped to the back wall of the room's closet, out of sight, and reach, of anyone who wasn't over six feet tall and standing on a stool.

He never knew for sure if what he suspected was true, that his father had intended to confiscate the return ticket so that Mack and Irene would have no escape. But his suspicion that not everything was on the level was soon borne out in another way. His father kept postponing appointments to discuss Mack's new publicity writing job; kept telling him to be patient, that these things took time to arrange. As the excuses piled up, it became clear to Mack that no writing job actually existed. He was ready to untape the return ticket from the closet wall and flee.

On one promise at least, John Kantor had made good: He'd found them an obstetrician, who confirmed that all fees had been paid in advance. Both Mack and Irene came to like the doctor, and trust him, so when he insisted that they could not safely travel back home until six weeks after delivery—a common belief of that time—they listened.

They were stuck, for at least a couple more months. When Irene complained she was going stir-crazy in the small hotel room, John arranged for them to move to a one-bedroom apartment. He even paid for yet another surgery to address the seeping wound on Mack's thigh (it failed to improve the situation). But still without the promised job, Mack was dependent on the emasculating $25-a-week allowance. What reason his father might have had to lure them with yet another false promise, Mack could not guess.

In any case, now that he had Mack and Irene there, John didn't see them much—always too busy with important meetings—except when he was parading them around town to social occasions, where everyone seemed to adore Mack's father, almost bowing down before him. Sometimes, after yet another big fancy meal, one of the guests would sing a song or play the piano. Then almost inevitably, someone would beg John to recite a poem or a story, as he had done at some previous gathering. "Oh please, Mr. Kantor, you tell it so beautifully," they would say. John had taken to responding to these requests with a preamble, noting that now that his son had achieved some notice as a writer of stories, people would ask him if he, too, wrote stories. "My answer is invariably the same," John would intone. "I do not write stories, I live them."

And then he would melodramatically recite some alleged experience of his as the assembled hung on his every word.

Earlier, I had come across a photograph that, absent context, was merely puzzling: a very young-looking Mack sitting glumly at the end of a long banquet table festooned with flowers and beaded lamps and lace as if for a society wedding. To his right, unmistakably, was Irene, looking similarly grim, but otherwise, at a mature twenty-three, astonishingly as I remembered her at a youthful sixty. Standing behind them, and filling the seats to either side of the long table, were an assemblage of elegantly dressed worthies—high collars, pearls, broaches—with pale moon faces all rounding at the camera, registering a range of expressions, from polite to blank to annoyed.

Now that I was learning about the stay in Montreal, that photo flashed in my mind. I dug through the box of photos until I found it and looked at it more closely: sure enough, in small white type—scratched on the negative by a professional photographer's pen—it said, *Dinner given by John Kantor for his son MacKinlay Kantor on occasion of his twenty-fourth birthday, Feb. 4th, 1928, Mount Royal Hotel, Montreal.*

When I flipped it over, I noticed faint blue-ink lettering on the heavily stained back:

John Kantor tall dark haired man standing 3rd from left
Poor sad Mack at head of table
Poor sad Irene to his right
I.L.K.

I recognized I.L.K. as the initials in the gold monogram on the towels in the Siesta Key guest room I had stayed in as a child, which also happened to be my grandmother's painting studio.

So the author of these notes knew for sure how poor and sad both Mack and Irene had felt that night—in the photo they look as if someone had just run over their puppy.

A man in his late forties stood behind Mack, his heavy-lidded eyes leveled at the camera with the emotionless focus of a shark circling its prey. The face had lost that lean, masculine definition that had been so compelling in younger days, his cheeks and chin filling with soft but still smooth flesh. But his hair, that relentless dark wave parting down the dead center of his scalp, made John Kantor instantly recognizable.

On the back of the photograph in ink of a different color, probably written also by my grandmother at a later date as a retrospective comment on the scene around John Kantor's show table, it says: *Horrors! What people! What a daddy!*

Six days after the photo was taken, poor sad Irene Layne Kantor gave birth to the fetus called Calliope, who became Carol Layne Kantor, my mother.

After I'd spent the better part of a year shoveling through the material at the Library of Congress, I thought I had every significant piece of the puzzle of my grandfather's life and it was only a matter of fitting them together.

But my sister kept urging me to fly down to visit her home in Atlanta and look through a dozen large boxes filled with photos and letters my mother had kept in storage for years, presumably ever since my grandmother had died in 1982. My mother died twenty-seven years after that, and my brother and I, left to our own devices, would have probably thrown them out, but my sister couldn't bear to do it. Neither could she find time to take on the massive project of sorting through them all, so as happens with so many boxes stuffed with the precious mementos of previous generations, rendered increasingly opaque by the passage of time, they just sat in a dark closet, slowly disintegrating.

When I told my sister I would be working on this book, she peeked in the boxes enough to believe that at least some of the contents might be of interest to me. I doubted that. The Library of Congress curator who had organized my grandfather's papers said she had sent a great deal of the material, either duplicates or irrelevant documents, back to my mother, and guessed that the boxes my sister had were filled with the rejects. But I couldn't take the chance I was missing something important.

Feeling pressed to make progress on my writing, I made reservations for just a quick visit. My plan was to fly from my home in Northern Virginia to Atlanta one morning, spend the day going through the boxes, and possibly the following morning as well (if I found anything), then fly back to Dulles that evening.

The afternoon before the flight, when I sat down to print out the boarding pass, I was in for a shock. The departure time was 10:30 the next day, all right: 10:30 *p.m.* I had made the reservation hastily, simply assuming that any 10:30 flight would be a morning flight without looking closely enough at the itinerary. How I hate nonrefundable tickets.

Wanting to avoid several hundred dollars in change fees, I decided to go ahead with the tickets I had. Though I wouldn't arrive until after midnight, I would still have much of the next day to go through the boxes.

Susan and her fiancé, Randy, gamely picked me up at the airport, then drove me the forty-five minutes to their suburban home, where she had thoughtfully stacked the boxes—big plastic bins—in the guest room. It was way past my bedtime, almost one a.m., but as the bins were literally stacked beside the bed, I decided to open a lid or two and just take a peek before turning in.

I didn't sleep that night.

The most unanticipated result of my exploration thus far had been the size of the shadow cast by John Kantor. Through century-old newspaper accounts, obscure passages in obscure books, and my grandfather's letters, annotations, and published memoirs, I'd been able to discover that my great-grandfather was not only a horrendous father, but the possessor of an unusual charisma and, in his own warped and minor way, even a historic figure. I'd seen no photos of John Kantor while I was growing up, and found none in the Library of Congress files, but had been able to form a surprisingly complete visual image of him from youth to old age owing to his habit of popping up in newspaper microfilm. And thanks to Mack's phenomenal memory, and his writing skills, I had developed a vivid mental image of John Kantor's personality as well—at least through my grandfather's eyes.

But what I didn't have and couldn't find in the files at the Library of Congress was anything—save a lone notation in a children's book—from John Kantor himself.

Which is why I gasped aloud when I saw the large overstuffed envelope, brown-spotted with age, marked in an antique-looking script: *Correspondence from and concerning John Kantor.*

Praying that the contents were in fact as advertised, I pulled out the first of the stacked envelopes inside. It was brittle, the once-white paper now a walnut brown with small tears around the edges and a large crescent moon torn from the side, but the address, "A. D. McKinlay, Webster City Iowa"—no street address necessary—was intact. The A stood for Adam, Effie's father, John's father-in-law, my great-great-grandfather. On stationery marked OCCIDENTAL HOTEL, EAGLE GROVE, the letter begins, "My dear father, will you please do me a favor and deposit at once with the First National Bank of Webster City ($15) fifteen dollars for me. . . . I regret much to ask you to do this for me but perhaps some day I will be able to return the favor. It is necessary you deposit the $15 at once. Please do this for my sake.

"I am yours obedient," and there it was, the run-together signature with gigantic, showy initial letters and great descending loops on both the *J* and the *K*: *JMKantor.*

I had only to open the second envelope, also to A. D. McKinlay, postmarked 1903, to discover that the favor from his father-in-law had never been returned.

For an envelope 112 years old, it was in surprisingly robust condition. Inside were six rag-paper pages that began, "My dear husband . . ."

The letter was from Evalyn McKinlay, Mack's grandmother, who was writing with obvious fear and loathing about an onerous "he" who was clearly John Kantor. I knew from another letter in the bin, dated weeks earlier, the circumstances that led Eva to be away from home and her husband in Webster City. Seriously ill with uterine cancer, Eva had been visiting Effie and John in Chicago to see doctors who had only grim prognostications. She had decided that instead of undergoing the risky surgery they proposed, she wanted to go home, possibly to get better opinions from doctors she'd known for years, more probably to die. But apparently, next to her fears about John Kantor, cancer was barely worth mentioning.

"He telephoned up a few minutes ago that I could not go home tomorrow for he did not get the money!" she wrote. Adam had sent her a bank draft for $44 to pay expenses for the trip home, which John claimed had never arrived.

> He pretended he would get it for me. It's my opinion that he has had it and spent it. I am so worried. I don't know whether to say anything to him or not. He asked me last week if I thought you would loan him more money. I said you might, if you will pay him what you already owe him. He didn't have much to say. How I hope that he has not gotten himself into a scrape. It would nearly kill Effie. . . . She thinks he is just most perfect. . . . She was very indignant when I told her you had asked her to come home. She said she loves her own home. . . . She does not understand John, I know.

Another antique envelope, this one dated several weeks later, confirms that John was indeed in a scrape. It was a letter from the offices of the Illinois Life Insurance Company, a personal note to Adam McKinlay from one of the company's officers. It seems John Kantor had written numerous bad checks totaling $315, which sounds trivial until you account for more than a century of inflation: It would be the equivalent today of more than $8,000.

The letter presents a grim choice for Adam—either make good on his son-in-law's fraudulent checks or watch the husband of his very pregnant daughter get carted off to jail:

> The defense which Mr. Kantor makes in this matter is that he was hard pressed for money, and as you on previous occasions paid his checks at your end, he thought that you would in these several cases. . . . Mr. Kantor has without question committed a crime, which would place him in the penitentiary for a term of years, and while I regret to cause you any financial burdens at this time, I do feel that it is a case where the future of your daughter and her babies would suffer from the stigma and disgrace that attached to them and to you, her father.

One of Effie's babies, Virginia, was then three years old, and the other would be born in less than two months and, initially if only briefly, be given John's name.

That baby, who would become MacKinlay Kantor, was born in his grandparents' home in Webster City, because John, fleeing the consequences of his accumulating misdeeds, had left his wife and daughter no choice but to return home shortly after Eva's letter. When the baby was born, Eva got up from her presumed deathbed and said she had no intention of lying about when there was so much work to do. She lived, vitally, defying all medical opinion, for another twenty-six years before dying . . . of uterine cancer.

As I went through these envelopes from those first years of the twentieth century, I discovered that this was hardly the first—or the last time—Adam had faced cleaning up after John's mess. Another letter dated two years earlier from another insurance company:

> *I advanced personally to Mr. Kantor $40 which was the payment of funds misapplied. Mr. Kantor has made repeated promises to return the money to me but has seemingly shown no effort to fulfill his promise.*

Yet another insurance company, yet another letter on Adam McKinlay's doorstep:

> *If you will guarantee the amount of Kantor's indebtedness, I have faith that he is very sorry for what he has done and I feel sure that he will be a man and pay every cent he owes and never again write checks on banks where he has no money.*

Ah, but he did.

From the district manager at John Hancock Mutual Life:

> *When Mr. Kantor came here, I investigated to some extent and learned of some acts of his that were not right, but he seemed to be in earnest and desired to establish himself here and make a home for his wife and baby. We talked with him very frankly, and also with the pastor of our Christian Church, and we decided to let the past be forgotten, and to support him as long as he lived a proper life. For a time he seemed to be right, but during the last month we discovered things in his way of living as well as in his manner of conducting business that could not be countenanced. . . .*

We are hoping that this may be a lesson to him and that he may profit by this awful experience, and apply his splendid faculties and his wonderful natural ability in better ways.

All those second, third, and fourth chances, all those Midwestern rubes charmed into thinking John Kantor sincerely wanted to reform and make better use of his splendid faculties, eventually led—through Big Bill's mobbed-up Chicago, through more and bigger scams, more serious scrapes with the law, and ever more remarkable resurrections—to 1928 and the overdecorated table in the Mount Royal Hotel, surrounded by sycophantic strangers supposedly in honor of Mack's twenty-fourth birthday, but actually honoring only the sonorous, ponderous man with the center-parted tsunami of hair standing at the focal point of the photographer's frame, looming above the gloomy youth at the head of the table.

Mack's gloom would not last. Within days of the birthday celebration, a letter arrived from the nearly forgotten agent in New York:

I telegraphed yesterday but notice returned that you were no longer in Webster City but at the address to which I am sending this. I hope so because I am the bearer of good news. DIVERSEY is sold.

Mack immediately wrote home with the news.

Naturally I was pretty much bowled over. And Irene, who was making a new pie of green apples, was so overcome that I think she put pepper instead of cinnamon into the pie. . . . It's only two or three hours since the letter came, and I'm still in a daze. When I consider movie rights, second serial and British rights, *my head swims. But I have been able to figure out that it is very unlikely that I will make less than $15,000. . . . Don't worry about my getting my hopes too high, but I'm just considering. At least everyone in the family won't have to worry about eating next year.*

Mack would soon be painfully reacquainted with the reality of the literary life. But allow him the explosive high of learning his first book had found a publisher. In the universal fantasy of aspiring writers, that long-dreamed of notice—"*Diversey* is sold!"—is the golden key to the gates of heaven, fame, fortune, possibly even a kind of immortality. When we imagine our book being published—our book!—we are imagining it will be like those books we grew up on, adored by the critics, imitated by the competition, worshipped by the masses. We are most definitely not imagining that it will join those endless Pyrrhic volumes whose indecipherable bindings fruitlessly wallpaper bookstores, libraries, and the dusty reaches of the neighbor's den; those anonymous, sparsely read, already forgotten legions of books that will never merit so much as a footnote in the history of literature and remain about as significant a year after publication as a back copy of *Dentistry Today*—only less profitable.

But in that instant of bracing affirmative response—they don't call it "acceptance" for nothing—every author-to-be has a Pulitzer Prize–winning best seller, a movie coming soon to a theater near you, and is the owner of a sprawling eccentric beach house with natural finishes, a bold-faced name in the celebrity magazines.

Mack wasted no time in this post-success world, hopping a fast train to Manhattan, five hundred miles to the south, and in a matter of hours found himself moving along the teeming sidewalks encased in a bubble of special status—picture the Good Witch of the North floating into Munchkinland—the new author on his way to meet with the person he would henceforth refer to as "my publisher."

For my grandfather, that person was Tim Coward, a product of Groton and Yale in his mid-thirties who had been a tennis and squash star in college, and who had recently been elevated to president of his own publishing house after a modestly successful career as office manager and salesman for the Yale University Press and Bobbs-Merrill. Mack later said that the firm was funded with the $11 million fortune inherited by Coward's wealthy wife. At the time, all Mack's agent knew about the brand-new firm was that it had "unlimited capital." And with that capital, astonishingly, Coward and his partner, James A. McCann, had chosen to make *Diversey* their first purchase.

Tim Coward's real name was Thomas—an otherwise insignificant fact that would have indelible implications for me. He became one of my grandfather's closest friends—so much so that Mack named his son Thomas after him, and called my uncle Tim—just like the original. I got the Thomas, as well, but by 1954 the "Tim" had worn off, along with my grandfather's close relationship with Coward. Thank God for the fickleness of friendship, or I might be Tim, a name I don't love, meaning no offense to the memory of my uncle.

Though Coward-McCann would survive in various incarnations into the 1980s, and in later years would publish John le Carré, Edward Albee, Jack Kerouac, Alexander Woollcott, Muriel Spark, Kate Millett, and William Golding, during Tim Coward's time it was a middling publishing house whose most notable author, aside from my grandfather, was Thornton Wilder. Tim Coward did not make much of a lasting impression in the publishing industry, as such things are measured. The only Thomas Coward recognized by Wikipedia is an unrelated English ornithologist, and even an aggressive Internet search of the publisher's name comes up blank, save for a mere sentence here or there in a thin smatter of esoteric books. You can learn, for instance, that he had a somewhat sophomoric poem (appropriately) in the 1917 *Yale Literary Magazine* (*I swore I'd be/True to myself. Let others have Life's praise!*) and that he was among a bevy of publishers pursuing Eugene O'Neill when the great playwright's original publisher went bankrupt in 1933: "After an exchange of correspondence, O'Neill had [Coward] fly down for an overnight visit. An affable, gentlemanly product of Groton, Yale and the squash courts, he charmed both the O'Neills, but his book list, which they received only after they had invited him, was disappointing."

That "disappointing" 1933 book list, by the way, would have included my grandfather's first three novels.

But in 1928, Coward-McCann had no list at all. I enjoy thinking of my barely twenty-four-year-old grandfather making his way to Coward's brand-new office, still in that bubble of specialness, on what was then called Fourth Avenue but is now Park Avenue South in midtown Manhattan. It would have been freezing in midwinter, but in my mind, it is a sun-warmed fall day, as it was for me on my first visit to a publisher, floating in that same bubble, the city spinning in its endless variations, a pageant for my personal entertainment, or better yet, a movie set in which I was the principal actor. For a writer, the scenario is the height of romance.

I found a wonderful letter from this time—wonderful because of when and where it was written: in Coward's outer office on that first visit in early 1928. Mack had been left alone for a few minutes, and pinched some Coward-McCann stationery to write Effie a note bristling with naive exuberance:

Dearest Mother,

Only time for a few lines this afternoon. Am sitting here in the publisher's office while waiting to have the matter of Canadian royalties thrashed out. . . .

Thus far I haven't taken a taxi anywhere but have found my way through this vast roaring maze all alone, and feel very proud of myself.

Canadian royalties! It sounds rather grand, but in practice, no doubt, amounted to very little. Yet there he was, an author now, hobnobbing in the world capital of publishing. That same day, he'd had his first experience with book editing.

"Both of the regular publisher's readers criticized my novel vigorously when it came to the ornate prose . . . one was almost violent on the subject," he reported. The other reader "enjoyed some of the passages as poetry at least," but still wanted to cut many of the sections Mack himself referred to as "interlarding."

"I can still remember the icy thrill as I read her summing up. . . . 'I'm not one hundred percent certain. In criticizing these passages . . . I may be just as stubbornly having the nerve to pass judgment upon a work of true genius.'"

Did someone mention "genius"? That was my grandfather as I had thought of him, firmly focusing on the latter possibility. *The nerve of that woman.*

I remember my mother telling me that he once threw such a vicious fit about a copyeditor suggesting an alternate positioning for commas that Coward sent an all-staff memo commanding that under no conditions should Mr. Kantor's punctuation be questioned. I discovered more than one of those in-house warnings in the files. Here's one alert sent to copyeditors at *The Saturday Evening Post*: "He can scream like a banshee if you change a title or delete a phrase or sentence which he particularly values."

But to be fair, every writer faces the dilemma of how much to be swayed by the opinions of others—including their editors. How can you be sure that a suggested change isn't simply a nod to convention, missing, blunting, or entirely undermining the point of something you've thought about far more carefully than anyone else?

I had never read *Diversey*. I didn't even own a copy of it until I fished through those boxes at my sister's house and found a frail red hardcover first edition, signed by Mack to my parents on an apparently random date in 1949. Why would he present the book twenty-one years after publication? I wondered. And then I took another look at the date and something clicked. My mother married my father when she was twenty-one. Doing the math—that would have made it 1949, the year of the inscription. In fact, stretching my memory to near the breaking point, I recovered a hazy recollection that my parents' anniversary had been June 12—which meant their wedding had been just a few weeks before Mack wrote the inscription in the book.

So this was a belated wedding present? But why *Diversey*? Had the bride's dowry included the complete works, signed by the author?

It took me a few days of head-scratching before I realized the obvious: *Diversey* wasn't just any piece of Mack's oeuvre—it was the book begun at precisely the moment he discovered Irene's pregnancy, and sold just days before my mother was born. In Mack's mind, *Diversey* and Layne were practically twins.

I began reading, not expecting much—both because it was a first novel and because it was dated by a stretch of nine decades. I surprised myself by enjoying it from the opening page. The reviews called it the first realistic portrayal of Chicago gangsters—which, if true, would be

THE MOST FAMOUS WRITER WHO EVER LIVED

quite a thing to be first at. *Diversey* was not only first, but remarkably prescient. Eight months after publication, in the very neighborhood where the book's main action takes place, six gangsters and a mechanic were murdered in what became known as the Saint Valentine's Day Massacre.

Diversey was ahead of its time in another way: The gangster characters were neither especially smart nor pure evil. They were human-scale—they joked, could be genuinely friendly when they felt like it, and were very much like the multidimensional, somewhat comic gangsters of those modern masters—Elmore Leonard or the Coen brothers. The hero/writer wannabe—obviously a self-portrait of the twenty-something Mack—had some depth and complexity, as did the office girl who became his love interest. Their relationship was sufficiently hard-boiled to avoid an aftertaste of saccharine. Interesting things happened, violent things happened, and I found myself eager to know what would happen next. The writing had a freshness, an originality and muscularity that still worked in another century—lush, but not embarrassingly so. His impressionistic description of a Chicago summer night really was poetic: "The wine of the evening was bitter fever in their mouths. . . . A bright limousine crowded with the giddy young fumed past them, some girl waving. An old-maidish woman with a tiny purple hat limped brazenly among snarling cars."

I found it amusing, and revealing of both the author and the times, that the book's triumphant climax involved the young writer turning his experience with Chicago's gangsters into a poem and getting it published in the daily paper.

"The gang wars! There was a steel which could take the edge he gave it, quivering like a stiletto under a staring sun. . . . They'd read it. Vast, troubled mobs in street cars, or libraries he might never know. . . . A sewing-machine salesman in Mattoon, Illinois. A thin-legged girl riding the El. . . . Bridal couples, retired farmers, violinists, domestic science teachers." The list of all those who would be wowed by his poem goes on and on. Was 1928 the last moment in American history a young man might dream of conquering the world through poetry?

In classical terms, a gang hit, followed by publication of the poem, was the peak of the rising action in the book's plot. The denouement that followed was more subtle, more intriguing. Our hero had spurned his girl for being too working-class, and then came to regret it. The girl had gone off to lick her wounds, and better herself—even learning to speak with a higher-class accent. It ends on a night when he is alone in his room, longing for her, while, unknown to him, she is walking toward the corner of the street where he lives, Diversey Street, of course. The final words, refusing to tie things into a neat bow, are: "She felt childishly nervous. . . . Her eyes watching the bright toes of her shoes beat evenly against the cement, and never knowing until she got there whether she'd turn in, or keep on going north."

I looked for the ornate prose that had triggered alarm in the publisher's office but it didn't leap out at me. Possibly that's because the most egregious examples had been excised in that long ago editorial meeting: Mack said he struck a bargain with Coward—he would keep five of the red-lined sections and let go of the rest. My best guess is that this description of the big-city newsroom may have been one of the five purple passages he kept: "A sleepy monster, shaking ink off its mane, yawning and stretching. Whining a little. . . . A bent 'boy' with sateen sleeve protectors hobbling back and forth from the brass maw of a shining tube. . . . Beneath that floor, the roar and rumble of breathing steel mammoths. Hairy men, sopped with pitch, running along steel shelves. Broad cylinders spewing out, faster and rumble, fastern-rumble, fassenrum, fassenrum, rum, rum, rum, mmmmmmmmmm—"

At that first meeting, Coward took Mack to the Yale Club for lunch.

Ironically, I had been taken, under similar circumstances when my first book sold, to the Princeton Club. Less than a third of a mile separates the two. Back then especially, New York publishing was all very Ivy League. I knew exactly what Mack meant when he wrote to Irene: "Somebody pinch me. Irene, truly this is how it feels to be sitting, ready for lunch with your publisher in New York City. I thought it would happen. We both dreamed it would happen. . . . But—But—this is how it feels. . . ."

It is, as a friend always reminds me, that magic moment, post-acceptance and prepublication, when all is yet possible.

Judging from Mack's reaction to that lunch, the conversation over the white-linen tablecloth was upbeat, even triumphal. This was the book that would launch not only Mack's writing career but the Coward-McCann company itself. Over multiple martinis, or perhaps rye whiskey—whatever 1920 literary types drank to excess at the Yale Club—Tim told Mack that Coward-McCann would push sales of *Diversey* to twenty thousand copies "if he had to go out and sell it himself." Every cent of *Diversey's* profits would be invested in advertising; "we'll get it all back on your next book, and the one after that."

"There's no doubt I'm hooked up with a wonderful bunch," Mack wrote, "and that in a few years from now we will all be on easy street, if such a place there is."

E asy Street had to go first through Montreal. On February 9, Irene went into early labor. Mack, back from his hiatus in New York, installed her in the hospital his father had paid for, and things proceeded slowly enough that the doctor assured him he had time to go meet his father for a meal. Mack had issued John an invitation, his treat, feeling "overcome with a sense of obligation," despite the false job offer. But lunch went badly after his father asked him what he intended to name the baby if it was a boy, an obviously sore subject considering Mack himself had briefly been named John. Mack said Kenny, after Irene's beloved dead brother.

"Did I understand you correctly?" John huffed.

"That's right."

John "sat in embittered silence . . . then glared at me with contempt as he got up slowly. 'There will be another John Kantor in this world if I have to make one myself,' he declared, and stomped out."

After my mother was born—a native Canadian, a fact we had always chuckled over with no understanding of the circumstances—Mack made sure Irene was resting comfortably and the baby blanketed warmly in the nursery, then walked to the hotel to inform his father, in conference as usual, of the blessed event. Mack stuck his head in the door and kept the news to a single sentence. He went to the American consulate to reassure himself that Carol Layne would still be able to choose to be a citizen of the United States—she could go either way when she turned twenty-one, it turned out. Realizing he hadn't eaten anything since the night before, he stopped at a cafeteria for a plate of hot food, then returned to the hospital.

Before he even entered the room he could hear Irene weeping.

Mack felt himself plunge into that black pit that is always waiting for us. He imagined a small casket, a tiny hole in the ground . . . until Irene managed to gasp, "He was here!"

"God almighty, *who* was here?"

Irene gulped and stammered through her tears until she got the story out. She had been asleep. When she awoke, John Kantor loomed high above her, chewing an unlit cigar. He plucked the cigar out and glared at her. "So you have a baby *girl*," he said coldly. "I know that, I was informed. Your husband is brokenhearted."

Mack wrote, "My father had given me many vile moments, but this was the first time I ever actually thought of killing him."

He half limped, half jogged back to the hotel, his fury driving him forward over the complaint of his bum leg. He interrupted his father in the midst of another meeting, and voice seething, asked to talk to him privately. His father refused to dismiss his associates—"Whatever you have to say you can say in front of these gentlemen."

Mack wrote: "In the middle of what might be called my discourse, he turned to the other men and said, 'I could wish that my son had my own voice, which has been compared to that of the great actor Boris Thomashefsky. But instead he talks more shrilly, like his grandfather McKinlay.'"

Mack's words burst from him in barely controlled fury. "My grandfather McKinlay is a poor old man, weak and crippled. All he has left to him is his reputation for unclarified honesty. I have in my possession some letters which he received in 1901, 1902, and 1903. There are receipts as well, for monies which he paid out in bail, or in making good on bad checks signed by another man."

As Mack spoke, John Kantor sat there making faces, then broke into crude mimicry of his son's speech in a whiny, nasal tone.

Mack turned to leave. "At a cry from my father I looked back to see him bursting into glee, his face demoniacal as he beat his fist on the desk. 'By God!' he cried, 'how I love to burn him up.'

"This was my last scene with him then, nearly the last that I ever had."

The new family fled Montreal with a wailing baby and a total of $30, not counting the $10 Canadian bill in Irene's purse. A cabbie dropped them off at Irene's childhood home in Chicago, collected an exorbitant fare, then took off with Irene's purse—Canadian bill and all—still in the backseat. They would have to start their career as parents with $20 to their names.

Mack hustled downtown and managed to sell ideas for some short crime fiction to *True Detective* magazine at a cent a word. He then solicited an assignment for a slightly more lucrative sketch for *College Humor* for which the editor had specifically requested "purple language." Mack had never thought of himself as a "hack writer," but now he would have to find a way to fit that into his self-image—at least until *Diversey* came out and produced that $15,000 he was expecting.

All my life I've heard the story of my mother's infancy, of the dirt-poor apartment in which her poor mother struggled to keep a semblance of peace so that Mack could tap out the stories that might keep them in baby food, while diapers hung on a line above his head and dripped on him as he worked. In its awful purity, this tale always seemed like a fable to me. I heard it as one might hear "In my day, I walked three miles to school uphill in the snow."

But now I knew the specific reality of the moment; that this was their first apartment as parents in an iffy north Chicago neighborhood with hookers and street kids loitering on the sidewalks, a third-floor walk-up with a hole-in-the-wall kitchenette, a crib improvised from three chairs tied together and one cramped bathroom, the tiny sink the only venue for washing the diapers, which they tried to dry on the fire escape until they discovered that the unsavory pair of gangster's molls who lived above them liked to drink out there and didn't bother going inside to pee. Having nowhere else to string that infamous laundry line, Irene placed it above the small dining table—which also happened to be the lone surface that could accommodate a typewriter.

One day Mack came home—if you can call the dump they inhabited home—from making the rounds of editors downtown to find a silver-haired man cooing over baby Layne as Irene made tea. This was Joseph Kantor, my great-great-grandfather, the grandfather Mack barely knew. When the subject of John came up, my grandfather remembers his grandfather saying, "So you hate your father . . . that is too bad, but nobody should blame you. Jan (he pronounced it Yan in a still thick Swedish accent) was always so."

Joseph, a slim, modest, courtly man descended from multiple generations of rabbis, blamed John's propensity for selfishness and self-aggrandizement on a pampering, overindulgent mother, and an inclination since childhood to build himself up in the eyes of others by lying. He said that when John was barely ten he disappeared one day and was finally found down at the docks, surrounded by a crowd of rough laborers listening to the little boy tell outrageous lies.

Mack walked the old man back to his tiny apartment. Joseph dug through some papers and pulled out official-looking documents written in Swedish and pointed to his name, Joseph Kantor, which was all Mack could make out. "You cannot read it," Joseph admitted, but he wanted him to know that the papers said that Joseph Kantor was empowered to sell clothing and other merchandise to the Swedish royal household.

A lot of good that did him in Chicago.

"Again he donned his threadbare blue topcoat—brushed until the seams stood out—and walked me to the corner," Mack wrote. "I spoke once more about my father, but Grandpa Kantor was musing in abstraction. . . .

"'Who? Yan?' he spat. 'Bah!'"

Two months later, Joseph Kantor was dead.

"He suffered no pain at all," Mack wrote in a letter to his mother. "I for one have not shed a tear. The vision of a lonely old man, living in a single room and bereft of his companions of earlier years, with sons in whom he could put little or no trust, is much more painful than the thought of that same man serenely asleep."

I assume that, despite the state of their relations at this point, Mack wrote some consoling words to his own father, because John wrote back in a rare mood of humility, thanking him and Virginia for their "words to comfort and cheer some weary, tired, worn-out soul."

He went on to deliver a mini-sermon (ever the phony preacher) on the commandment to honor thy mother and father, concluding on a shockingly uncharacteristic note: "I try to be good and to so live that in my life I will reflect honor and credit upon my parents. I have not succeeded and perhaps I will not succeed, but I hope that you, my children, will benefit from my shortcomings, learn from my frailties and so strengthen yourselves so that where I've failed, you will succeed."

Future letters would not be so self-denigrating.

It must have been after four a.m. that morning in my sister's guest room that I came across a thick envelope addressed to my grandfather, care of the Layne family in Chicago. The multipage letter inside it, typed on posh, personalized Mount Royal Hotel stationery, was dated March 28, 1928.

No doubt, Mack would have tried to brace himself before opening the bulging envelope, but even so, he couldn't have anticipated what he would find on those three single-spaced pages.

"This is written to my son," John Kantor begins. "So there will be no misunderstanding I am sending a copy of this to his Mother and his sister. . . .

> By the time this reaches its destination, Mack will be gone from Montreal, and in leaving he has committed the most refined cruelty that has ever been done to a human being. If he had planned for twenty-four years to do what has been done, it could not have been done any better and yet I do not blame him at all. For Mack is a paradox. In some things he is extremely brave, in

other things a dismal coward; at times a spine as stiff and rigid as Cleopatra's needle and then again, as weak and limber as a thread; in a few things unselfish, in most things the most selfish person I have ever met . . . a real ingrate . . . a conglomeration of ideas without any substance. . . .

For almost twenty-four years, through no fault of his own, he caused a void in my mind and soul which only he could fill. He came to fill it, he did fill it completely and then unfilled it, dug out the tree he had planted, roots and all, creating an emptier, more dismal, more hideous emptiness than ever before. Weak, volatile, melancholy hypochondriac. . . .

This gush of self-pity goes on for many more paragraphs. All largesse lavished upon Mack and Irene during their stay in Canada is itemized: the luxury hotels, the dinners, the apartment, the hospital stays . . . "at a cost of thousands and thousands of dollars, all trampled underfoot because his wife cried and said she was lonesome. My God!"

John even suggests that Mack owes the sale of *Diversey* to him: "Mack, conduct a little investigation now and find out just how you got that contract," he says between parentheses.

Finally, he compliments himself for his restraint. "I feel I could write a lamentation greater than Jeremiah's but have studiously avoided anything that would smack of asking for sympathy."

Despite these grievous wrongs, he says to Mack, "I would be glad to hear from you often. Under no circumstances do I wish to hear from Irene, directly or indirectly."

He signed it, "Lovingly and sincerely, Daddy."

My grandfather did not include an account of receiving this remarkable document in his autobiographical writings about this period. Perhaps he just tossed it in some box where he kept all those other letters, the ones from 1901, 1902, and 1903, and tried to forget about it. In time, other letters from other unhappy acquaintances of John Kantor would add to that cache.

Those letters would reside together, in various containers, over the course of three generations. For decades, they had been as good as lost among the fading context of lives ended, and well on the way to being forgotten. Given my grandfather's penchant for broadcasting his feelings about John Kantor—"I hated my father with the hate of hell!"—I couldn't explain why he'd never sent these envelopes to the Library of Congress curators—who surely would have recognized their importance—with the rest. But as my plane lifted off from Atlanta, barely ahead of a tropical storm that would shut down the airport, I had those same envelopes tucked securely in my carry-on ("*I have in my possession . . .*"). I wondered what John Kantor would have thought if he could have had a vision, as he stuffed those tightly packed pages in the envelope, of the circuitous journey they would make, in whose hands they would end up, and for what purpose they would be used.

TEN

Diversey was published to notice in newspapers around the country. Mack estimated the total at more than 150 papers— an astonishing amount of attention by contemporary standards, when even a single review in the mainstream media is difficult to come by. And many of those reviews, if not most, were very positive. The Philadelphia *Public Ledger* called it "The first novel of a promising young author and the first publication of a promising young firm. An auspicious debut for both."

The Washington *News* said, "This novel marks the appearance in the literary world of two forces that promise to be important."

The *Buffalo Times* added, "Superbly vital and virile and shot through with galvanic shafts of poetry."

But, as is still true today, critical praise is no guarantee of big book sales. And clearly there were no big sales in this case. The $15,000 in royalties, foreign rights, and movie deals that Mack had imagined in those heady moments after Coward-McCann purchased the book—which would have amounted to about $210,000 today—never materialized. I could not find out, and it may well be impossible to discover, exactly how many copies of *Diversey* sold. Whatever the number, it wasn't enough. His difficult living circumstances persisted, as did his drive to produce, and his optimism. In a 1929 letter he wrote:

> *It is difficult to work in such small quarters as we have here, with Layne-o kicking up a hell of a racket half the time—laughing and cheering—so I have to spend a lot of unproductive hours in front of the typewriter. But I beg to report that I have completed nearly 8,000 words or about one-tenth of the total of the new book. It is going to be different in many ways from DIVERSEY— much more subdued in tone, but none the less realistic. . . . It is called HALF JEW. We think it's a bear of a title—one that will mean much more from a sales angle than the more mysterious DIVERSEY.*

Half Jew! A bear of a title, indeed. This was a book I'd never heard of, and a quick Internet search came up blank. And then I found it in the Library of Congress index—not just a reference to it, but the actual mess of a manuscript. ("A young woman in Des Moines agreed to type it for me," Mack explained in an annotation. "She wasn't a very good typist. And also charged too much.")

The book was about a cigar-puffing, purple-prose-spouting, Swedish-born Jewish con man with shady connections—a dead ringer for John Kantor. Coward-McCann loved it, and was all set to publish it, until Tim Coward realized the novel was autobiographical. "In the opinion of their attorneys," Mack wrote, "my father could sue, and collect. . . . Accordingly, they became adamant about refusing to publish."

No wonder I didn't know the title. After his father died two decades later, clearing the way for lawsuit-free publication, Mack said he no longer considered the book good enough to publish.

But at the time, having just suffered through the painful process of writing a novel—especially such a personal one and one needed so desperately to pay the bills—I would have thought such a last-minute derailment would have crushed him. Writers have given up hope for far less severe reversals than that.

I see no breast-beating or hand-wringing in the letters from that time. Instead, it appears he simply went back to work on another Chicago novel—one that he would eventually consider "the weakest and most confused" he ever wrote, but still.

It's impossible to overstate the iron will (and iron ass) it takes to forge ahead with writing under such circumstances. As I write these words, it's all I can do to force myself to remain sitting upright and continue to press the buttons on the keyboard, rather than slouch forward into a face-plant on the desk, or stagger away to the couch for a little nap. Nothing is flowing, no thoughts seem sharp enough, no words apt, and my gut seethes with despair. I know from experience that despair is always the first stage of writing—or as Ernest Hemingway put it, "The first draft of anything is shit." But no matter how many times I manage to push through that first stage and emerge with something I might eventually be proud of, it never gets any easier to believe it will happen *this* time. The revulsion of the moment is so intense I am not exaggerating to say that it feels as if you are trying to force yourself to eat the substance Hemingway so colorfully described. I'm awed by my grandfather's ability to press on through the disappointments and deprivation.

Unfortunately, he had chosen a bad time to launch a writing career. In October of 1929, just a year after *Diversey* came out, the stock market crashed, the entire nation's economy cratered, and book and magazine publishing collapsed like a soufflé in an earthquake. Desperate, Mack wrote a letter to his publicist at Coward-McCann, describing his sorry state and feeling her out on the possibility of asking Tim Coward for another advance. "I sympathize," she responded. "If you write, you've got to eat and you can't eat unless there is something to pay the grocery bill with. . . . Write to Mr. Coward and tell him that you're awfully anxious to finish your new book but simply can't do it unless you have financial security."

Mack must have done just that. Coward agreed to provide a stipend of $50 a month to provide groceries while Mack wrote. Helpful, but hardly enough for a growing household. Mack arranged a deal with the newspaper in Des Moines to write a daily column for another $50 a month.

Effie, whose heart was acting up again, had to give up her own literary pursuits—she had recently won a short story contest under an assumed name—to come live with Mack and Irene in Des Moines. By now, she had reconciled herself to her son's marriage and had cordial, if not fond, relations with Irene. The previous year, she had written Mack a letter on his twenty-sixth birthday: "I know that many times in your childhood, you were not happy. . . . I have not realized how very many times you were miserable until you told me yourself, for in my ignorance, or in my great desire to make you happy, I thought you were. . . . So now I am wishing for you more happiness than ever you have had before. You have so much ahead of you, both in the enjoyment of Irene and in the dear possession of your darling baby. To say nothing of your great possession—the genius and talent which are yours."

The house in Des Moines was not large, and Effie had to share a room with my mother, not yet four. Every night she'd lift little Layne-o out of her crib and bring her into bed with her, and tell her stories about the black cat they had at the time, who—in the stories, at least—attained magical powers after dark and could fly all over, including to the moon. On Thanksgiving Day in 1931, Effie had a major heart attack, then suffered through four painful weeks before lapsing into a coma on Christmas Eve. On the day after Christmas, Effie's large and oft-broken heart gave out.

I don't remember ever hearing about Effie's death from Mack, or even my mom. The whole memory must have been too painful even decades later. So I was especially interested in one of the items discovered in the boxes my sister kept in her closet; a short article Mack wrote about the immediate aftermath of his mother's death for a magazine appropriately named *Fate* ("True Stories of the Strange and the Unknown").

After the undertaker took her body away, Mack and Irene thoroughly cleaned the room, aired the mattress, and washed the sheets. That night, with some trepidation, they told Layne-o she'd be sleeping alone in her room again. They marveled at her innocent glee in returning to the room, absent all morbid fear of death's shadow. Just a few nights later Irene was getting my mother ready for bed, or trying to, as Layne was jumping all over the bed joyfully. "Oh, I love to go to bed!" she said.

"Do you?" Irene said, amused.

"Yes. I like to come to this room and get into my nightclothes and get into bed. For then the Pink Lady comes."

Irene, beginning to get a little spooked, tried to appear only casually interested.

"What does the Pink Lady do?"

"Oh, she sits on the bed and she talks to me and tells me stories. I just *love* the Pink Lady."

A ghost of a different sort appeared within days of Effie's death in the form of a telegram from Chicago. Mack opened it with reluctance. The message said, "Now she is a saint."

It was signed *John Kantor.*

However it was intended, that meretricious sentiment only inflamed Mack's wound. Ultimately, he would be the one to have the last word on his mother's passing, writing in her obituary: "Whatever troubles came to her, she faced with a calm and steadfast faith in the eternal goodness of things, and was a tender giver of inspiration in the joy of living."

It was, I think, exactly the epitaph I would hope to deserve when I die.

I took another look at that photograph from Christmas Day in 1959 when my grandfather was teaching me how to ride a bicycle. I studied the singular intensity of his gaze once more. Now I felt I finally could read his thoughts as he watched me ride off down his driveway—not only was he certainly remembering his father's cruel betrayal, the bike promised but never delivered, but also he must have been thinking of his mother, and the Christmas in 1931 that was her last full day of life.

When I collected all the letters I had photocopied at the Library of Congress and arranged them by date, Effie's death was a clear line of demarcation. It may have simply been the deepening Depression, but it was hard to miss the fact that, after Effie died, all optimism vanished from my grandfather's letters. Mack quit the Des Moines column—the daily deadline had sapped his creativity and eaten up the time he needed to produce fiction, which he thought could make more money than the column, and was really what he wanted to do, in any case. He packed his four-year-old daughter and his pregnant wife in a mortgaged Chevy and headed east to New York, center of the literary world, once again with only a few dollars in his billfold. They couldn't afford New York real estate, of course, and rented what he called "a series of ever shabbier apartments" in Westfield, New Jersey, where he tried to type his way out of trouble, without much success.

In the three years following the aborted *Half Jew,* he wrote two more novels. One was another novel about contemporary Chicago life and the other about a broken-down Civil War vet who takes his granddaughter on the road to look for a runaway mother. Mack describes both as "flops," and they certainly did little to help the financial situation.

One of Mack's annotations dealt with this period, the fall of 1932, in gruesome detail:

> *I was having severe tooth trouble, and naturally could not go to a dentist. I had cavities—some new, some in which the fillings had come out. I kept these stuffed with cotton: tight little wads of it, packed in with a toothpick, so that the guck from decaying teeth would not ooze constantly into my mouth. Later I'd remove the cotton, saturated with decay, and put in fresh. Sometimes during that autumn and winter, the teeth would begin to ache unbearably. I worked out a routine to deal with this situation. I didn't want Irene to know that I was having any aches in the teeth, because she might have been reduced to tears. So I'd retreat to our toilet in that crazy, scrabbled together apartment in the old house on South Ave. in Westfield. I'd lock the door, sit on the toilet seat, and hang my head away down below my knees. In this position the blood would pour into my head, and apparently swell up tissues until the nerves which transmitted the toothache impulse to the brain would be squeezed off. That's the only way I can account for it. Perhaps it wasn't sound medically. Anyway it*

relieved the ache and I could go back to my work for a while without suffering.

As he was working on new novels, always hoping for the big payoff, he also labored ceaselessly on stories that might pay the household bills. His letters are filled with the ins and outs of his efforts:

> *The* Rotarian *just called and told me that they would get a check off to me for the Christmas story in a few days—$150. That's five cents a word. Our income is certainly creeping up perceptibly, which is fortunate as we must get a high-chair soon and don't want to have the payments on Irene's [winter] coat hanging over us for very long! If I keep steadily at work, another month will see us cleared up as to immediate crucial expenditures and debt.*

And then there were the long-term debts, not only his, but his mother's and grandparents':

> *I want to take care of as many debts as possible before my royalties come in, so I won't have to immediately beggar myself paying old debts. I will pay Dr. Wyatt then, also the old small bills. Richardson has a five year note and can wait another year. The notes in the old First National can also wait indefinitely; some day I'll go in and square up the entire $745. . . . We will take care of the tax debts on the house and Irene and I want to do a number of nice things for you folks. God knows you have waited long enough and invested enough in me.*

And God also knew he was trying. But even the acceptance of his third novel, the road-trip story about the ancient Civil War vet and his granddaughter, called *The Jaybird*, only highlighted how bleak his prospects had become. Just four years earlier, after that grandiose luncheon with Tim Coward, toasting to future fame and riches over cocktails at the Yale Club, Coward sent what must be one of history's grimmest acceptance letters: "We are publishing *The Jaybird*. . . . Times are terrible and I don't want you to anticipate very much. It is the devil to get orders."

By the winter of 1932, Mack did not even own an overcoat. What he did have was a second child—Thomas MacKinlay, whose middle name represented not only self-tribute on Mack's part, but an homage to Effie's maiden name. My uncle insisted that his conception occurred as a conscious act, his father's way of seeking solace during the paroxysm of grief that followed his mother's death.

When I came across my uncle's full name in one of those eighty-year-old letters for the first time, I felt my head jerk back in a literal, physical double take. Thomas MacKinlay . . . I was looking at my own name. I'd known my uncle Tim had been born Thomas, but I'd never known, or somehow forgot, that his middle name was the same as my own. It was odd to contemplate: at the age of sixty, I was discovering that my most personal attribute, the name I signed on formal documents, the identity at the root of memory, was all tied up not only with the beginning of my grandfather's career, but with the death of the great-grandmother I'd been born twenty-three years too late to meet.

The months that followed the move east were an extended flirtation with disaster.

When my mother told me stories of the desperate poverty of her early childhood, I wondered why my grandfather didn't feel compelled to find a job, any kind of job, rather than keep pounding his head against the wall of publication. While I marveled at his persistence, I thought the less of him for—as I imagined it—allowing his ego to prevent him from doing what was necessary for his family.

A passage from one of Mack's letters from this period showed me what shallow, uninformed thinking that was: "Of course it's next to impossible to get a job in New York now, though I've been trying hard. Came near a couple of things, but they dribbled out. . . . Existence means nothing if it is saturated with poverty, pain, discouragement. I've spent hours walking up and down New York, trying to figure some way out of it. Perhaps it is lucky that my accident & life insurance lapsed last fall. I would have been tempted to ease matters with those. . . . One man can't pull off a stick-up successfully, or that would have happened long ago. . . . Consequently—well I didn't do anything about it. Just hung on, tried to write, waited."

In the cold early months of 1933 he wrote to his sister, "We have just passed through the most crucial and devastating period in our history. Everyone had been sick, Baby Tom had colic, they all had flu." Irene had to have some unspecified "minor operations."

"Three magazines owed me money, and I could not collect a cent. From Christmas until Jan. 30th, we only had $65, and that was borrowed. On Jan. 14 we got an eviction notice to be effective Feb. 15. There were plenty of times when it seemed like there was nothing to do but turn on the gas."

For years we have had photos of my grandparents—and my wife's, as well—looking out from dust-collecting frames on the less prominent walls of our home. You spend an hour hanging them one day, then notice them on the wall for possibly a week. Ultimately, you walk past them, perhaps a dozen times a day, thousands of times over the course of a year, and barely give them a thought.

Possibly because you know so little about them.

That changes, I can attest, when you begin poring over nearly century-old letters filled with these people's most intimate thoughts concerning the detailed dramas of daily life. It becomes almost impossible not to compare your own experiences with those—previously unknown to you—of the people who made you, both figuratively and literally.

Reading about my grandparents' early poverty made me consider my own upbringing in a way I had not done before. I did not grow up poor—we were solidly middle- to even upper-middle-class. My father was a builder/developer, working in a firm founded by his father. We grew up in a house with a pool table in the basement and a swimming pool backing up to wooded hills in the famously upscale New York suburb of Scarsdale. I became aware, as I approached my teens, that my father had suffered some business reversals. In fact, that was a large part of the reason we would leave New York for a more modest home in Sarasota, less than a mile from my grandfather's house. I constantly felt the financial tension in the background, a fog of anxiety, impossible to pin down but permeating everything. We always seemed on the brink of penury, but the trap we lived in never sprang shut.

My state college was inexpensive, and my salary for working at the college newspaper, as pathetically small as it was, paid the better part of my expenses—sub sandwiches and beer, mostly. After college, I expected to be, and was, fully self-supporting. Within a year of graduation, I had married my college girlfriend, and a year after that I became a father at twenty-three. Though I didn't consider this at the time, I was within six months of the age my grandfather had been when my mother was born. A reporter making just $8,000 a year—minimum salary at the medium-size newspaper on Florida's Gulf Coast—I had no more business than my grandparents in starting a family with such limited resources. Oddly, accounting for inflation, my income—or lack of it—was almost identical to what my grandparents had been making jointly in 1927.

Initially, we lived in a $125-a-month apartment in the city's decayed downtown area. The second-floor, one-bedroom apartment had some down-at-the-heels architectural charm—high ceilings and tall, plentiful windows overlooking coconut palms. But when our downstairs neighbor was raped at knifepoint by a random intruder, we moved to a bare-bones three-room cottage a block from the beach. There was still such a thing as beach-access funk in those days (the cottage is now an unrecognizably upgraded remodel; what was a sandspur- and morning-glory-vine-covered path to the beach is now buried beneath something called the Diamond Head Beach Resort), but even then it was twice the rent of the downtown place. I was always conducting triage on overdue bills, and we couldn't even think of the occasional movie or dinner out. I picture one night in particular from those years when the ancient, oil-burning heap that was our only transportation seized up and stopped dead six blocks from our place. When I opened the hood, the engine was hot and smoking. I yanked the dipstick: bone-dry. I hiked to the nearest gas station and found a mechanic who guessed from what I told him that the engine gasket had blown. Worst case, the engine was destroyed. Even in the best case, he said, it would cost $600 to get it running again. I remember the figure exactly, because it seemed to me the definition of unobtainable. There was no way I could come up with that kind of money, and yet I had to have a car to work. The world squealed and ground to a halt, leaving my brain to spin pointlessly like tires buried in mud.

Because I could think of nothing else to do, I bought a few quarts of oil—it took all the money I had on me—hiked back to the car, and poured it in. With my heart clutching in my chest, I turned the key in the ignition. The engine hummed to life—I was saved, at least for the moment. But the memory of that vertiginous sense of teetering on the edge of a fiscal cliff, a precipice from which any unanticipated expense could send you tumbling, has never faded.

All this was trivial, of course, compared to what my grandfather faced. But I couldn't help thinking of it when I got to a letter describing his last-minute reprieve from eviction, if only because of this ironic detail: The week they were to be evicted, Mack got news that *Redbook* had bought one of his stories for the amount of—wait for it!—$600.

Deep in one of the Library of Congress files, I discovered yet another irony. I happened on a 1964 mail-order request to FAO Schwarz for the purchase of one pool table, seven feet long by three and a half feet wide, to be billed to MacKinlay Kantor and delivered, before Christmas Day, to my childhood address.

Finding that particular mail-order document in the Library of Congress conveyed a peculiar kind of recognition shock. It was a little like watching the president taking the oath of office on TV only to realize that he was wearing your favorite T-shirt from the summer camp you attended when you were twelve. I had spent (wasted?) countless hours of my early adolescence banging colored balls around that pool table's felt surface. Still, I had no memory of it having been a gift from my grandfather. I wondered: Why on earth would he have included that in the papers he sent to Capitol Hill?

My first thought was once again uncharitable—that it was a crude boast, an ostentatious flaunting of his generosity. But once again, as I learned more, as I read more deeply into Mack's financial struggles in the early years of his marriage, I became more sympathetic. That pool table, to him, was not merely a boast, but a symbol of what he had achieved: the ability to provide a kind of childhood environment that would have seemed a fantastic dream to him then. I would not have to mingle with the wastrel crowd at some sleazy pool hall, as he had. I could learn to shoot in the comfort and security of my own home!

The pool table had been one of those undeclared markers of ascendant middle class that defined our home life, a symbol. I would soon discover that Mack had played a more substantial role in my family's financial well-being than I had ever imagined. That sense of economic uncertainty I'd lived with may have been more accurate than I knew.

Later, I discovered a letter that Mack wrote to a friend in which he discusses having signed over all royalties from one of his books to my mother. "I'm hoping it sells well," he wrote, "mostly because I want it to generate enough so they can pay back the substantial sums they've borrowed from me."

That trap that always seem poised to snap but never did? In part, I have my grandfather to thank for that.

He certainly couldn't rely on *his* father's generosity to escape financial calamity. He had only his own talent, and fortunately, in 1933, that turned out to be just enough. The $600 sale to *Redbook* enabled him not only to avoid eviction and pay the most pressing bills, but also to move to a summer rental in an art colony called Free Acres in the mountains about thirty-five miles west of New York City. "A kind of hunting lodge in the woods," as Mack described it. For a while, things were looking up again. He had impressed the editors of some of the crime-fiction pulp magazines and was able to sell a series of short stories that Mack himself considered to be hackery. One of the magazines included a small profile to acquaint its readers with this frequent contributor, and it provided me with a wonderful glimpse of my grandfather at the age of twenty-nine, as others saw him: "Mr. Kantor is an extraordinary young man, and probably the one writer we know who really looks like a writer. Tall, loose-jointed, horn-rimmed glasses, long brown hair, he emerges periodically from New Jersey with a brief case under his arm and a pipe in his mouth."

The manuscripts in that briefcase had dug him out of a hole, but by the fall of 1933, he was feeling strapped again.

In a letter home he wrote, "In April we got a small shot in the arm from the sale of a full-length detective tale . . . a thousand dollars, less commission. But by the time we had paid up the Westfield bills, traded in the car on a less rusty hack, it was all gone. Our furniture is still in storage in Des Moines, and God knows when we will get it here. I haven't sold anything worthwhile since April and the pinch is getting us down. We had knocked off one or two Des Moines bills, but the rest are still howling mournfully. The worst is that old man Kantor had to go and seduce himself with a new novel, and with that on my hands, I haven't been able to think of anything else."

Actually, he'd been thinking of it for quite a while, at least since he'd visited Tim Coward in 1930 for a literary blowout that morphed into something more important. "Coward-McCann threw a drunken orgy for us," Mack reported in a letter to an old friend, "and I think Burton B. wanted to make Irene, but a swell chance he would have had. . . . Well, I didn't sell a single story while I was in town, and that made me pretty blue. We came back by way of Gettysburg, Harper's Ferry and the Blue Ridge Mountains. I got quite an emotional wallop out of Gettysburg, and material for an article which helped pay the expenses of the trip. . . . Quite an emotional wallop . . ."

Later, in a newspaper interview, he said of that experience, "I saw the headlights of my car washing over the rows of grave stones along the Chambersburg Pike. I didn't sleep much that night and at dawn I was up and tramping over the battlefield."

He began writing on January 1, 1933—thanks to a New Year's resolution "to begin work that very day, and to write at least something on it every day despite poverty, creditors, toothache, my new son's colic, and all hell and high water."

ELEVEN

———

As history turned out, Mack began his new novel at the precise nadir of the Great Depression—for the nation, and for the young Kantor family personally, only six weeks away from the looming eviction.

He later claimed that he'd been wanting to write about the pivotal battle of the Civil War "since boyhood," inspired, he said, by his great-grandfather and his great-grandfather's brothers, all of whom fought during the Civil War.

This stopped me. I'd been fascinated by the Civil War since childhood—an interest I never attributed to my grandfather. When I was about eight, and my brother ten, we both got Union uniforms for Christmas—blue cap, jacket, pants—and toy muskets. We waited until the first thaw. Then, for some reason I find difficult to reconstruct,

TOM SHRODER

we decided to stay awake until our parents were asleep, put on our uniforms, drop the muskets out our bedroom window, and climb out after them.

Maybe we imagined that in the shrouding darkness, absent any adult presence, our fantasy world could flare to life. For hours in the strange void before dawn, we crept around the suddenly unfamiliar landscape of our neighborhood, pretending to be tramping through a battlefield. We crouched behind boulders, crept along fences, moved tree by tree through the woods, almost believing that every shadow, every creaking branch, signaled the advance of Johnny Reb.

I can't say exactly why the Civil War moved me more than World War II, in which my father participated (he was a Navy seaman in the Japanese invasion fleet that was spared combat by the atomic demolition of Hiroshima and Nagasaki), and which occupied the fantasies of most boys in the early 1960s. Maybe it was the idea that the battles had occurred on my native soil, contested among soldiers, on both sides, who sounded like me. That doesn't really seem an adequate explanation, but I was hooked on Civil War history enough so that I am quite sure if anyone had told me I'd had direct ancestors who'd fought in the Civil War, I would have remembered. That I didn't remember anything of the kind left me surprised, then skeptical, when I saw my grandfather's claim in that 1930s newspaper interview. Maybe he'd just been feeding the reporter a line for better publicity.

What I did recall—one of the few stories of any sort about previous generations that I knew—was something my mother told me about my great-great-great-grandfather, Effie's grandfather, Joseph Bone. The topic came up one day when my mother was rolling out some dough with a rolling pin that she said had been handcrafted from wood from an apple tree by Joseph Bone's father and handed down through the generations. The story was that Joseph Bone had been wounded or became ill fighting Indians on the Great Plains. An Army surgeon, who thought he might die, sent a telegram to Joseph's wife, Rachel Bryan Bone, saying he would send an escort of soldiers to collect her in Iowa and bring her to her ailing husband in western Nebraska.

The message couldn't have arrived at a worse time. Rachel, fevered and in agony from an abscessed tooth, was driven to desperate measures.

Now comes the part of the story that guaranteed I would always remember it: Rachel put down the telegram, heated a steel knitting needle in a lamp, and jammed it into her swollen gum to lance the abscess and kill the nerve. She then traveled the 350 miles to the Nebraska Territory with her cavalry escort to retrieve her husband and bring him home.

I'd often wondered if this wasn't a melodramatic family myth— possibly embellished by my grandfather, the professional inventor of stories—rather than reliable oral history.

Besides, this was a tale of the Indian Wars, not the Civil War. When I began wondering if my grandfather had also exaggerated his Civil War antecedents, I did some searches and hit on something surprising. The name Joseph Bone popped up prominently in the history of an infamous massacre of settlers by Indian warriors. According to a half-dozen histories, on the morning of August 8, 1864, Lieutenant Joseph Bone of the 7th Iowa Cavalry was traveling with a small platoon on a ranch near Plum Creek in central Nebraska, when "he spied . . . a crescent-shaped formation of about one hundred Indians thunder down the bluffs to the south upon a wagon train." The wagons, about a mile and a half from where Lieutenant Bone watched, formed a circle as the drivers tried to take defensive positions. Armed only with pistols, they barely slowed the far superior Indian force. All Bone could do was race for the telegraph office at the Plum Creek station and tap out this message to his superiors at Fort Kearney: "Send company of men here as quick as God can send them."

God was otherwise occupied. The reinforcements didn't arrive until ten that night. By then the thirteen men on the eleven-wagon train were all dead—scalped, shot through with arrows, and partially burned. One woman and a boy had been taken captive (the boy would eventually die of typhus; the woman, rescued after a year of captivity, would write an account of her ordeal). By the time the soldiers arrived, all they could do was dig graves.

This left unsettled the question of how much truth was in my family's story of Rachel Bone and the white-hot knitting needle. I found some intriguing, if not definitive, clues in a book called *Massacre Along the Medicine Road: A Social History of the Indian War of 1864 in Nebraska Territory*. Joseph Bone is introduced as a "red-haired, fiddling lieutenant." I don't know anything about the red hair—the one picture I have of Joseph Bone is as an old man with a John Brown–style pointy white beard and white hair. There's no conspicuous red hair on my mother's side of the family, except, as a younger man, I had mysteriously abundant red highlights in my beard. And fiddling? I found another record indicating that before he was promoted to lieutenant and transferred to the cavalry, Joseph enlisted in the infantry as a drummer. Maybe he was musical in general.

But the key assertion was this: When his company had left for a new posting in Kansas, Joseph was "left behind because of a chronic disability which caused him to be unfit for rigorous duty. Now he was on his way home and out of the Army."

With him, multiple accounts agree, was an escort of ten men. None of those accounts mention an attendant wife. Why, after all, would a soldier's wife be summoned all the way to Nebraska to pick him up if he had an escort of ten soldiers to see him home?

And yet I eventually found, in an envelope stuffed in the back of my own closet, a particularly vivid account written by Mack's sister, Virginia, who heard the story from Effie, who heard it from her mother, Evalyn Bone McKinlay, who heard it from Rachel Bone herself.

Virginia confirmed the story about the knitting needle and the abscess, and confirmed that the homeward-bound group, "consisting of two sick officers, their wives and a small escort of soldiers," witnessed the massacre from behind some rocks at the crest of a hill. When the Indians had galloped off with their captives, Rachel and the rest of the party descended to look, fruitlessly, for survivors. And then there was a gruesome endnote. "Great-grandmother Bone attempted to secure an arrow that had been shot into one man's chest. He had gripped it so hard in a futile attempt to remove it that, in death, his hands could not be released. Great-grandmother Bone broke it off and brought the feathered handle home as a reminder of their danger. . . ."

My triple-great-grandmother was one tough broad. If the story is true.

The historical record's confirmation of some of the details of the family oral history (Joseph Bone's involvement in an Indian raid, his disability and trek homeward with an escort) and the vividness of the handed-down tale (white-hot knitting needles plunged into swollen flesh and arrows yanked from the chest of a corpse are, after all, hard to forget) make me think that it probably is.

As it turned out, my grandfather would prove reliable in his assertion that the men of his great-grandfather's generation had served in the Civil War. Joseph Bone wasn't just a fighter in the Indian Wars, I belatedly realized. The date of the attack he witnessed in the summer of 1864 was deep into the four-year war between the States. Many soldiers from the upper Midwest were fighting Confederates to the south, but some had to stay home to protect settlers. So Joseph had indeed been a Union soldier—even if he fought Indians instead of rebels.

I quickly found confirmation that at least one of Joseph's brothers had also enlisted. Samuel Bone, a year older, enlisted in the infantry in the same place on the same day as Joseph. Unlike Joseph, who got promoted and transferred to the cavalry, Samuel remained a corporal in the infantry, moving south with his regiment, eventually participating in the siege of Vicksburg and the capture of Mobile. In the family genealogy I'd found, there was mention of only one other brother, Moses, and all I could find on him was a long how-to article he contributed to a 1905 book on mink trapping. (Another published author in the family! Sample handy trapping tip: "If you wish a good scent to draw mink, collect the scent bags of muskrat and preserve them in alcohol.")

Only as I was writing this did I come across a Civil War record for a Thomas Bone. Because there had been no Thomas in the genealogy, I wondered if he was unrelated. But his birthplace was the same as Joseph's and Samuel's, and his parents had same names. Joseph was not listed as a brother, but Samuel and Moses were. And then there was another surprise, a fourth brother I hadn't yet seen: Addison Bone. Clearly, these were my triple-great-uncles, and I would soon discover that all fought in the Civil War. The least fortunate was Addison, who was with the 28th Iowa Infantry for just seven months before being injured in the Siege of Vicksburg, then dying of his wounds on a hospital ship in the Mississippi River. Thomas Bone's war record was perhaps even more dramatic: He, too, fought at Vicksburg, was wounded severely, had his arm amputated, but returned to service and was promoted despite the lack of limb. Within another few months he was severely wounded a second time, in some unspecified but horrible to imagine way, and finally discharged in February of 1865, three months before the war ended.

All that is leaving out what may be the most significant detail: On July 14, 1863, during the Siege of Jackson, Mississippi, Thomas Bone was taken prisoner by Confederate forces.

To me, all this is just history, but to my grandfather it would have been living memory. His grandmother, Evalyn—three years old when her injured father returned from Nebraska and the Indian Wars, and four when her uncle Thomas came home from the Civil War and recent captivity with one empty sleeve—would surely have remembered such dramatic events. She would have no doubt told my grandfather all this, and almost certainly it retained a strong hold on his imagination, considering what was to come.

I know for sure that Evalyn had kept the buttons from Joseph Bone's Union uniform, because my mother showed me those buttons. She gave one to me to hold. I can still feel it, the coolness, the density of weight. I remember circling the flesh of my thumb around the engraved surface, wondering where those buttons had been, what they had seen.

I felt a thrill of recognition when, in *But Look the Morn*, I came across this passage:

> *The Civil War lived in Grandma's button-bag. . . . On rainy Sunday afternoons I used to take the Civil War out of the button-bag and play with it on the floor. There were the large brass buttons which had fastened [Great-grandpa] Bone's blouse down the front, and the smaller ones which had adorned his sleeves. There was a shoulder-strap, too, with its single bars of stiff gold braid; and upstairs we had a picture of him which would have terrified me if I had not known that, in spite of his angry eyes, he was an old soldier. And all old soldiers were kind to little boys.*

Mack knew that because he didn't just play Civil War as I had, though he did that to excess. He taught himself to play a fife, and actually joined a fife and drum group consisting of himself and a constantly shrinking contingent of Civil War veterans, who played on commemorative occasions in town, when they weren't attending one another's funerals.

"I can remember parading through cemeteries on the Fourth of July, the old men of the town and me, a skinny kid in his teens with a fife. Sometimes the Civil War seemed closer than the time I was living in."

Even as his financial situation continued to be desperate, my grandfather sensed as he worked deeper into *Long Remember* that this was the beginning of a new phase in his life.

"Have about 23,000 words done . . . ," he wrote in a letter to his sister. "Two years ago I wouldn't have been in any way capable of doing what I'm doing now. . . . Sometimes I wonder if it's my peak—if I can ever feel anything so tremendously again."

He was still only twenty-nine years old.

That summer he wrote to Dick Whiteman, his best friend from his Webster City childhood, who had gone into advertising and was living in Southern California:

> A week or two ago I delivered Books I and II to Tim Coward.
> He was somewhat bowled over by them. He dug into his pocket
> for a little money which has kept us out of the breadline at pres-
> ent while I try to go ahead with Book III. . . . I know it's about
> 400 times better than anything I've done before . . . a dead ringer
> for Hollywood, what with the Confeds and the Yankees and the
> hottest love affair that ever breathed itself this side of Hades.

Where did that kind of confidence come from? Might it have helped having a mother who called him a writing genius on his twenty-sixth birthday and could say, "I believe in you as I believe in a supreme being"?

Apparently he hadn't always been that way. I discovered a 1930 essay written by Effie herself on her son the novelist for a Boone, Iowa, newspaper. "MacKinlay Kantor is seldom pleased with his own writing," she wrote. "I have seen him more often sad, depressed over his inability to express what he feels, than happy or elated at accomplishment."

Now, that sounded like me.

I don't recall ever having the certainty, as my grandfather did in 1933, that I was in the process of hitting something out of the park. Reading my grandfather's words of exuberant self-belief forced me to wonder about my own lack of it. Maybe I'm just being realistic.

And as amazing as it seems, so was he.

The completed novel, about 120,000 words, was published in April of 1934, and the gates of heaven opened, pouring out the reviews of an author's dreams.

Jonathan Daniels, writing in *The Saturday Review of Literature*: "It is an understatement to say that Mr. Kantor has written a historical novel. For in *Long Remember*, far from being background, history is the actor and the men and women of the story are swept irresistibly before it."

Another reviewer declared it an instant classic: "*Long Remember* can stand shoulder to shoulder with *The Red Badge of Courage* as a romantic-realistic presentation of one of the great dramatic moments in our history."

Some years later, Edith Walton would write in *The New York Times Book Review*: "The solidity and brilliance of *Long Remember* gives it a lasting quality lacking in *Gone with the Wind*. . . . It made one feel like a shuddering eye witness; it flamed with life and imaginative insight."

For contemporary readers, some dated language will stand out. (In a spasm of lustful inner dialogue, our hero appraises the love interest's hotness thus: "Oh, you woman!") The final resolution of the book is vague and a little disappointing. But the vitality of the characters and situations remains undiminished.

Following the pattern of Hemingway's A Farewell to Arms, which had been a huge best seller five years earlier, in Long Remember, readers experienced the horrors of war in unrelenting close-up, through the eyes of an iconoclastic but realistic and ruggedly appealing anti-hero with a semi-nihilistic worldview. Visceral depictions of battlefield action intertwine with a doomed romance only the more passionate for being set against such a grim background.

If anything, Long Remember was even easier for readers to relate to than Hemingway's World War I novel, as the protagonists were not soldiers fighting in Italy, but civilians going about their lives in an American small town until the crest of war broke on top of them.

And readers did relate, by the droves, wallets in hand.

Long Remember remained high on national best-seller lists for months, Paramount eventually bought the screen rights, and Cecil B. DeMille, impressed with the book, invited Mack to come to Los Angeles to work on the screenplay for a biblical drama, which, though never produced, paid him the 2015 equivalent of $6,000 a week. In the first eight months after publication in 1934, Mack's total revenue went from $30.20 over a similar period two years earlier to $12,622, the equivalent of $226,000 today.

Almost overnight, he transformed from an obscure writer barely able to make the rent to someone whom newspapers referred to as a "celebrated young novelist" with more money flooding in all at once than he'd made in the previous thirteen years combined. Magazines that had paid him $100 for a story were now forking over $1,000.

"Although I never lost hope, there were times I thought fate had forgotten me," he told a reporter at the time. "But it's all over now."

It sure seemed that way. His next book, a short (128-page) novel called *The Voice of Bugle Ann*, about a feud over the killing of a beloved foxhound in the Missouri hills, was rushed out less than a year later. It became an instant sensation when it was serialized in *The Saturday Evening Post*, bringing tears to the eyes of dog lovers everywhere. And dog lovers were *everywhere*. *Bugle Ann* sold better even than *Long Remember* and again sold to Hollywood, where it was almost instantly made into a movie starring Lionel Barrymore and Maureen O'Sullivan.

That same year, still living in New Jersey, but suddenly flush with money, Mack inevitably decided to spend some of it. I'd never known exactly how my grandparents had decided to build a home on a Siesta Key beach until I came across a 1950s interview with Mack in a Sarasota newspaper.

"The children were both sick all the time. . . . They had colds, always out of school. 'Take the children down to Florida,' I told Irene. They had never been south of Des Moines."

Irene made the long road trip alone with the kids—which must have rivaled the hell of living through the Depression—an eight-year-old and a three-year-old, on those pre-interstate highways. In Punta Gorda, one of them—Mack didn't say which one, and of course it was too late to ask my mother—stepped off a steep ledge in the surf and nearly drowned. So, back on the road. Driving through Sarasota, Irene crossed a rickety wooden bridge onto Siesta Key, a narrow barrier island between a sparkling blue bay and six and a half miles of sugar-white sand beaches on the Gulf of Mexico. In that whole slice of sub-tropical heaven lived just 250 souls. She stayed the night in a motel on the next key to the north.

I found Irene's account in yet another newspaper feature. "I often think of that first night," she told the interviewer. "I looked out of the hotel window at the pure white sand, which looked exactly like fresh-fallen snow."

She was hooked, and I knew exactly how she felt.

One night in late 1967, my parents informed us that we were moving to Sarasota. It was after dinner in our Scarsdale dining room, dishes still on the table, when my father cleared his throat and made the announcement. You would think I would remember the reasons he gave, but I don't. I remember the shock—my entire life, almost fourteen years, in one house, one school district, one set of friends, and now it would all just end? I don't even remember that it helped knowing Sarasota from all those winter vacation trips to our grandparents' house on the beach. I loved those trips. I loved the palm trees, the fishing trips, the sun, and the warmth. I loved my grandparents. But Sarasota was not home.

We didn't move right away. My parents and my sister waited a few months until school was out and went south, while my brother and I headed north to a two-month-long summer camp in New England. When we returned on the camp bus to New York, family friends picked us up and drove us to JFK International. We flew on our own—my first flight without my parents—to the then tiny Sarasota regional airport. I remember standing on the curb just outside the terminal, watching the palm fronds undulate in an ocean of wind, waiting in a kind of suspended animation for someone to pick us up and a new life to begin.

The house my parents bought was on a man-made canal on Siesta Key in one of the subdivisions that had pumped up the Key's population from 250 to 5,000 in the thirty years since my grandparents had built their house—the kind of development my grandfather loved to rail against and wrote a raunchy, rambling protest song about that he was only too happy to perform. I felt lonely and isolated at first, but as the fall months rolled into winter and the steamy heat gave way to the most delicious soft breezes, I began to see the advantages. One November afternoon, friendless and nearly literally bored to tears, I took off on my bicycle, tires crunching along the crushed-shell road that led from our house toward the beach. I stopped beside an orange tree, noticing that the fruit had seemingly puffed up overnight to the size of baseballs and had turned from dark green to bright orange without so much as an intermediary phase. They were hanging there like living Christmas ornaments, free for the plucking. I think the moment I bit into that sweet pale flesh, the burst of flavor exploding in my mouth, I began to see life in Florida differently.

Not long after, I was sitting at a beachside restaurant with my father for a late dinner on a night with a hint of chill in the air—Sarasota did have some cold snaps in the winter, but they were about as threatening as vanilla ice cream. I looked up from the table, and my attention was captured by a penetrating glow, radiating through the large windows that circled the dining room. A full moon had risen above a stand of Australian pines, whose trunks made feathery shadows on gleaming, pure-white sand, which looked exactly like a field of freshly fallen, completely undisturbed snow.

Memory is an odd beast. That was an otherwise ordinary night, undistinguished and unremarkable in any other way. But as I read my grandmother's description of her first night in Sarasota, the image of that driftlike sand came back so powerfully I could feel the chill, smell the mingled scent of pine and sea salt, and see the glow that I suddenly realized had always been with me, not merely as a visual memory but as a marker of transcendence, a moment of feeling complete and unshakable peace in the present moment.

So I understood why, in 1936 with their newfound wealth, they quickly snapped up an acre of jungle with fifty yards of beachfront, bought additional acreage of jungle to either side as a buffer, then commissioned Ralph Twitchell, the architect who had supervised the construction of John Ringling's opulent mansion on Sarasota Bay, to design the sprawling, eccentric, and—for the time—radically modern beach house of their fantasies.

I also understand, given Mack's rising wealth and visibility, why the letters began to arrive.

CORNING, NEW YORK, 1935

My dear Mr. Kantor:

I want to tell you how much I enjoyed your story The Voice of Bugle Ann. *I have been interested in your success since your father made me one of his victims to the amount of six thousand dollars. I have in my possession your book* Long Remember *he inscribed as follows: "I hope you will enjoy reading this book of my son's as much as I enjoy giving it to you, John Kantor."*

At the time I thought that inscription described in a few words the type of man I believed your father to be—kindly, generous, and extremely proud of his son's success. It was his fondness for books and garden and his pride in you that inspired my confidence and it has been the most cruel thing that anyone has ever done to me—to find that a man who appeared to be a friend of our whole family had deliberately robbed me of nearly everything

The main street of
Webster City, Iowa,
as it appeared when a
young Mack delivered
newspapers there.

ABOVE: My great-grandmother Effie McKinlay in her
wedding dress, on the day of her ill-advised marriage
to John Martin Kantor in 1899.

RIGHT: In 1905, a year after fleeing Iowa a step
ahead of the law, John Kantor popped up at a leftist
think tank and was billed as a lecturer in
the organization's magazine.

Effie, thirty-five
here, had been a
single mother for ten
years. Mack was ten
and Virginia fourteen.

My great-grandfather John Kantor (with cigar in mouth and hat over heart) was among the inner circle of Chicago mayor Big Bill Thompson, one of the most corrupt politicians in American history. This rally celebrated the collection of 100,000 pledges to vote for him.

Mack at seven, circa 1911, the year
he met his father for the first time.

Mack in 1915.

Mack and Virginia in 1916.

Mack in 1921.

A young Peggy Pulitzer (née Margaret Leech), probably around 1920, in her mid-twenties. Leech would marry the publishing magnate Ralph Pulitzer in 1928 and have an affair with my grandfather in the late 1930s. She went on to win two Pulitzer Prizes for history.

Mack at a bookshop soon after he moved to Chicago in 1925, hoping to become a famous writer.

A portrait of my grandmother Irene Layne Kantor at age twenty-one in 1926, the year she married my grandfather.

Irene and Mack in Chicago, probably in the fall of 1926, a few months after they eloped.

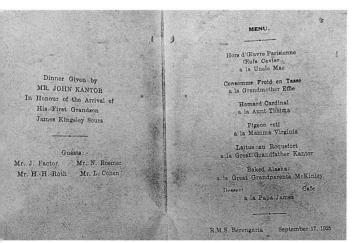

MENU.

Hors d'Œuvre Parisienne
Œufs Caviar
a la Uncle Mac

Dinner Given by
MR. JOHN KANTOR
In Honour of the Arrival of
His First Grandson
James Kingsley Sours

Consomme Froid en Tasse
a la Grandmother Effie

Homard Cardinal
a la Aunt Thelma

Pigeon roti
a la Mamma Virginia

Guests:
Mr. J. Factor   Mr. N. Roemer
Mr. H. H. Roth   Mr. L. Cohen

Laitue au Roquefort
a la Great-Grandfather Kantor

Baked Alaska
a la Great Grandparents McKinley

Dessert   Cafe
a la Papa James

R.M.S. Berengaria   September 17, 1925

This is a menu for a shipboard dinner thrown by my great-grandfather, allegedly for his first grandchild. But the only guests were his cronies, including John Factor, a historic Prohibition-era gangster and con artist.

This is the party John Kantor threw for his friends and associates supposedly honoring my grandfather on his twenty-fourth birthday in Montreal. Mack, looking miserable, is seated at the head of the table. Irene, nine months pregnant, is seated to Mack's right, and John Kantor looms behind him.

ABOVE LEFT: Mack at thirty-one. He always said he was no good at ball sports but was an excellent marksman.

ABOVE RIGHT: A publicity photo of Mack in 1936, after his first critical and financial success as a novelist.

RIGHT: The photo of a sixty-year-old John Kantor that appeared in the *Baltimore Sun* in December 1938, describing him as a "suspected swindler in oil stock."

The Kantor family around 1941. From left to right, my uncle Tim (six), Irene (thirty-six), Mack (thirty-seven), and my mother, Layne (thirteen).

I thought Mack was *in* the Air Force, and so did he. But actually he was a war correspondent who went native.

Mack posing with a B-17 he flew in on bombing runs over Germany during World War II.

A page from a 1946 publicity release for the movie *The Best Years of Our Lives*, based on my grandfather's novel *Glory for Me*. Producer Samuel Goldwyn (left) and Mack (right) look pleased with each other, but some accounts and my family's oral history contend that Goldwyn was apoplectic when Mack delivered the screen treatment in the form of an epic poem.

Air Force Chief of Staff General Carl "Tooey" Spaatz pins the Medal of Freedom on my grandfather in 1947 for distinguished contribution to the war effort by a civilian.

Grant Wood sent this woodblock to Mack in January 1941, but he titled the image of three apocalyptic horses *February* as if he knew that he would die just eighteen days after Mack received the note.

Ernest Hemingway sent this letter to my grandfather in 1952 after Mack and my parents visited him in Cuba over a wine-soaked luncheon. In the letter, Hemingway begged my grandfather not to fly in any more combat missions over Korea, and promised to send two copies of what he called "just a little book," *The Old Man and the Sea.*

My grandparents dancing at my parents' wedding, held in Mack and Irene's New York apartment in 1949.

This photo of Irene from the late 1950s or early 1960s, around the time of Mack's maximum fame, is the "Grandma" I remember.

Mack and Irene barbecuing on the porch of their beachfront home on Siesta Key soon after the house was enlarged with the huge royalties from *Andersonville*. The canine is Lobo, who adopted them while they were living in Spain.

When MacKinlay Kantor, noted American author of the current best-selling novel Andersonville, entertains his friends, Lord Calvert helps to make them welcome. Above, the candid camera catches Mr. Kantor (second from left) sharing a good anecdote and good Lord Calvert whiskey with fellow-authors Stuart Cloete (seated on sofa), Temple Fielding (standing at right) and other friends.

HALLMARK OF A GRACIOUS HOST

Wherever entertaining is an art, there you'll find Lord Calvert... the acknowledged aristocrat of American whiskies. For of all the millions of gallons distilled by Calvert, only the finest are set aside to bear this proud label... and not a drop is released, regardless of demand, until it has achieved true *perfection* of smoothness and flavor. Make Lord Calvert your whiskey... for friends, for honored guests, for yourself.

Lord Calvert

American Whiskey

For Men of Distinction

This advertisement will appear in LIFE magazine on stands May 24, 1956.

The Lord Calvert whiskey ad featuring Mack, second from left, in 1956, at the height of his fame.

My grandmother puffs on one of her favorite little cigars while entertaining company on her Siesta Key patio in 1957. The man at right looks to me suspiciously like Ernest Hemingway.

In Havana's Sloppy Joe's bar on the trip where they visited Hemingway at Finca Vigia. From left, Bill Shroder, Layne Kantor Shroder, Mack, Irene, and Tim Kantor.

The photo on the jacket of my mother's 1957 book, *The Four of Them*.

Mack watching me ride my favorite
present on Christmas Day, 1959.

Mack in the late 1950s with Bill Dog,
named after my father.

My favorite photo of my grandfather,
as he looked in the 1950s.

Immediately after discovering a letter in the Webster City library archives attesting to Irene's pain over Mack's many affairs, I turned a corner and almost literally bumped into one of her paintings hanging on the wall.

This is my grandfather's study overlooking Big Pass in Sarasota, as I remember it.

Mack drew this card for me on my fourteenth birthday.
"O God!" he wrote. "We fear he may become a writer!"

A contemporary photo of the house where my grandfather grew up in Webster City. It is little changed after 110 years.

My last photo of Mack, in 1976, taken at my first wedding, with my two grandmothers, Mildred Shroder (left) and Irene (right). He would be dead in less than a year.

I owned in the way of securities. The title of your book, Long Remember, has turned out to be so sadly significant.

Since then I have read every story you have written. I want you to know that there is a woman in Corning who will read each new publication with interest but with a little stab of pain as well.

KENMORE, NEW YORK, 1936

Dear Mr. Kantor,

Your father called on us in 1934 and because we thought a man who could be so sincerely proud of his son was trustworthy, we gave him one thousand dollars from our savings for investment in oil wells (leaving only a balance of $42.17 which unfortunately is still the balance as I have been to the hospital, we lost our only son, and have been unable to add to our account). We have received no return of any kind, although your father did keep in touch with us, even writing through an attorney after he was arrested. However, I still have faith (not my husband, he hasn't even read a line of yours because of his prejudice) that your father will return, not an increase, but just the amount we entrusted to him.

Where is your father now? Can you give us any hope to cling to?

CHICAGO, 1936

Dear Mr. Kantor:

I am writing to inquire whether you can tell me the whereabouts of your father, Mr. John Kantor. About five years ago, at a time *when he seemed to be in real distress financially, I made him a personal loan of $600, accepting his note for the money. This was at a time when he was trying to promote a campaign to bring back beer. Shortly afterward, the campaign fell through and I lost track of him; but reports coming to me in the meantime were not reassuring.*

Now I find myself in really urgent need of the money. On the off chance that you will be good enough to tell me where he can be located and whether in your judgment I have any chance to collect, I am writing you this very frank letter. I like your father and have a genuine admiration for his ability. I believe he would want to reimburse me if he knew my situation. . . .

NEW JERSEY, 1937

Dear Mr. Kantor,

One Friday afternoon a tall imposing looking stranger entered our delicatessen. While I was getting his order ready, his eye wandered around the store and hit on a bag of Kantor's coffee.

"Is this good coffee?" he asked.

"It has to be," I said. "It bears our name."

"Have you ever heard of MacKinlay Kantor?" he queried.

"The great American writer? Why yes, I've read a few of his works."

"Well I am MacKinlay Kantor's father. . . ."

The next morning the telephone rang. A lady's voice said, "Hello, this is Mr. Kantor's sister-in-law. . . ." When she hung up, I tallied up her order—something over $10 which is a good size order for a small store, especially in these times when every dollar

counts. When I delivered the goods they told me that Mr. Kantor
wasn't in, but would come to the store early in the week to pay
the bill.

A week passed and no Mr. Kantor. A few more days, and I
began to get fidgety, so dad suggested I go up to the house. I
found the place deserted, with a note on the porch reading "no
more papers."

Weeks have passed. I hate to think that the name of a great
American writer should be besmirched by his own father, who
contracts debts using his son's good name as a key to the heart of
trusting citizens, and fails to redeem his honor. . . . If there is any
way that you can see to the payment of this obligation, it will be
greatly appreciated.

As awful as this barrage of letters must have been—and there were
many more, equally heartbreaking—they weren't entirely unexpected.
Nor was it surprising to see the baffling range of crimes, from defraud-
ing a trusting couple of their life savings to cheating a deli owner of a
lousy $10 worth of cold cuts, nor was the unflagging energy of his
malfeasance.

As soon as *Diversey* came out, letters of the type once directed at
Adam McKinlay—stories of bad checks and bad faith—had come to
Mack. He hadn't seen his father since their encounter that February
morning in 1928 on the day my mother was born, but in December of
1933, when he was in New York to put the final edits into *Long Remem-*
ber at Coward-McCann, he was in the lobby of the Commodore Hotel
when a man about his own impressive height touched his shoulder.
Mack must have felt quite a jolt when he turned to find his father's
bejowled intensity aimed in his direction.

"He wanted me to have dinner, etc.," he wrote to his sister.

He had his wife with him. I wouldn't come for dinner, but dropped in during the evening and chatted with them. They were living in Hartford, Conn. The wife was a pretty redhead about twenty-eight years old [John was fifty-four then], and seemed to have the knack of handling him. He seemed older, somewhat subdued, but just as full of lies and fine speeches as ever. I wouldn't invite him out to visit the children. Later however, I did go with Irene and have dinner with them at the Biltmore. We were both very much amused, but didn't care to pursue the acquaintanceship.

Some time later while we were down south he read in a New York paper that we were gone and promptly drove out to see the children. Mrs. Keyes was quite bewildered to have a self-announced grandfather come marching in. He stayed an hour or two, made a long distance call, and Mrs. Keyes found him spying over my mail when she came into the room. He asked where my clippings were kept, but she wouldn't allow him to penetrate my workroom, so he left.

That was all we heard of him until April, when he called up full of congratulations and fulsome phrases about Long Remember. *Needless to say, I didn't send him a copy.*

About six weeks ago, I received a letter from a psychologist of Columbia U. It seemed that my father had cheated the prof out of some $22,000 and he was trying to get it back, wondered if I had any influence with my father etc. . . . I learned to my astonishment that he had been using my name as a lever, talking about the money I would make from Long Remember, *and finally he begged the prof not to prosecute as it would REACT UNFAVORABLY ON MY BOOK. I immediately wired the old devil to get the hell away from me and never mention my name again in any of his nefarious enterprises. I also communicated with the* *prof and volunteered any aid I could give in order to bring about a speedy prosecution, but he's likely fled the country by this time. I wish they had got him and stuck him in the pen where he has belonged these many years, but apparently he was born to die with his boots on, cheating somebody merrily up to the last gasp.*

I couldn't find any mention of John's dealings with the Columbia professor in searches of newspapers, but I did find a brief article in *The Webster City Freeman* from less than a year later that answered both Mack's conjectures about whether his father had fled the country and the sad query of the man who had purchased some oil wells from John wondering if there was any hope he would ever get his investment back. The answer to both questions was negative. The news account reads:

John M. Kantor, who police say posed as 'a senator from Iowa' when making allegedly worthless oil deals, was lodged in jail Monday, charged with larceny.

I don't know if my grandfather saw that story, but I know he found out his father had landed in jail, because I have a letter dated a month later, a torn half of yellow notebook paper with a CENSORED BY SHERIFF'S OFFICE stamp and a folded notice about the rules of the Rockland County Jail. "My dear Mack," the note began. "As Marie is absolutely without funds will you please send to her all or any part of the $200 you borrowed from me on your note in Montreal for your trip to your publishers seven years ago. If she had any money at all I would not ask."

My grandfather—who at the time of the alleged loan had been living on John's meager allowance—never said how he had paid for that train trip to New York after *Diversey* was sold. If indeed he borrowed money from John, then it would be rich irony to think his father had been taken in by a promise to repay that was never fulfilled. More likely, in a fit of self-aggrandizing parental pride, John had simply bought him the ticket (which would have been far less than $200 back then—the entire trip with hotel and food included couldn't have been more than $50 or so), and now was choosing to call it a loan.

Just over a month after the first pleading letter, another arrived from the same address with a very different tone. This was typed instead of handwritten and began: "Dear sir: Some time ago I wrote you a little note asking to please send the $200 you borrowed from me. . . . The money I spent on you and Irene for clothing, food, shelter, hospital bills and making it possible to bring your first-born into the world in comfort I don't mind. But the $200 that you borrowed as a business proposition I need. I need it so badly that unless you voluntarily send it to Marie at once I shall be compelled to take such steps as I am entitled to under the law, for no other reason than at the present time it is blood money."

Again, I found no record of a response from my grandfather, and quite likely there was none. Just over a year later my grandfather received a letter that tells the story well. It is from the John Kantor fraud victim who became a MacKinlay Kantor fiction fan, a woman named Emma who had been robbed of her life savings in part because she'd been impressed with John's glowing pride in his son.

My dear Mr. Kantor:

Thank you so much for your letter. I knew that John Kantor—I do not like to refer to him as your father—has been out of jail since last fall. His attorney and mine decided to gamble in this way. They knew that if he stayed in jail no one whom he had defrauded would ever get any money, while if he was released and allowed to go to work there might be a little hope of his making restitution. Of course I have no faith in him at all, but am grateful for anything that may offset my loss. I really believe the man is unbalanced when I remember him as he appeared in our house and then realize how he schemed to defraud me. . . . Someday I should like to describe John Kantor's technique in establishing a friendly footing in our house. Such finesse! Such histrionic ability and careful attention to detail to represent himself as the type of man he wanted us to believe he was.

Then, sometime later, Emma updated the situation:

Court was called for May 1st. I set out feeling it was a complete waste of time. But I was mistaken. John Kantor himself was there with his attorney. I hadn't seen him in nearly five years and dreaded facing him because in all my life no one had ever done such an unkind thing, to use us as he had done. But nothing could have been more charming and easy than our meeting. He was looking very well and was his most polished self, without a trace of embarrassment. We fairly outdid each other in our exchange of pleasantries and you would have thought it was one of the happiest moments in his life when he saw his attorney count out the stack of $100s and $50s and place them in my hand. I couldn't bring myself to thank him but instead said, "I am very glad indeed to have this money," to which he replied with a bow and a charming smile, "And I am glad to have you have it." All was Sweetness and Light and I made what I hope was a graceful exit and I almost broke the speed laws getting back to the bank.

Another letter from the same correspondent dated a year later:

Be sure to read the January 16th copy of The New Yorker *which describes in detail the latest activities of John Kantor. Now all is clear on why he was able to pay restitution.*

The *New Yorker* piece, "Death Without Sting," for the column A Reporter at Large, drolly describes a meeting of "a remarkable organization" called Associated Cemeteries Corporation. The reporter, Jack Alexander, explains that it was remarkable because it has brought to the usual sobering experience of buying cemetery plots "a technique that blends joy with mortality and music with salesmanship."

An auditorium full of marks, lured by acts including "a man who plays a musical saw, a vocal soloist, a recital by kiddies of a dancing school," were softened up for the big sell. The article made it clear this was a pyramid scheme. People were solicited to buy plots, but even more so to solicit friends and relatives to buy plots as well, who were to entice *their* friends in turn. In so doing, they all became "coworkers" entitled to a cut of the action.

After the kiddies danced and the sawist sawed, the crowd was treated to a series of speakers on economic topics, but all was a preamble, a mere tease, for what was to come.

"'And now,' the emcee cried, 'I want to make way for the man everybody is waiting to hear, the man everybody loves!' . . . There was a ripple of applause," Alexander wrote. "I turned and saw a towering, Lincolnesque man moving down the aisle in slow, deliberate strides. He ran a hand through a mane of jet-black hair and smiled paternally. 'That's Mr. Kantor,' my neighbor said. Mr. Kantor had a deep rich voice, and as soon as he turned it on, he seemed to take everyone right up on his lap for an intimate chat. His delivery was easy, except when he was emphasizing something. And then he roared. He was definitely a personality lad, frankly conscious of his power and appeal."

According to *The New Yorker*, John Kantor had created Associated Cemeteries in February 1936. What they didn't know was that this was the same month that he had been released from jail upstate, with the idea that he could then go to work and make his restitution. Go to work, he did.

After warming up with a few fables and Bible stories and homilies—"I know a lot! It would be false modesty for me to say I didn't!"—he talked about the immense profits to be made in burial-plot speculation. It was a simple matter of supply and demand. Considering the huge numbers of Jews dying every day in New York, and the shrinking supply of space in nearby Jewish cemeteries, someone wisely buying up plots now could sell them at jacked-up prices in the near future. "Jerking his head back and looking ceilingward, he raised a hand aloft and cried, 'Why I can see vast funeral trains moving through the air for the Jews of New York—who must be buried before sundown! . . . After all, man is born to die, is he not?'"

What the *New Yorker* piece missed was this: Aside from the questionable sales technique, the naked greed and callous eagerness to take advantage of the newly bereaved, something was not quite right with Associated Cemeteries. Apparently, John Kantor was so enthusiastic about the sale of these burial plots that he sold them two and three times over—to the chagrin of the second and third owners. Or maybe he only sold the plots a single time, plots he didn't happen to own or that didn't happen to exist.

Here's another in the fat pile of letters to Mack, begging intercession with his father:

Dear Mr. Kantor:

Would you be so kind as to inform me as to how I could get in touch with your father, Mr. John Kantor. I bought some plots in the new Montefiore Cemetery from a firm of which Mr. Kantor was a member. Since then I have been unable to contact anyone with whom I did business.

In a biographical sketch of my grandfather, I came across an amazing quote about John Kantor that Mack attributed to a major figure in American history. I was skeptical of it at first—how would this man have known my great-grandfather at all, much less well enough to have a strong opinion about him? Then I discovered that both had been active in Chicago's tight-knit Democratic political machine in the early 1900s, both sought-after orators on the party's behalf. So it's probably true that Clarence Darrow once said, "If John Kantor had been content to climb slowly, he might have risen to one of the highest offices in the land."

In 1938, a remarkable scandal broke, often called one of the biggest financial scandals of the twentieth century. Here's what I pieced together from dozens of articles about it: An Italian-American named Philip Musica had made a fortune many times over, each time fraudulently. First, he cornered the market on imported Italian food products by underselling his competitors—something he was able to do by paying bribes to avoid taxes at New York ports. He was finally caught, but served only six months before using political clout to win a pardon from President William Howard Taft. He then went into the hair business—long natural human hair for wigs was a valuable commodity. Musica assembled a vast inventory of crates filled with the stuff, but only the top layer was actual quality hair. The rest: sweepings from barbershop floors. He used the fake inventory as collateral for large loans and as paper assets to sell stock in his company until he again made millions. When the fraud was uncovered, Musica was nabbed in New Orleans on the way to Panama with steamer trunks filled with ill-gotten loot. But he wheeled and dealed his way to a suspended sentence in return for making partial restitution (about ten cents on the dollar) and informing on others.

Now Musica thought it prudent to change his name. As Frank Costa, he went into another hair-related business: the manufacture of shampoo. Shampoo containing alcohol. During Prohibition, hair-product companies could still legally buy the alcohol they needed to manufacture shampoo, and Musica bought all he could—then sold it illegally at hugely inflated prices to bootleggers, covering up the sales with phony paperwork.

When someone tipped off Treasury agents, they raided the company, but its owner, Frank Costa, had disappeared.

Musica/Costa reappeared with yet another alias, F. Donald Coster, claiming to be a physician-turned-businessman. He used the wealth accumulated in two decades of scamming to buy another hair product company, again to act as a front for sales to bootleggers, including some of the biggest in the country. This time his efforts were more sophisticated, and he used his profitable bootlegging operation to support and develop the legitimate side of the business. By 1926, he'd become successful and respected enough to buy the century-old pharmaceutical company McKesson & Robbins. He placed three brothers, his sister, and his mother into company management, all under assumed names. Using his usual bookkeeping tricks of fake inventories and bills of sale, he made the company look like a profit magnet. Wall Street fell in love and Coster and friends prospered mightily.

McKesson became one of the largest pharmaceutical companies in the country. Under Coster, the firm put together a national product-distribution chain, and even managed to break up foreign monopolies on raw materials, to public acclaim. He became popular with socialites and politicians, and was even asked to run for the Republican nomination for president. (He humbly declined.) He bought an eighteen-room mansion on a seven-acre estate in Connecticut, a large yacht, and a dozen chow show dogs.

When McKesson's treasurer became suspicious about the operation of a Canadian subsidiary controlled solely by Coster, it all began to unravel. Supposedly a center for the purchase and storage of exotic materials used in pharmaceutical manufacture, the subsidiary turned out to consist of a single secretary in a mail room, whose sole responsibility was to route incoming mail to Coster's home address. The exotic-materials stockpile didn't exist. The money supposedly used to buy the stuff had ended up in Coster's pocket. Altogether he had stolen the contemporary equivalent of $50 million.

Coster denied everything. Of course his photo appeared prominently in the news. A veteran investigator recognized the man in the photo as twice-convicted fraud Philip Musica. Fingerprints confirmed that one of the country's foremost corporate execs was actually a career criminal.

As federal agents moved on Coster's mansion to bring him in, he fired a bullet into his brain, leaving a note blaming it all on bankers, lawyers, accountants, and auditors.

The scandal unfolded across front pages for weeks as Coster/Costa/Musica's bizarre web of lies and deceit spread in unexpected directions, including a gunrunning scheme to foment a revolution in Honduras.

Naturally, John Kantor was involved.

A *Chicago Tribune* article on December 21, 1938, nearly two years after the *New Yorker* article about John's cemetery plots, contained this revelation: "John Kantor, a stock promoter, who said he had been approached by representatives of McKesson & Robbins to aid them in a gun running deal involving a foreign power, was held on bail of $25,000 in the Tombs prison. . . . Kantor, regarded as 'an important witness' by the government, is also wanted in Connecticut in connection with stock fraud."

In 1945, ten years after John Kantor had walked off with her life savings, and nine years after he'd been forced to make restitution, my grandfather heard once again from Emma, and once again her letter included a clip. Another scandal story, this one about Elliott Roosevelt, son of the recently deceased president of the United States.

Elliott had been a good soldier in World War II, but a bad businessman. In 1939, hoping to curry favor with President Roosevelt, John Hartford of the A&P grocery chain made Elliott a large loan to buy a Texas radio network. The younger Roosevelt's network quickly went south, and two years later, again under White House influence, Hartford agreed to forgive the $200,000 loan for a measly repayment of $4,000—then promptly wrote off the $196,000 loss on his taxes.

This all came out, and was investigated by Congress, in 1945, shortly after FDR's death. One name popped up in the middle of it. The name was there in the clip Emma had sent, in a column by muckraking journalist Westbrook Pegler. The name was: John Kantor.

Kantor, Pegler said, had been hired by Elliott to solicit loans for the station and sell airtime. When the project began to crater, John tried to buy Hartford's bad debt for pennies on the dollar.

"Kantor, who is a hustler, might have figured that some loyal Democrat with the interests of the administration at heart would buy them from him at face value to avoid a scandal."

As an aside, Pegler noted, "John later had to go away for twenty months for some monkey business about cemetery plots."

Along with the clipping, Emma had sent a note:

I have often wondered what had become of John Kantor and if he was still in circulation—What a man! Well, the best thing your father ever did in his life was to pass on to you his great gift as a story-teller, and you glorified it into something worthwhile.

TWELVE

After months of research, I had grown used to having assumptions about my grandfather reversed. But this one I never could have seen coming: As I read through an otherwise mundane letter from Mack to his sister from 1936, I came across this: "I flatly declared all along that I didn't want to build in Florida. It cost far more than [the contractor] said it would cost, even counting his revised estimate, and I told him to call a halt on any expansion when I was in England, but he went ahead sublimely."

I had always thought of that house as his haven, the calm center of the creative storm, the one place he could retreat from all the demands of mundane life—editors, agents, publicists, producers, even family, and especially children—to hunker down in the cedar-scented, memento-crammed, surf-soothed writing room overlooking a wide slice of tropical paradise. It just didn't add up that the man who wrote his first book under assault of dripping diapers and a baby's wail could tell his sister of that seemingly ideal setup: "I can't work down there in the way I need to work and want to work."

He wasn't just venting. Despite his concern about the cost overrun on the house, he rented an apartment in New York, and furnished it, so he could stay and work while Irene and the kids went down to Florida.

"It means that Irene and I will have to be separated much of the time this winter, but in the circumstances it is a necessary evil."

I would soon begin to think the phrase "necessary evil" was only half right.

It turned out that even in the solo New York apartment his literary production remained negligible. Now he decided what he really needed was . . . a solo Central American vacation.

Another letter to his sister from late November or early December of that same year of 1939:

> *Wednesday—I think.*
>
> *One rather loses track of days down here. . . . I am having a lazy week—too lazy perhaps—but at least I ought to be saving up a lot of emotional energy, since I'm not spending any. I got sold on Costa Rica when I met a gal on the boat coming down—a native who gave it quite a boost. In fact, if you only looked at her you'd get quite a boost! We had one of those week-long, fleeting, provocative shipboard things that occur sometimes in life, and so I stopped over. Not on her account. . . . I needed to go to the end of the earth if I were ever going to write another line, and this is a good three-quarters of the way there.*

At the bottom he wrote, "By this time I trust you've decided this letter isn't for general family consumption."

And I knew what he meant. As a member of the general family, this was genuinely difficult to swallow, even three-quarters of a century later.

Though these exact words never formed in my mind, I knew my grandmother and grandfather as the perfect couple. He always portrayed their marriage as a great love story—and of course he even named part two of his autobiographical volumes *I Love You, Irene*. My grandmother always paid tribute to Mack's genius, but he seemed even more eager to praise her youth and beauty. In fact, the few photos of Irene in her twenties and thirties reveal her to be plain, almost homely—a too-narrow face, a too-wide mouth, a scrawny figure, and crimped hair. But Mack never described her as anything other than mystically alluring.

Maybe those ancient photos didn't do her justice. In any case, she indeed became more comely with increasing age—her face and figure grew rounded but never heavy, the green eyes that showed only gray in the photos sparkled intelligently under perfectly arched eyebrows and hair colored to a polished bronze. My mother told me that her parents' romance had always come first, even before her and Tim. They traveled the world together, leaving the kids behind with a succession of nannies, boarding schools, and summer camps. ("Don't worry about the kids, because we're not going to," Mack wrote to friends when he and Irene were boarding a ship for a months-long trip to Europe the year Tim turned four.) They attended glamorous parties, exiting the house in a swirl of pipe tobacco, silk, and Chanel. To balance the writer's lair on the southern end of their house, they built a high-ceilinged studio on the north end where my grandmother worked in oils and watercolors. She eventually got good enough for her paintings to appear in juried art shows and sell occasionally to private collectors. Enthroned in their creative redoubts, they were two oppositely charged poles of a battery that kept the electricity flowing, figuratively, and also literally through the wires of the intercom that crackled from studio to studio.

I remember more than once cringing as an adolescent when my grandfather very pointedly announced he was retiring for a midafternoon "nap," then minutes later impatiently began calling—"Reno! Reno!"—from the bedroom. They would have both been pushing seventy then.

So the casual, jovial reference to a shipboard dalliance—and in a letter to his sister, no less—floored me.

I had only to read deep into my uncle's memoir to see this letter was no fluke. When Tim was eighteen, he says, he confessed to his father that he had recently lost his virginity. Mack's response: celebrate with drinks at the neighborhood bar.

Tim's account of their remembered conversation is clearly created, not actual. But even stripped of Tim's probable embellishments, it is astounding enough.

Mack begins: "You know, sex is wonderful. It's a hell of a lot of fun, as you've discovered. And . . . most real men need women. And no matter how much we love a particular woman, many of us can't be satisfied with just one. Man's a hunting animal."

Then Mack leveled his still teenage son with the revelation that, though "I love [your mother] more than any other woman I have ever found" and Irene is "the most desirable woman I have ever known . . . I've screwed a lot of other babes as well. Hundreds. . . ."

"To court a pretty babe, to charm her, win her, and have her laughter and her flesh to comfort you during the empty nights . . . is one of the greatest joys in this world."

Even if Tim embroidered his father's actual words, no doubt he captured his attitude. "He once told me," Tim wrote, "that he'd been faithful to my mother during the first years of their marriage. 'For four long years,' he said, 'I never even looked at another woman. . . . But your mother was so goddamned jealous. After every party we went to Irene would be all over me. "What did you say to *this* girl? Why were you talking to *that* one?" . . . Finally I decided that, if she was going to be jealous anyway . . .'"

In other words, "Look what you made me do!"

I later found something Mack himself had written, a more elevated view—if even more shocking for its mention of a possibility of divorce—reflecting on the innocence of the early days in his young marriage: "Of the strains which dissolve most early marriages among creative folk we held no awareness, no indication that such exertion would come snapping into our lives. Neither of us had ever looked at another with desire since the moment we met. In ignorance we assumed calmly that we never would. We had not one inkling of those complex passions which baffle the mature of our kind, and which would goad us to the brink of divorce again and again."

So: This wasn't just about men being men, driven to the hunt by their masculine nature. It was about the complex passions of creative people. It was about his needs as an artist. Or so he told himself.

Ever since the first photos of Mack had appeared in newspaper stories about his literary success, he'd fit the part of the tall, dark, romantic poet—sensitive yet entirely manly. He had thick, abundant hair, like his father, only far less absurdly unruly; a smooth, broad forehead; those hooded, penetrating eyes; a full, firm jaw; and, despite his gimpy leg, a tall, lean, athletic figure. He inhabited an age in which literary novelists became full-fledged celebrities—especially if, like Hemingway, they exuded the masculine energy that suggested a world of adventurous activities not remotely related to the reality of sitting around in an empty room all day pressing keys on a typewriter. That trifecta of looks, image, and success made it certain that no shortage of women would find him attractive. It couldn't have hurt to have inherited his father's mesmerizing gift of gab. And having grown up with a mother who worshipped him, Mack no doubt felt that an unlimited ration of female attention was his due.

There was nothing to be ashamed of! He was forthright, honest, merely expressing his true nature, the true nature of manly men.

The day I discovered the Costa Rica letter, I told a friend about it, who said, "He was a complete narcissist! You are lucky you didn't inherit that trait."

Hmm.

As easy as it was for me to scorn the narcissism, the selfish and careless way he handled the people he claimed to love most, I found myself forced to face an uncomfortable truth. I had been that guy, once, many years ago. Although I was not the classic tall, dark, handsome lothario who drew attention in a packed bar as Mack almost certainly did (I am five nine, not six one, for one thing), in close quarters I did have an intensity of focus that conveyed sincerity and depth. It was not an act. I did not put out some glib line. When I turned my focus on a woman it was because I was truly interested in her, in who she was and how she thought, not just romancing her—though, often that, too. And women responded. I could sense the effect it was having, like a tractor beam, drawing them in. Who knows, maybe it was the last diluted magic descended from John Kantor's ability to mesmerize large crowds.

I recognized something deeply familiar in Mack's self-interested enthusiasm for women. You often hear that womanizers act out of antipathy more than desire, and I'm sure that's often true. But Mack belonged to a class of philanderers motivated by an abundance of appreciation for women. Like him, I loved the thrill of discovery, the peeling of the layers down to the intimate core, both intellectual and physical. And I wanted to believe that this was mutual exploration, nothing selfish about it. I remember trying to persuade a college girlfriend that jealousy, not promiscuity, was the real problem; that feelings of love could never be a bad thing, wherever they might lead, even if that was to other lovers.

But by the time I found the woman I wanted as my lifelong partner, I had learned, through pain and with great difficulty, that what I really most desired, and needed, was not an unending series of lovers, but one human being in the world I could unquestioningly trust with my most naked self, all barriers relaxed, knowing that she would forever have my back, as I would have hers. And I knew in my gut, sure enough to act on it, that if you were lucky enough to find that person, the one person in whom you could imagine having infinite faith, nothing gained in another relationship could possibly outweigh what would forever be lost.

Mack remained focused on what he could gain and didn't worry so much about the cost—especially the cost to Irene, who at times, I discovered, he felt to be crimping his social style by being the type who was "reserved, somewhat distant, and never put themselves forward to get acquainted."

On the second page of the letter from Costa Rica he casually describes Irene left at home alone, dealing not only with the kids and the famously insane-making preparations for Christmas, but also laboring to furnish a new house with an insufficient budget ("too hard up at the moment" to afford store-bought curtains, Mack reported, leaving Irene to make them herself). "No doubt she is up to her ears," Mack told his sister, apologizing for the fact that her Christmas present might be late. "Irene may be able to handle it single-handed, but don't count on it; she's a wonderful gal who has a hard time doing the routine things that other people (some not so wonderful) find very easy to do."

A comment that would be infuriatingly dismissive and patronizing in any circumstances becomes almost unbearably so, considering that while Irene labored at domesticity Mack was kicking back in the eternal Costa Rican summer, still simmering from his "fleeting, provocative shipboard thing" with the señora.

If the Costa Rican was one of the "hundreds" of Mack's dalliances (Tim says Mack later amended that number to "many"), at least she merited mention in a letter. Unless his claims were outrageously exaggerated, the great majority of Mack's women went undocumented— casual flings consumed and forgotten. But, I discovered, at least a handful of these relationships had been quite serious.

One letter caught my attention at first for other reasons. Mack, routinely reciting family news, mentioned "Layne and Bill," my mother and father. They were "blissfully happy," he said, and spoke of nothing but their baby son (my brother, Michael) and the near completion of the house they were building in Scarsdale—the house I would spend the first fourteen years of my life in. "All you can hear is Mike and the house, the house and Mike," he wrote, and then added as an afterthought: "Also talk of another small Shroder they expect to start manufacturing in the spring."

That would be me. Undoubtedly the first mention of my (potential) existence ever put to paper.

The letter was written to someone I'd never heard of, a woman my grandfather addressed as "Ginny-wabbit" (and in another letter, "Ginny Angel"). I wasn't puzzled for long. After he announced my near existence he wrote:

> *Ah, me. Kids are wonderful. How I wish life had let you have your own. Better than that, I would have had it that I, by circumstance, could have guv them to you.*
>
> *Right now I wish you were sitting in the chair by the window telling me all sorts of gossip and yarns and making your mulish laughter. Better than that, I wish that Riverside were in the immediate future, and not many months in the past. First chance I ever get to strike a deadly blow at California again, maybe we could take a trip or something or something—IF you could subtract yourself from your regular existence. There is no ignoring the fact that we profit, each to the other and for the other. To you, my eternal respect and joy and admiration and appreciation: spell it L-U-V.*

I assumed that "Riverside" referred to a town in Southern California where they met for a tryst. Less ambiguous was a passage in a letter he wrote to his friend Dick Whiteman. "Ginny was here: we had about eight days together, and despite the failing currency in my private coffer, we flew to Cuba for two or three marvelous days."

All the above would have been enough—a long-term, substantial relationship carried on with passion (obviously), expenditure of scarce resources (by implication), and great regret at what could not be (explicitly).

It didn't stop there. A paragraph at the bottom of page 2 of the letter to Ginny sheds light on the particularly murky mystery of Irene's role in Mack's meanderings, if "sheds light on" can be taken to mean blasting it with a white-hot klieg.

"Irene is painting calmly and steadily and with all determined passion," he tells Ginny-wabbit. "Her water colors are really going places. She has sold two—no, maybe three—within the past few weeks. . . . She has a lot to give and tell, and only her own sense of inferiority has restrained her. Certainly it's a lot smoother, domestically speaking and from my standpoint, to have her heart and soul occupied by painting than by some guy like Hark. She goes out at times when I am away, but there are no longer any conflicts or demands or affirmations between us: just a contemplative and harmonious relationship."

A guy like Hark?

From another letter, I discovered that Hark was the nickname of an Air Force officer whom Mack would fly with in World War II and remain close friends with after the war. When I did some basic research on Hark, something puzzling emerged. He was fifteen years younger than Mack (and fourteen years younger than Irene). Could that be right?

Apparently it was.

My uncle said he remembered Hark staying at their apartment in New York when Mack was away. Hark was by then a loan officer at a bank—a career progression Mack would base one of his most memorable characters on, and in turn be immortalized in the history of American film. What Tim remembers from those visits is Hark staying up late talking to Irene. When Tim awoke in the middle of the night, he'd find Hark asleep on the other bed in his room, and in the morning they'd all have breakfast. Except, a few times he woke up in the middle of the night, long past midnight, listening for the sound of conversation. Nothing: a silent house, and the other bed still empty.

This sent me hustling to the Library of Congress index. Sure enough, Hark merited his own file folder. The letters ranged from 1944 until his very premature death at forty-three in the 1960s.

The early letters reflect a glib-talking relationship between Hark and Mack in which they come off as old frat brothers. Talking about a trip Mack took to Havana that apparently was less than satisfactory, Hark says, "I warned you about a visit to that fabled city with your family. It is rather better accomplished alone, as are the opportunities for compounding the felonies which in turn make the penicillin or sulfa or Bloody Marys all the sweeter, to say nothing of the memories and the mammaries."

Then there are several letters that would have been extremely puzzling if I hadn't known Tim's stories of Hark spending extended time with Irene while Mack was away. They were chatty accounts of Hark's adventures with Irene in Mack's obvious absence. Just one example: "I seem to have collapsed into a state of almost uninterrupted siesta. Irene has borne the overdose of sheer boredom with the most unflagging patience. . . . I can guarantee nothing more constructive for next week, although at the first sign of combat fatigue I am prepared to rush her into town for dinner."

If it is not a smoking gun, evidence of 1) an affair, and 2) an open marriage sort of relationship, with the knowledge and consent of the absent husband who possibly handpicked one of his closest friends to be the other man, it is damn close. Another letter comes even closer to revealing an "arrangement" gone bad, while still leaving room to wonder. Does the "blunder" in the following note refer to Mack arriving back home at an inopportune and compromising moment?

Mack, I deeply regret not having written you sooner, the more so because our last meeting began as a blunder and ended in complete fiasco. For this I can offer only profound regrets, and if at this point you feel inclined to dismiss them, I hope you will do so without a sneer. As you already know, I have deep and abiding

affection for you, which I reiterate. I hate to imagine that recipro-
cally it has gone down the drain, not 'with a bang, but a whim-
per.' . . . Between the lines was the perceptible suggestion of your
own tacit (at least) acquiescence in all this.

Ah, of course: Mack, at least in his own mind, was no ordinary philanderer, but a progressive, "creative type" who was open about his affairs and open-minded about the affairs of his wife—the "tacit (at least) acquiescence" Hark mentioned. That acquiescence bought him something: as he told Ginny-wabbit, an occupied Irene allowed for a much smoother go of it on the home front—and presumably made it easier for Mack to justify his various girlfriends. All good in theory, but in practice, well, it could lead to sneering and conflict. Better after all for Irene to lose herself in her painting rather than in one of Mack's buddies.

I unexpectedly discovered the ironic denouement of the Irene-Hark relationship in a 1951 letter my grandfather wrote to Dick Whiteman. I'll let Mack tell it:

Remember my old girl friend, the blond who used to be [my
agent's] secretary? At the time that she and I were especially
friendly, I introduced her to Sid L. and Sid, in turn, introduced
her to Hark. Believe it or not, she and Hark are now married. Isn't
that the damnedest thing?

Mack managed, despite the tangled quadrangle of relationships, to remain friends with Hark, exchanging chatty, intimate letters, until Hark's death in 1962. I'll never know how Irene reacted to Hark's marriage, or if she knew the bride had been a former girlfriend of her husband. All I know is that the entire soap opera situation was a recipe for agony—a reality Mack's breezy recounting seems to miss completely.

And as for Ginny-wabbit, that didn't end as Mack had imagined, either. Another letter to Whiteman, this one from 1953:

> *Have you run into Ginny anywhere? The damndest thing happened. When I was there in March '52 relations were easy-goingly cordial. I didn't write, as per usual, but last fall I wrote her* [the "wish I could have guv you a baby" letter] *and had Random House send her my two new books. Stopped in at Random on my way abroad and the guy in charge of shipping gave me a peculiar look, and produced the two books sent to Ginny. On the wrapper it said, "Refused by addressee." Ain't that something?*

I had to admit, it really was.

Then he went on to his other California girlfriend: "As for the dainty Barbara, she up and married Dick Whats-his-name last spring. So I am fresh out of girlfriends when and if I get out your way."

As a postscript he added, "Irene has been painting like a whiz; she gets better & better."

Good for Irene. And good for Mack.

Much later I found a further postscript in the California girlfriends saga in a letter from 1956, when he was fifty-two:

> *Occasionally I get a letter from Barbara. She's so erratic. I think she is still in love with me, despite her marriage, and that is very stupid. As for the other one—Ginny—I am told that she is very happy, although I don't know her married name.*

Mack's letters made it clear, or at least possible, that he believed his adventures had not ultimately damaged his marriage—Irene remained the "most desirable woman I've ever known," the one he would always come home to.

It frustrated me, as details of Mack's long history of adultery revealed themselves, that though I was getting an astonishingly intimate glimpse inside my grandfather's mind, I could never get even the slightest sense of how Irene saw things. I assumed it all had been horribly destructive to her, but was I in fact being narrow-minded?

And then I visited Webster City.

Lisa and I stayed in an old mansion, restored as a bed-and-breakfast, just a block away from what had once been the home of Adam and Evalyn McKinlay, where Effie Kantor raised her two children. Glorious in my grandfather's memory, this was the place where he heard his father's voice for the first confusing time through the receiver of a telephone, where he wrote his first short story and completed his first novel. To us, it appeared to be little more than a shack, paint shedding from the once whitewashed siding, weeds encroaching where a lilac-covered arbor had stood a century ago, sheltering Mack as he wrote in fine weather. We'd been told that until recently the house had been inhabited by a hoarder, stuffed floor to ceiling with junk. Now it stood empty—except for the junk, which still filled the rooms where Effie once played the piano and Mack sifted wonderingly through the bag containing buttons from his great-grandfather's Civil War uniform. I circled the house, hoping for some sense of magic, but all I got was an overwhelming blast of melancholy.

Webster City, population nine thousand, is no bigger than it was in 1904. What had been a prosperous farming and business community when my grandfather was a boy gradually hollowed out, losing almost all of its industry. Oddly, the declining downtown still contains an absolute gem of a public library, donated by Kendall Young, a wealthy nineteenth-century cattleman, and completed the year after my grandfather was born, with no expense spared. The large, two-story beaux arts building has gold marble columns imported from Africa, mosaic terrazzo floors, and stained glass coloring both large windows and an impressive dome. My grandfather, never an avid student, always said this was where he got his education. And now the library has a room set aside to contain a collection of his books, and letters that the Library of Congress is missing.

Some of them had been donated to the library by Dick Whiteman after Mack died. Perhaps nobody screened the letters before handing them over, or maybe whoever did decided that, given that everyone involved was dead, there was no reason to hold back.

I was glad for that lack of discretion. Because, finally, here was the smoking gun, the clear evidence of the impact on Irene of Mack's philandering, and it wasn't pretty.

Addressed to "Friends in the Know," Mack described a tour of France during which Irene won a bet for "a unit," as they called it, giving her the right to set the day's itinerary, compelling her husband to range far afield to a small town with a four-star restaurant she'd seen in a guidebook. Mack grudgingly obliged, but ended up enjoying the meal.

> *Come morning, Irene was morbid and kinda sullen, so I says Whatsa matter? . . . She said: Well, I dreamed about—Ugh, how could you?*
>
> *How could I what?*
>
> *You were writing to That Creature again!*
>
> *Which Creature? (Since there have been a galaxy of Creatures in my life, I can be pardoned for being obtuse. But she always has a most fearful intonation when she says those two words.)*

The one out in Los Angeles. Nasty little thing . . .

Oh, Barbara?

No, no, no . . . That nasty Ginny. Ugh . . . dreamed you were corresponding again, then you were meeting her and then . . . What a horrible woman!

By no means. I was very much in love with her, once. How could I not be? You were in love with Hark; I was shopping around, met Ginny. . . . We had perfectly marvelous times together, until she got so disturbed . . . so jealous of You, and my devotion to my family; she saw I would never get a divorce in order to marry her. . . .

Ugh. What a ghastly dream I had! Well, I can tell you this: If I ever hear of your seeing That Creature again, I'll . . .

Mack assured her all was in the past, and went out to pay the hotel bill.

So, there in the hitherto-unheard of town of Vienne, France, on the morning of 2 June, 1959, I closed the door, walked about eleven steps, saw a woman with dark glasses, heard her scream my name—And there I stood, face to face with . . . Ginny.

It was an odd feeling, holding that letter in my hands, knowing it would forever change the way I remembered my grandparents, and feeling a retrospective pity for my grandmother, both for a life of almost total dependency, and the pain of maintaining this illusion of a storied, everlasting romance.

I thought about something that had hovered in the back of my mind, a slight uneasiness I had felt when I noticed that in almost every "Dear Everyone" letter my grandfather wrote, he'd go on at great length about his doings, catch up about the kids, then the grandkids, and then finally close with a paragraph about Irene. It was always about her painting... "having fun this week with water colors" ... "doing some of the best work of her life" ... "sold two paintings last month" ...

Now I realized why it bothered me: It seemed too pat, a little patronizing, part of the elaborate maintenance of the myth of equal partnership, both creative and sexual. It was a myth that suited Mack's purposes. My uncle wrote that his father "thought it was wonderful that she was exercising what he privately, only privately, considered to be her modest gift, and so he praised each painting she made. 'Irene! That's magnificent!' And she would pause, eyes straining at the canvas; the brush held, uncertain, in her hand."

I put the "Creature" letter back in its folder and returned it to its rightful place in the MacKinlay Kantor collection of the Kendall Young Library. I exited into the main library and turned to leave. I walked about eleven steps when something caught my eye. There on the wall was an oil painting, a scene of a nun in a white habit walking down an unpaved street in a Spanish village. The colors are muted, somehow dyspeptic, and the houses to either side tilt inward. It's all a little dizzy and claustrophobic. The nun's eyes seem empty, holes in her soul.

I recognized the style, and glanced at the artist's signature in the lower right corner: *Irene Layne Kantor, 1954.*

B elieve it or not, I've so far omitted what could be the most significant of my grandfather's affairs, mostly because it takes some telling.

The night eighteen-year-old Tim Kantor sat in a bar "celebrating" his first sexual experience, when he got over the shock of his father's revelation, he remembered a time in his early childhood when Mack announced, "Now I'm going to take you to see one of the loveliest women in New York."

This lovely woman was Peggy Pulitzer, born Margaret Leech, the newly widowed second wife of Ralph Pulitzer, publisher of *The New York World* newspaper and heir to the great publishing fortune of Joseph Pulitzer. "Lovely" was no exaggeration. She had lustrous brown hair; a flawless peaches-and-cream complexion; large, luminous, wide-set eyes; and a perfectly proportioned nose and mouth—beauty saturated with a grave intelligence. She was ten years Mack's senior, and an accomplished writer in her own right: three well-received novels and a best-selling biography of New York anti-vice crusader Anthony Comstock, cowritten with legendary journalist Heywood Broun, to her credit. She was accomplished and clever enough that she became a recognized member of the famous Algonquin Round Table, which, if nothing else, indicated she could hold her own among the sharpest, wittiest conversationalists in America.

Tim's childhood visit with Mack to her home—which Tim chose to remember as a perfect echo of the time John Kantor took little Mack to see Sophie Tucker, "the most lovely woman in Chicago"—can be dated by Tim's age in the anecdote: six. That would make it 1939, the same year Mack had met the hot Costa Rican babe aboard the ship to Central America, and the same year he'd taken his solo apartment in New York—allegedly because he couldn't write in Sarasota.

Based on the dates of letters Mack had kept in a file marked, ambiguously, PULITZER, Mack and Peggy had been having an affair since 1936, when Peggy was researching her first solo book of nonfiction, an ambitious reconstruction of the Civil War in Washington, DC. To do so required daunting amounts of research at the Library of Congress, something at which Mack was already an expert. He had begun his prodigious sessions at the Library years earlier while researching *Long Remember,* and continued them for another Civil War novel that followed called *Arouse and Beware,* the tale of two escapees from a Confederate prison. As one reviewer said of the book, "There is, as with *Long Remember,* a note of authenticity in the manner and matter of telling."

No wonder. When Mack decided one of his characters would swim across the James River in early March under cover of darkness, he drove to Virginia and, in the middle of the night, found the location that matched his story, stripped off his clothes, and plunged in, banging against rocks and shuddering in the cold: "I thought to myself, you could get killed this way."

He had also consumed the kind of maggot-ridden food prisoners at Andersonville would have eaten. These stunts aside, most of the authenticity in his historical novels owed itself to the countless hours he'd spent in his private study carrel at the Library of Congress.

When Mack wasn't in DC researching, he was gadding about New York in literary venues, and sure to have rubbed up against his Algonquin peers if not been invited to sit at the table himself on occasion. It's easy to imagine that, if so, he would have paid especial interest to members of the female persuasion. That speculation isn't much of a stretch considering Mack's description of his lunches with his publisher Tim Coward at that other famous venue for publishing types, the Oak Room of the Plaza Hotel.

He was an inveterate gossip; so was I, and how we loved to sit at the corner table and chew over everything which had happened in the past week or month—which had befallen us or had befallen others whom we knew. Wearying of this gentle sport, we would then privately, and with due meditation, appraise the ladies sitting nearby, then each would come up with his selection A) for marriage B) for a solitary week-end upon some tropical island C) a one night stand, pure and simple. . . . All the time the poor innocent women would be laughing and chattering or drinking and dining utterly unaware of this profanation. . . . We were children at these times, sophomores if you will, but we were reasonably healthy and reasonably happy and we both had good imaginations.

He clearly didn't always stop at imagining things. Between Mack's good looks and rising talent, and the happy fact that he had lots to teach about research and the Civil War, Peggy, a sophisticate if there ever was one, must have either overlooked the mile-wide sophomoric streak in him or found it somehow endearing, presenting the intriguing challenge of polishing the rough edges off this boyish man with so much potential.

In any case, the letters make it clear that she accepted that charge with relish, and pleasure.

"Not the least of the things that have happened in the last year is, for me, the ability to excite your mind a little sometimes," she wrote to him. "I don't mean dragging you to *Othello*, or putting on a disk of Beethoven, though they have a relation to what I mean. But I like to strike an occasional spark from those dim recesses. . . . It's not completely different from the excitement of sex, just the same sort of emotion permitted to invade the entire personality."

Mack had never been to college, never even read some of the classics of literature. It was Peggy who urged him to read Tolstoy, the Russian master whose ability to write about characters in vast historic panoramas as if he had access to X-rays of their souls wowed Mack. In a letter from that same year to Virginia, Mack reported, "Have read *Of Human Bondage* and *The Way of All Flesh* this summer. Am now boring stubbornly and willingly under the vast weight of humanity in *War and Peace*."

So, progress! In one letter, Peggy wrote: "Sweetheart, you've got the makings of a great person, and I like the way you're doing."

What would it take to mold those "makings" into the man Peggy imagined?

Well, they had plenty of opportunity to practice the polishing, with both of them making trips to DC to labor at research in the Jefferson building.

(That research, carried on periodically over the course of two decades and several books, would result in both authors winning Peggy's father-in-law's little literary prize. In 1942, Peggy would become the first woman to win the Pulitzer Prize for history for *Reveille in Washington, 1860–1865*, and eighteen years later would become the only woman ever to win that prize twice. Given her married name, it's necessary to add that, sixty years after that first award, prominent book critic Jonathan Yardley wrote, "No one who has read *Reveille in Washington* can believe that the prize was won on anything except merit.")

In those early days, when all such accolades were yet undreamed of, Mack and Peggy spent their time dreaming of each other. After one joint research trip in 1938, soon after a novelette by Mack called *Writing in the Sky* had been published in *The Saturday Evening Post*, Peggy wrote, elliptically but evocatively:

"The yellow church on the corner brings back a luminous grey morning, with all the branches wet and black and the girls hurrying their way to work. The writing on the sky says Mack. It's a miracle."

For all I knew, Peggy was referring to somewhere in New York, but living in Washington, I instantly thought of St. John's Episcopal

Church in Lafayette Square, near the White House, which every president since James Madison has attended at least once, for no other reason than that it is the most strikingly yellow church on a corner I know. This thought was nothing more than passing fancy, of course, until I came across a note in Mack's short story collection mentioning that when he was conducting research at the Library of Congress in 1937 he stayed at the Hay-Adams hotel, which is . . . directly across the street from St. John's.

I found it easy to imagine the two of them, steeped in pheromones, inhabiting that snow-globe world unique to completely entwined lovers, cosseted in the lovely Italian Renaissance confines of the Hay-Adams, with its vaults and arches and dentil moldings and floor-to-ceiling windows overlooking the yellow church on the corner.

It took me a surprisingly long time to realize just why it was so easy for me to imagine, and so vivid in the imagining. In some nearly forgotten time decades ago—a moment that might as well have been another life—I met a woman under similar circumstances: illicit rendezvous, cozy historic hotel, research trip to Washington. Okay, *identical* circumstances: She was also a writer, introduced to me when we had both been awarded the same prize for our work. Such an odd, chill-inducing parallel served well enough to remind me how little standing I had to judge my grandfather harshly.

In my grandfather's case, it's clear that Peggy, older and wiser, never imagined that their "miracle" would ever include them leaving their spouses for each other, even after she was widowed in June 1939. She saw his marriage—which no doubt in frankness, Mack would have characterized as a happy one—and their age difference as net positives:

It is even an advantage that our birthdays are so disparate, for the high unsuitability of our ages frees us, without the restless intrusion of hope, to preserve the quality of our love. Does that sound like a lot of words? I mean that it is normal for two people who love each other deeply to look forward to that fulfillment which must be the end of romance. Well, we have our romance, and are permitted to keep it longer than more fortunate lovers do.

It didn't turn out to be all that long. In 1939, she wrote him one last letter as his lover—there would be other letters through the remaining decades of his life, but they would be polite, distantly fond. Obviously, she had grown weary of her pupil lagging behind.

You are at a Parting of the Ways, and, though startlingly undeveloped, won't be able to keep on growing up—even you!—much after thirty-five. So unless you take a brace and look about you and associate with people of more background and broadmindedness and procure a modicum of education and get curious and take some cognizance of the great culture of Western Europe, on which everything we have and are is based and which until now you have tossed aside like an old brochure on the wall-paintings of Southern Tibetan lamaseries, as something too esoteric and unrelated to your experience, as well as too complex and formidable, as well as something you don't feel quite up to bothering with, like typhoid fever shots—I say, taking a long breath, unless you do all these things and set about them hard this very afternoon, you are presently going to turn into one of those elderly Pucks, those superannuated Peter Pans, these elfin, quaint, dear old special Characters, who grow old without ever having grown up.

It was a snooty and insulting (also literate and amusing) takedown. Certainly, it was memorable—how many breakup letters have you gotten from a Pulitzer Prize–winning writer? But perhaps the most amazing thing about that letter is that Mack kept it—this brilliant lecture on his immaturity—ripped from the rest of the letter, folded and tucked into an envelope marked PEGGY in that no longer so ambiguous PULITZER file.

THIRTEEN

———

A s most of America languished in the Depression through the mid-1930s, my grandfather prospered. Though the books that followed *Long Remember* and *The Voice of Bugle Ann* would not become top sellers, between continuing book royalties and advances, movie-option deals, and ever-increasing rates for short stories, he managed to make $35,000 in 1937, which incredibly is the equivalent of about $600,000 today. In 1938, he made $27,000 ($460,000 equivalent).

Consider how astounding it is, then, that after making the contemporary equivalent of about a million dollars over two years, in the first month of 1939 he wrote this to his sister:

"Since I sold my first poem in 1923 for two bucks, I have made one hundred and thirty-two thousand, nine hundred and one dollars. . . .

To my intense delight, I find myself not at all baffled or broken-hearted because I haven't any of it left."

For someone who'd grown up in poverty and only briefly glimpsed the luxury purchased by the tainted wealth of his father, Mack had a real talent for spending. I saw one letter from this period where he discussed the impossibility of getting by without servants—cooks, maids, and a full-time nanny—despite the fact that Irene did not work. He rented houses in Manhattan, and in upstate New York, and even in Webster City, where he funded a summer archaeological expedition to excavate Indian mounds he'd always been curious about when he was growing up. He paid off ancient family debts, repurchased his childhood home as a summer place (he never used it), and put Virginia's daughter, born with cerebral palsy, through five years of an expensive private school for kids with disabilities. There were cruises to South America and multiple tours of Europe, complete with first-class cabins in the ships that brought them there and luxury hotel rooms in the places they traveled. And he built the (too expensive) beach house on Siesta Key.

He tried to put a positive spin on it all in that January 1939 letter: "Irene and I have kept ourselves through a combined quarter century of life, and we have had fun. We have learned, seen, looked, laughed, cried, growled, cheered, whined or enjoyed. We have driven cars, we have sailed and flown and fished and danced and drunk and eaten. We own nearly twenty thousand dollars worth of palm trees and sand and beds and tables and curtains and hibiscus bushes, even if we can't do much with it right now."

A year later, finances had only gotten worse.

In January of 1941 he wrote Dick Whiteman: "1940 was a hell of a year and so was the last part of 1939. Couldn't write and was oppressed with bills and financial necessities . . . had a nervous breakdown."

A nervous breakdown?

I had never heard nor imagined such a thing about my grandfather. As I had always understood it, through sheer cussedness and almost superhuman perseverance, Mack had banged his head against the wall of literary success until he broke through with *Long Remember*, and then never looked back. I'd even found a newspaper interview where he'd made exactly that assessment of his own career.

Now it appeared that wasn't the whole story. Nor was writer's block the entire cause. The breakdown came right about the time Peggy Pulitzer told him to grow up. The timing is unlikely to be a coincidence.

He continued: "Went to Central America twice to recuperate. . . ." I had to assume he considered the hookup with the hot señora on the first of those voyages part of his therapy. He found a different kind of heat on his next trip: "I caught a recurrent fever which started hitting me in a regular menstrual cycle. . . . Well it's one long tale of woe up to December of 1940. Last year I earned less than half of what I earned in 1937. I simply couldn't work and there was an end to it. . . . We got a lucky break by not selling our house down here when we had actually tried to and I hoped to, so now we are comfortably installed and I am really doing some work and enjoying it."

Looked at another way: Now that Peggy had dumped him, the apartment in New York no longer seemed so necessary. Suddenly, Florida was the perfect place to work.

In 1941, he indeed began to turn things back around. He made $17,000—same as $275,000 today—but it still wasn't enough to pay his debts and support his lifestyle. He'd gone through the earnings, including the advance on a novel he'd whipped out in two months, and was still behind on his phone bill.

The novel, *Gentle Annie*, was a shoot-'em-up Western with a twist.

The bandits were sympathetic, and the sheriff not. Again, Mack was ahead of his time with this moral ambiguity, anticipating *Butch Cassidy and the Sundance Kid* by twenty-eight years. He hoped to attract serial publication in a major magazine and the interest of Hollywood. But the Japanese had just bombed Pearl Harbor. War was upon America and nobody knew what the coming years would bring. Certainly nobody knew what Americans would want to read, or what movies they'd want to see, in wartime.

Mack's agent had bleak news: Magazine editors had been infected with caution. His plot was too immoral for their readers, they'd decided. From Hollywood, there was only silence.

My uncle's memoir tells what happened next: Just after New Year's 1942, Mack decided to use his dwindling funds to travel to New York himself and see if he could do any better selling his stuff than his agents had. After a few days of hotel bills and bar tabs, he had to admit failure.

Feeling down and defeated, he boarded a return train to Florida at Penn Station. He'd taken his seat, no doubt thinking grimly of starting all over again with new ideas for new stories that might well not sell, either, when a boy holding a slip of paper in his hand came walking toward his seat calling, "Mr. Canton? Mr. Canton?"

Close enough. Mack took the paper from the boy and unfolded it: a message telling him to call Tim Coward. What could be so important that he'd be called off a train? He felt a brush of alarm. Irene? The kids?

"Oh," the messenger added, belatedly remembering his instructions. "Mr. Coward said to tell you it was good news."

Very good news. From the stationmaster's office he called Coward, who told him Donald Friede, Mack's new Hollywood agent, had telephoned to say that he'd been offered $20,000 for the film rights to *Gentle Annie*—and turned it down. Friede felt certain they could get even more. Mack should find somewhere he could talk comfortably and call Friede back.

Mack had been staying in a cheap hotel downtown, but to hell with that now. He told Coward he'd be at the bar in the Algonquin, and that's where Friede reached him.

The offer was now $25,000 for movie rights.

"But the deciding point," Friede explained in a letter he wrote to Mack that same day, "was the offer of a twenty-seven week writing contract. . . . You will have an opportunity which I feel you need very badly, namely the opportunity of learning motion picture technique. . . . With what you will learn out here—being paid for learning it at the rate of $1,000 per week—you will be able to quadruple your income in the future."

Since he'd sold the rights to *Long Remember* in 1934, Mack's experience with the movies had been mixed. *Long Remember* got kicked around from studio to studio, but never filmed. *The Voice of Bugle Ann* had become a fairly successful movie. But mostly his relations with "the Coast" had been so much sound and fury.

"I've had three series of negotiations with those people which came to anything, and about fifteen which came to nothing," he wrote in a 1936 letter.

In 1938, he said he had been approached to come to Hollywood to rewrite the screenplay of *Gone with the Wind*, but "we scared them out by asking for too much money."

Well, now the money was on the table, the equivalent of nearly $15,000 a week in 2015 currency for twenty-seven weeks over a two-year period.

Let the spending begin.

Once in Hollywood, he rented a big house on Beverly Glen Boule-
vard in West LA, overlooking a pool, a patio bar, changing rooms, and
landscaped hills beyond. He labored there, between parties where he
palled around with stars including Gregory Peck and James Cagney,
mostly in futility. *Gentle Annie* got made, with Donna Reed as the
romantic lead, and earned modestly positive box office and reviews,
but someone else wrote the screenplay.

That would be the case for most of his books that made it to film.
Eventually, in 1950, he would get a significant screenwriting credit.
The movie, *Gun Crazy*, was based on a short story he'd written and
is now considered a noir classic, the inspiration for Arthur Penn's
famous film version of *Bonnie and Clyde* with Warren Beatty and Faye
Dunaway. Even today, noir buffs know and love *Gun Crazy*. The
aggregate critical rating on the Rotten Tomatoes movie website is an
almost unheard of 97 percent. One typical review from a critic reads,
"One of the most distinguished works of art to emerge from the B
movie swamp."

I bought the DVD and watched it one night, not knowing what to
expect. I was riveted. The plot centered—as the original story had—on
a sympathetic bad guy, a reform-school kid who had a passion for
guns. When he ages out of state custody, he really is reformed, a decent
sort who can't even bring himself to shoot a rabbit, until he hooks
up with a femme fatale in the form of a carnival sharpshooter à la
Annie Oakley, a temptress with all the moral fiber of Lucrezia Borgia.
She leads him into a life of bank robbing, then murder, and finally
doom—the inevitable unwinnable dead-end shootout, surrounded by
heavily armed police. The characterizations are grabbing, the dialogue amusingly hard-boiled, and the direction way ahead of its time,

including a famous scene of one of the bank robberies filmed entirely from the lover/robbers' point of view, using a single camera in one unbroken take.

I thought it exceedingly odd that my grandfather had written a cult-classic movie that I'd never known about. As I dug deeper, I discovered why Mack had never mentioned it. In *Who the Devil Made It*, Peter Bogdanovich's 1997 book of movie lore, *Gun Crazy* director Joseph H. Lewis told him: "The King brothers came to me. They had a script written by MacKinlay Kantor—quite a fabulous writer, as you well know . . . about 375 pages [roughly five hours of screen time], and the task was given to me to cut it down to about 140 pages. . . . Now, in so doing, maybe I took out some of the things he liked. . . . He has never forgiven me. . . . He's the only one I ever spoke to who said he thought the picture was horrible."

The final script was attributed to my grandfather and Millard Kaufman, who wrote an Oscar-nominated script for *Bad Day at Black Rock* and, later in his career, co-created the character Mr. Magoo. As I dug deeper, I discovered that actually Kaufman had nothing to do with the script, except agreeing to serve as a front for the writer Dalton Trumbo, who had refused to "name names" in the House Un-American Activities Committee's communist witch hunt and was declared in contempt. He served eleven months in prison and was blacklisted from Hollywood movies when he got out.

I wanted to credit my grandfather with the noble deed of offering to front for the unjustly treated Trumbo, as some sources indicated. But Kaufman shared Trumbo's agent, and said that he was the one approached with the request. I ultimately concluded Mack's only contribution to helping Trumbo out was in writing a script so massive it needed a rewrite in the first place.

I don't know if Mack always wrote so overlong in his Hollywood efforts, but I do know this: Though he spent good portions of a number of years laboring in Hollywood and eventually a dozen of his books would be produced as movies or television shows, other than one forgotten B Western and *Gun Crazy*, his screenwriting credits are nowhere to be found. Even *Long Remember*, his big best-selling hit, kept failing to make it into theaters. Mack's hopes kept being raised, then dashed, the classic Hollywood two-step. In 1939, he wrote to a friend that Merian Cooper, who'd directed *King Kong*, had expressed strong interest in *Long Remember*, then backed off.

"If *Gone with the Wind* is successful," Mack wrote, "he may take another crack at the Civil War."

Gone with the Wind came out the following year and became the highest-grossing film of all time. I guess you could call that successful. But *Long Remember* was never produced.

"I think I can call myself about the most unproduced writer in Hollywood," Mack said in a newspaper interview. "They buy a lot of my stuff, and get me out there on special writing jobs, but most of the time they seem to lay my work in files and forget about it."

It probably isn't all that unusual, then or now. Hollywood is famous for many things, including its profligate waste of both talent and money. One of my closest friends and his writing partner were assigned by a famous director to write a screenplay and were paid a lot of money for it. When they finished, all the director's minions oohed and ahhed about how great it was—Number One for Takeoff! Totally green-lit. Some A-list star just couldn't wait to make it!

And then, years passed in silence, during which, unbeknownst to my friend, the director gave the script to two other writers. Both did complete rewrites. Both cashed big checks.

Five years later, the famous director called again to say he'd recently reread all three scripts and decided that my friend's version was his favorite. With a few caveats.

So once again my friend and his partner were handed a big wad of cash to do yet another rewrite. Once again the minions cooed wildly over the completed script—totally green-lit! A big star cannot wait to make it! And then . . . nothing.

I've had my own Hollywood hijinks. My book *Old Souls*, about a psychiatrist who spent thirty years investigating cases of small children who appeared to remember previous lives, was optioned to the movies a half-dozen times, each time with energetic assurances that it would become a feature film or a documentary or a TV series. Once, someone worked on a script for a couple of years and then said that the story had been altered so much in the process, he no longer felt he needed the rights. Another time a producer used capital letters in an e-mail, saying how much she LOVED, LOVED, LOVED the screenplay that I'd finally written myself and how she was DEFINITELY buying it, after which she never returned another message. Finally, a big production company—also rabidly positive about the book—optioned it yet again. When I called to discuss how they were going to handle the adaptation, I discovered that they were turning a story about a researcher risking his career to explore the fringes of science into a story about a cult of serial killers who believed that reincarnated children might bring about the apocalypse.

It is oddly comforting to learn that my grandfather would have understood, and been sympathetic.

"No one knows better than myself that the picture business is cock-eyed," he wrote in a 1936 letter.

In any case, by 1940, Mack no longer wanted to be a screenwriter. What he really wanted to do, what he'd wanted to do ever since he was a child playing make-believe in Webster City, and as a teenager telling lies in Des Moines, was go to war.

A s the Nazi war machine trampled Europe, Mack was entering middle age and was physically unfit for service. Yet he'd been looking for a way to join the fight ever since, as he told his sister, British prime minister Neville Chamberlain had condemned Hitler's invasion of Poland in September 1939. Mack had already persuaded *The Saturday Evening Post* to sponsor his application for certification as a war correspondent by the relevant French and British bureaucracies.

"I was going in the middle of September, but realized that I had to get the family in proper financial shape before I left . . . also the leg was giving me trouble," he told Virginia.

It wasn't until the summer of 1943—after the sale of *Gentle Annie* to the movies filled his accounts once more and a surgeon at Johns Hopkins finally managed to permanently heal the seeping wound in his thigh, which had plagued him on and off, mostly on, for two decades—that he actually went.

To do so meant he would be leaving not only Irene, but his fifteen-year-old daughter and ten-year-old son. I found a disturbing mention of this aspect in my uncle's memoir. When my mother, understandably upset, asked why he had to go to war, Mack said he felt duty-bound, and then added, "You know, Layne-o, I kind of hope I don't come back."

Shocked and terrified, she asked why he would say such a thing.

"Well, hell, I'd make a lousy old man."

That last sentence leapt off the page and exploded in my brain. Forty-one years after Mack went off to war I was sitting with my father in his Siesta Key living room when he got the news that, at age fifty-seven, he had less than a year to live before lung cancer would kill him.

"What the hell," he said. "I would have made a lousy old man."

———

Mack sold his plan to write about the war to Ben Hibbs, the legendary editor of *The Saturday Evening Post*.

"I couldn't be sure how Mack would perform as a war correspondent," Hibbs wrote in a recollection, "but I suspected that the fire within him, his towering love of country, was something the American people could use in those anxious days."

Mack had a less altruistic intent. "I simply didn't want to miss out on this emotional experience as I did the last one," he wrote.

It made me think of all the old movies in which men exulted in cheers and hat-waving when they learned they would be going to war. Apparently it was what people did Back Then. Was it real? Or a mask to hide their fear?

I pictured my own dread, so vivid still after nearly half a century, lying on a bunk in a dormitory room, listening to a voice on the radio reading out birth dates and draft numbers, knowing that but for a quirk of luck I might soon be swept to the other side of the world, forced to kill, or be killed by, people against whom I had no grudge and who otherwise presented no threat I found credible. As I lay awake in the small defenseless hours after midnight, my mind endlessly looped around a puzzle with no solution. Would I go or would I run? Was I driven by conscience or cowardice? How different would I feel if I thought war could accomplish something, if not entirely good, at least absolutely necessary?

From the earliest time I can remember, war meant one thing to me, an unstoppable holocaust of nuclear destruction; cities flattened, walls blown away, bodies incinerated or cooked by deadly radiation; all the beauty in the world poisoned. I spent long nights of my childhood fearing I'd never have a chance to grow up, or that I'd sicken and starve in a postapocalyptic wasteland.

So I suppose that Mack had both a more clearly necessary war and a somewhat forgivably less nihilistic understanding of its consequences. All his life he had longed to be a hero. I'd seen it in his childhood fascination with the Civil War vets, the self-deluded belief that he had rescued a girl from a burning car, and his atrocious lies about serving in the First World War. The civilian hero of his imagination, the protagonist of *Long Remember*, talked his way past pickets, unarmed, into one of the most famous and fatal infantry charges in history, not only surviving, but somehow managing to kill a Confederate general with a borrowed bayonet in the process.

Even when he was in his late thirties, there remained an element of a boy yearning to prove he was a man—something he apparently hadn't been able to do, no matter how many women he'd had. He would be a correspondent only because he couldn't be a soldier. His goal was not to report whatever truth he could find—which is my understanding of being a war correspondent—it was to help in the fight.

"If I were any good, I would do something a little more pertinent," he wrote. "But I guess I'll have to content myself with propaganda."

At first, he did. And because his propaganda was effective, over time he managed to ingratiate himself with the standoffish American airmen he was more or less embedded with in the 305th Bomb Group of the Army's 8th Air Force, stationed at an airfield in Chelveston, seventy miles north of London. The commanding officer was a feisty colonel named Curtis LeMay, whom Mack instantly admired and whose favor he curried.

In August of 1943, Mack scored a hit with a heroic poem—aimed squarely at the tear ducts—about a tragedy all too common in an air war that was taking heavy casualties. On July 4 of that year, a B-17 bomber from the 305th was hit by enemy flak and set on fire. Seven crew members were able to parachute from the flaming plane, but one of those chutes opened too soon and caught fire.

Or as Mack put it so floridly in the poem:

> . . . a little flame chewing,
> Eating the glossiest silk of the chute.
> Who was it had waited not near long enough?
> Who let his hand tremble too eager and wild?
> Who managed his handle too soon, so the cord
> Tossed open the fabric to kiss the high fire?

There was some question as to which of the crew had died this way, and Mack played that uncertainty to effect by focusing on the plane's young navigator, Second Lieutenant William R. Bailey, whom he had met, briefly, in the barracks.

Based on the poem, he obviously didn't know him well, playing off instead on a sentimental stereotype of a Kentucky kid from the heartland:

> This is the way that I think of you always:
> Cocky and walking untrammeled and quick.
> Tough face and monkey mouth wrinkled and pert. . . .
> Childish forever you swagger and sing.
> Always your cot with its rumpled gray blanket.
> Always your pin-ups with lingerie leer,
> Always your silken-limbed blondes on the wall,
> Always your tongue running loose, and some
> Fellow hauling you off of the bed on your fanny,
> All the way down to the floor with a bump.

Like a drumbeat throughout the long poem, filled with insider jargon (*Broken the firing pin / Or broken the firing pin extension, / Or broken the belt-holding pawl arm*), was the repeated refrain *O Bailey—who burned?*

It didn't strike me as a great poem, but like the sentimental mourning-in-verse of spelunker Floyd Collins that launched Mack's literary career a quarter century earlier, it would hit a chord with a public eager to connect emotionally with the appalling losses.

Still, then as now, a heroic poem was an oddball way to reach the masses.

When the dispatch arrived at Ben Hibbs's desk and he saw that it was verse he thought, *Oh, God! What has this unpredictable guy done now?*

By Hibbs's account, he put the poem on his second-in-command's desk without a word. The number two "came back with his eyes glittering, and said, 'Let's give it the works.'"

Here's the telegram, now in the Library of Congress files, that Hibbs sent to Mack in Europe:

"HAVE DECIDED TO BREAK RULE LONG STANDING AND GIVE BAILEY TWO PAGES UP FRONT WITH FULL COLOR PAINTING STOP."

The big display, and even bigger response from readers, made an impression on the men with bars on their shoulders whom Mack depended on for access. Now that he had proven himself simpatico to his air squadron hosts, he managed to talk his way into the squadron's gunnery school, learning to shoot the big .50-caliber machine guns that provided a B-17's only defense against attacking enemy planes. He gained entry by saying he wanted to take the course to write about it, but he finished second in his class, a result that gave him the credibility to wheedle his way into actual combat missions, and even to fire the gun in anger when the navigator was otherwise occupied. This latter chore was expressly forbidden to correspondents under the Geneva convention, so I suppose that, technically, my grandfather was a war criminal.

I admired Mack's drive to get close to the story, even though close meant sitting in the freezing confines of a lumbering B-17 at altitude, flying into flak so heavy it could be mistaken for cloud cover while German Messerschmitts screamed through the sky, hunting them.

I don't even like to fly on supersafe commercial flights, and neither, I discovered, did my grandfather. In one interview, he said he had nearly lost his Cedar Rapids newspaper job by refusing to take a plane to a distant assignment. Yet he flew five combat missions, missions in which one of every twenty planes sent out didn't return. The sheer horror of combat in these flying coffins has been so well and vividly described in immortal novels like *Catch-22* and nonfiction masterpieces like *Unbroken*, I feel I can fully imagine the almost supernatural effort of will it would take for someone who didn't absolutely *have* to be there to nonetheless voluntarily climb up that ladder into the belly of the beast. Not just once, but five times (one source, less reliable, in my view, said he flew eleven missions). During one of these he claimed to have fired in the general direction of an incoming German fighter, and to have been awarded a "probable kill" when that enemy plane went down.

My grandfather would have had one more mission to his credit, I discovered, but the orders to allow him to board a B-17 nicknamed Polly Ann before dawn on September 23, 1943, were botched. Some junior officer failed to transmit Mack's authorization in time, which Mack regarded as nothing more than "a rank and annoying stupidity."

In due course, it became something far more significant than that.

I found his account in an author's note on a short story he wrote in

1944. The bomber had departed before dawn, without Mack, for a raid on Stuttgart, Germany. Mack was at the airfield when the squadron returned from the successful mission around noon.

As they were landing, "the plane went down; the crew died instantaneously in flames and in the hasty disintegration that comes with impact. I watched them smoldering for hours—watched the wreckage of the B-17 in which I had been supposed to ride and from which I had been saved by a microscopic, unpredictable defect in the machinery of Bomber Command."

Of the "ten boys" on the plane, there were no survivors, he said.

I have to admit, given my grandfather's history of embellishment of his military encounters, I wondered if perhaps he had made up his near miss. Correspondents have exaggerated their combat scrapes before and since, of course; Brian Williams and Bill O'Reilly being only the most recent examples. But what were the odds I could confirm or disprove, seventy years after the fact, the crash landing of a single B-17 out of 4,754 of the bombers lost in the European theater?

My grandfather had noted the date of the event and I knew the base where it took off and allegedly crashed. It turned out that was all I needed. With a little searching, I found a crash on landing on that date at the Chelveston air base, with ten fatalities, just as he'd said. That's how I knew the plane was nicknamed Polly Ann, and that it was flown by a pilot on his fourteenth mission by the name of Norman A. Drouin, just twenty-two, three years younger than my son.

The official report said Drouin was flying in the lead on the approach to the landing strip. When he peeled off to land, he slowed too much and collided with the planes on either side. The other planes, both damaged, managed to land without casualties, but Drouin went down just short of the strip. Polly Ann crashed and burned. It wasn't classified as a loss by enemy action. So, pilot error?

The reports I found made no mention of any other factor, but Mack said the plane had been so shot up with flak in the raid that it had become virtually unmaneuverable.

A few days after the crash, my grandfather went to where the men had been buried, Brookwood Cemetery, "drawn not by the magnet of affection (I did not know those boys well . . .) but rather by a grim personal curiosity. . . . Brookwood stayed in my mind. Each time I closed my eyes I saw again the patient trees . . . quiet lengths of clipped grass above the older graves, brown gravel on the new ones. Waking or sleeping, I saw those crosses."

I'd always been confused as a kid, seeing photos of my grandfather posing jauntily in his Air Force uniform, a pair of wings pinned above his breast, the thin line of a neatly clipped mustache above a huge grin, and a dazzling light in his eyes that I now see as an explosion of joy at finally inhabiting the role of his dreams. I'd been unaware that even war correspondents had uniforms in those days, so between that, all those mementos on the wall, his friendship with General LeMay, and the showy regimental insignia he wore on his blue blazer, I'd always assumed he'd actually been in the Air Force.

Now that I knew more about his war experience, I understood. As far as Mack was concerned, he had been.

And apparently, the Air Force shared that conviction.

Very early in my research I came across something online that said MacKinlay Kantor had won the Presidential Medal of Freedom. Stunned, I immediately texted my brother and sister. Turned out that none of us had ever heard that our grandfather had been awarded the highest honor the United States government can bestow on a civilian. How could that be? Mack wasn't exactly shy in pointing out his achievements.

I still can't explain it, other than as an index of our sheer inattention and indifference to matters of family history. The Web accounts were murky on the details of why it was awarded, and even differed—by a decade—on when he received it.

That all got cleared up in spades when I came across Mack's own typed account of the award presentation. He wrote it quite clearly while still giddy with excitement, wanting to share his moment with a long list of friends. "When the thing finally broke, it broke fast," he wrote. He'd been in New York in November 1947 when he got the call, two days before the proposed presentation ceremony in Washington, which would be presided over by General Carl "Tooey" Spaatz, recently appointed as the first chief of staff of the newly independent Air Force. Mack was asked if that would be convenient. "Since you don't tell a four-star general that anything would be inconvenient, I said Yes."

It wasn't convenient. The date chosen was the day before Thanksgiving. Mack yanked fourteen-year-old Tim out of school, and called my mother at college, telling her to come home a day early. On Wednesday, November 26, he took the 9:30 train to Washington's Union Station with Irene and the kids. There was one additional passenger in their party, of high interest to me given what I knew about the future of their relationship—his best buddy from the war and Irene's present and/or future lover, Hark. Then, irony upon irony, the man who had flown five combat missions said they were taking the train and "refusing to fly because of the pitiful and dangerous state of commercial aviation."

I guess it was an acceptable risk only if people were shooting at you.

The actual citation for the medal, which, contrary to what you can find online, was not the Presidential Medal of Freedom then, but simply the Medal of Freedom, initiated to allow the military to honor civilians who had made strong contributions to the war effort. "I think they have authorized fourteen of them to date—including Marlene Dietrich's," Mack reported. "I know my legs weren't as pretty as hers; but I can't tell you whether mine were shaking."

Spaatz read the citation, which Mack says he barely heard—"all I could recognize was Tooey's militant gaze, burning like tracer bullets."

The award, it said, was for "outstanding service . . . through his personal experiences and his participation in actual combat operations he became familiar with the problems and characteristics of the Air Forces and skillfully carried the soldier's story to the people . . . and contributed immeasurably to the morale of the Armed forces and to the enlightenment of the American people."

Digging through one of the boxes of family photos my sister had been storing, I came across the official news photo of the medal ceremony. The general is focused on the breast of my grandfather's tweed coat, where he is attaching the medal, a humble medallion back then. Mack is staring straight ahead, appearing for once more frightened than proud. He is standing at attention, but his rounded shoulders and a slight wedge of fat beneath his chin announce middle age. As I thought about the date, I realized that this is how Mack would have looked when my father encountered him for the first time, courting my mother after they met at a college party given by mutual friends.

Also in my sister's boxes were a clutch of old envelopes, bound by a rubber band that disintegrated at my touch, containing letters my father had written to my mother in the year between when they met and when they married. They consisted almost entirely of an elaborate catalog of his longing for her, written in a classically adolescent style by a young man just out of the Navy and barely out of his teens. More intriguing, and surprising, were some other envelopes containing evidence of my father's early desire to be a writer, unknown to me. "The stories I want to write, the things I love and hate," as he put it in an unintentionally amusing prose poem: "Whistling in the oblivious world upon a rainy street. Living life and being lived by life. Trying to delve into the incomprehensible, and finding nothing but my own personal thoughts . . . the joy of putting your ideas on paper as you wish them to be put down, and the keen and bitter disappointment when you fail."

In fact, my father went into his father's building business, which he never loved, and often hated. He completely lacked the ability to sit in one place alone for more than a few minutes, much less to struggle with the eternity of writing, so he channeled his desire to express himself artistically into directing community theater productions, at which he grew expert enough to secure a brief gig directing a professional off-Broadway production of an Arthur Miller play.

His desire to write, if it still existed, was never mentioned while I was growing up. But I would find out, late, when he knew he was dying, just how essential it had been—not to him, but to me, to my very existence.

One of the main things that attracted him to my mother, he told me, was that her father was MacKinlay Kantor.

In my adult life, whenever the subject of my grandfather came up, I would begin, "You've probably never heard of him," and most people hadn't.

They were impressed by the mention of a Pulitzer Prize, of course, but the title *Andersonville* most often produced a squint—the name seemed kind of familiar, though possibly because of the unrelated recent Turner Broadcasting movie of that name or the historic prison camp itself.

The one thing that almost always rings at least a faint bell is *The*

Best Years of Our Lives, a 1946 movie that killed at the box office, swept the Oscars, and still makes most lists of great American films. When humanities scholar Stanley Fish did a top ten all-time movie list for *The New York Times* in 2009, *Best Years* was number one—the greatest American movie, period. Fish's blurb: "Regarded as producer Sam Goldwyn's masterpiece . . . filled with thrilling and affecting scenes."

I always hesitated to mention it, though, because this was one aspect of my grandfather's career I had always known, or thought I had known, and it was complicated.

The story I remember my mother telling was this: Mack wrote a novel about vets returning home from the war. Against his editor's strenuous objection, he wrote the entire book in blank verse. When Sam Goldwyn asked him to turn it into a screenplay, he got halfway through the script, then said he was quitting to go back to the war. Goldwyn, enraged, brought in another screenwriter. When the movie came out, he vengefully changed the title to *The Best Years of Our Lives*, chosen by a focus group. Mack hated it, thought the internal irony would be missed or misconstrued. He had named his book *Glory for Me*, after a hymn his mother had loved (*When all my labors and trials are o'er, / And I am safe on that beautiful shore, / Just to be near the dear Lord I adore, . . . / O that will be glory for me*). Goldwyn refused to even mention the name of Mack's novel in the film's credits, leaving my grandfather feeling bitter and betrayed.

My research told a far more complete, and significantly different, story.

Articles written when the movie came out said that either Goldwyn, or Goldwyn's wife, became fascinated with a story that appeared in *Time* magazine in the summer of 1944.

As a Goldwyn publicist put it in *Dramatics*, a glossy publication distributed to promote what was then considered a big-budget film ($2.5 million), the story was "a moving and factual account of a trainload of

American Marines coming home on a furlough to a country that seemed unfamiliar and occasionally hostile. [Mr. Goldwyn] saw in the news story the subject for a film at once novel, important, and tremendously human. So, with the instinctive gesture of the man who knows he is right and goes ahead, he put in a call to MacKinlay Kantor. . . . Mr. Goldwyn himself might not be able to explain why this name sprang immediately to mind."

The PR piece went on to speculate that perhaps it was because in books like *Long Remember,* Mack had shown himself to be a "writer with deep sympathy and understanding of the American scene," or because several of his books had already become successful movies, or because he'd just "lived through a particularly intense period as virtual member of a heavy bombardment group."

Anyway, Goldwyn called, and Kantor came. "Within a week he was in Hollywood. ('A few minutes of conversation with Goldwyn,' his biographer Alva Johnson once wrote, 'and writers go to California as if extradited.')"

A month later, the account continues, Mack entered Goldwyn's office not with the requested fifty-to-sixty-page screen treatment, but one hundred typed pages that covered only the first quarter of the story—*"in blank verse!"*

"Whatever consternation the producer experienced he managed successfully to conceal, and Mr. Kantor was instructed to continue his 'treatment.'"

I found an annotation in a Library of Congress file that sheds light on Mack's odd approach to this assignment. A year before Goldwyn called him, during his first return home from the war, Mack made a journey around the country "to call on the next of kin of a number of the boys I had known who had gone down. From this highly emotional experience" came the idea of writing a story about a returning vet forcing himself to visit his fallen comrades' families and confront the altered landscape of home. It didn't go well. "It seemed that I couldn't write about anything except the war, and yet somehow I couldn't get started properly." He put aside the few aborted pages he'd managed, and returned to Europe and the 305th.

When Goldwyn called, Mack, just back home again, saw an opportunity to begin afresh on the very subject he'd been forced to abandon. It went no better the second time around. He worked for a month in frustration, hating everything he wrote, until he thought of the success of the Bailey poem, and decided to try verse once more. After all, what subject could be more Homeric than coming home from the wars? Suddenly, something in him unlocked. He pounded out the first hundred pages in a fever, and that's what he brought to Goldwyn. Either Goldwyn took it in good grace as the publicist claimed, or he didn't. Some other articles cite allegedly eyewitness accounts of Goldwyn's reaction to the manuscript. "What the hell am I going to do with this?" is one. "This is utterly useless" is another. But whatever Goldwyn's reaction, it didn't stop Mack from finishing.

By the time he handed the completed screenplay to the movie mogul, it had mushroomed to 434 pages. The publicist's account concludes in astonishment, "Mr. Goldwyn had bought a poem!"

The most complete account comes in an extensive 1996 piece in the VQR literary journal by Philip D. Beidler. Beidler says that, first of all, it wasn't true that Mack "came immediately to Goldwyn's mind," as the publicist would have us believe. The producer would have preferred to have had Lillian Hellman write the treatment, but the two were feuding. His second choice would have been Sidney Howard, who wrote the screenplay for *Gone with the Wind*, but Howard had been dead for five years.

So, Mack.

What Mack delivered to Goldwyn, "a homey conflation of verse modes" according to Beidler, "seemed so eccentric . . . he gave up on it at once as unfilmable and prepared to write off the whole business as a bad $12,500 self-indulgence."

Beidler asserts that the director William Wyler, just back from the war himself and still owing Goldwyn a film on his prewar contract, was the sole reason that *Glory for Me* didn't end up in the trash heap. Goldwyn tried to interest Wyler in two other projects without success. In desperation he pulled Mack's poem out of the circular file.

I found a 1946 interview with Wyler in *The New York World-Telegram* in which he describes his reaction: "I told Mr. Goldwyn I didn't want to work for a long time. He asked me to read some stories, and I read a good many of them. Then when I hit this thing of MacKinlay Kantor's it really set me on fire. Whatever anybody contributed to this production, the primary thing is that it was Kantor's inspiration that made the picture possible. He is really responsible for the whole thing."

(The glossy-paper account written by Goldwyn's press agent entirely reversed the poles of the story. Wyler, it said, "soon became as enthusiastic about [Kantor's] story as was Mr. Goldwyn himself.")

I was struck by something Wyler was quoted as saying at the end of Beidler's essay. Talking about why his war experience had so affected him, Wyler said, "The war was an escape to reality. . . . The only thing that mattered were human relationships; not money, not position, not even family. . . . Only relationships with people who might be dead tomorrow were important. It is a sort of wonderful state of mind. It's too bad it takes a war to create such a condition among men."

In Wyler's words, I understood for the first time why my grandfather's identification with the Air Force, the surly colonel who commanded him, and the slouching men posed beside planes painted with naked women in those group photos on the wall of his study had become a primal force, perhaps *the* primal force, throughout the remainder of his life.

If that interest in, and identification with, the military by my grandfather influenced me in any way, it was to push me in the opposite direction. I grew up anti-regimentation (I was bounced from the Cub Scouts for wearing the wrong color socks to a "jubilee"), antiwar, and extremely suspicious of all men in uniform. Yet, when I found the love of my life, it just so happened that she was an Air Force colonel's daughter who grew up on air bases around the world. And when I wrote my most recent nonfiction book, *Acid Test*, I chose as the emotional focus a Marine veteran of the Iraq War and his painful struggle to return to civilian life. In the scores of hours I spent getting to know the most intimate details of his combat experiences and their painful aftermath, and the weeks and months I spent writing about it, I never once considered the glaringly obvious connection between my work and my grandfather's efforts in writing *Glory for Me*. Until. Just. Now.

N ow I had a fairly complete picture of Mack's involvement in the film, except for one thing: None of the accounts—except my mother's and my uncle's oral history—mentioned anything about Mack starting, and then abandoning, a screenplay.

I was forced to wonder, Was that a fantasy? An artifact of a story too often told?

Then I found it—in a bulging file stuffed into box 71 at the Library of Congress: the screenplay itself.

At 226 pages, it is twice as long as most movie scripts, and it ends with a synopsis of unfinished scenes—which, fleshed out, would have made it even longer. So it seems that the "half-finished" screenplay idea my mother had told me about was an understatement.

I found Mack's explanation, once again, in his annotations: "I didn't proceed any further with this because I quarreled with Goldwyn, who insisted I come to Hollywood and take a seven-year contract with him . . . at a suggested salary of $2,000 per week. I think that this was a lot of money for any young-middle-aged writer to turn down, but I had my complete fill of Mr. Goldwyn. All I wanted to do was to go back overseas, and when Goldwyn said somewhat sneeringly, *Well, what good could you do over there?* that really clinched the deal. Incidentally, Frances Goldwyn, his wife, told me that she considered this the greatest screenplay she had ever read in her life, even in its incomplete form."

Given the above, and the actual existence of the screenplay by my grandfather, the complete lack of any mention of it in the accounts, both from the 1940s and from recent retrospectives, is puzzling. The official press agent account says Wyler and Goldwyn were already hashing out "who should be cast in the principal roles and how certain scenes should be played. And then they remembered that they still lacked a screenplay."

It's possible, even likely, that despite Mrs. Goldwyn's alleged high opinion of it, Goldwyn and Wyler considered Mack's script so unsuitable that it was not even worth mentioning. They hired four-time Pulitzer-winning dramatist Robert Sherwood to write the screenplay, and the contemporaneous articles say quite clearly that he based the work on the original story, not the first draft of a screenplay. In her 2007 biography of Sherwood, Harriet Hyman Alonso says the initial reaction of the playwright (and more recently FDR's speechwriter) to the story was "negative. . . . He found Kantor's emphasis on the veterans' isolation and their 'bitterness against civilians, whom they considered slackers and idlers'" too depressing. He said he'd work on the film only if he could make it clear that the vets realized that those on the home front also had had a tough time, and so would they as civilians. "Kantor was very amenable to the revisions," Alonso wrote.

Sherwood would win a Best Screenplay Oscar for his effort, and even Mack praised his work. But he clearly believed he deserved some of the credit.

"I will not venture to estimate how much or how little Sherwood depended on my screenplay when he came to write his own," he wrote. "I do know that I saw a copy of my play on his desk several times when I had business with him at the Goldwyn studio. Let me say, modestly, that I suppose it would be difficult for two accomplished writers to write their respective screenplays about the same story and keep them entirely dissimilar.

"My own approach, I am now confident, was entirely too melodramatic. I am glad that this melodrama was finally discarded. . . . I have always had enormous respect for the talent of Bobby Sherwood."

In newspaper features on the opening of the film and its blockbuster success, Goldwyn, Wyler, and Sherwood all say kind things about Mack, and Mack lavishes praise on the film and everyone involved in making it. Nobody mentions the odd absence of the name of the novel *Glory for Me* in the movie credits, though later correspondence make it clear that Mack and Tim Coward conducted a campaign to correct that. Unsuccessfully.

Goldwyn's advertising director blew off their objections, saying, "Using the title *Glory for Me* would have been confusing to readers of the ads."

That's about as clear a "fuck you" as I can imagine.

So, despite the lovefest in the papers, there was bitterness, even infighting. Tim Coward wrote to Mack and threw a roundhouse at Donald Friede, Mack's Hollywood agent. "Any agent who allows you to make a contract which is a means of putting out one of the greatest pictures in years without reference to your name and to the title of your book in public announcements should be bounced on his head."

The novel, which came out well before the movie release, had been reviewed viciously and sold poorly—at one point Coward sent a telegram warning that sales had come "to an absolute stop." It seems that even in 1945, epic poetry was a hard sell.

Now that the movie was such a hit, Goldwyn's revenge on Mack—and surely it was revenge he intended, either for writing a poem instead of a treatment or for walking out on the screenplay—assured that *Glory for Me* would remain a relative failure.

What should have been a high point in Mack's career was actually the beginning of another decline. After *Glory for Me*, Mack worked on several small books that Coward rejected, and then wrote another Western novel Coward didn't believe in and refused to publish without extensive revision.

In the spring of 1947, Mack wrote back in anger, saying he wanted out of his contract with Coward-McCann.

Coward responded with a letter that not only echoed Peggy Pulitzer's breakup letter, but cited it. It must have been almost unbearable for my grandfather to read:

Dear Mack,

*   . . . I'm sorry indeed you are gone from us. It marks the end of an epoch. . . . I think you have been on the wrong track for years & I blame myself for not facing it & risking a showdown. I probably owed it to you, but whether you would have paid any attention I doubt. . . . Peggy criticized, but not the right things &, of course, Irene has never had the courage or perhaps the knowledge to stand up to you in things that really count. . . . You surrounded yourself with inferiors or people who so admired you personally*

they were incapable of a sound critical attitude toward you or your work. . . . All those who didn't like your work were bastards with some axe to grind. . . . You have resolutely refused to grow up so that a remarkable fresh talent has been put to little use for the past ten years. Glory for Me, *thoroughly thought out and with four times the time given to it that was and written in decent straight-forward masculine prose might have been a great novel. It's getting late & the discipline of a full length novel is going to be harder & harder to suffer. A few more years of Hollywood & its quick silver written under high pressure will be all you will be able to do. . . . I'd like you to make a smashing success with a full length, fully thought out, digested creation worth divorce from any thought of Hollywood, that graveyard of serious literary talent. No one would shout Hosannas louder or be more pleased to point to the fact that C-McC first published you. . . . I have too much respect for the writer I once knew who WAS a writer and not an appendage of the movie industry. If this letter makes you grind your teeth and swear "I'll show that x-xxx?@ so & so" I'll be delighted.*

Given how things turned out, Tim Coward must have been delighted, indeed.

FOURTEEN

———

In the summer of 2014, after my very first visit to the Library of Congress manuscript reading room, I took the Metro home and started digging through the hard-to-reach cupboards, the ones where we stuff the boxes of family photographs we can't bear to throw out but will probably never look through again. It took me a while, but I found the box of my mother's old photos, including many of Mack and Irene. As I shuffled through, one jumped out at me—Irene entertaining company on the terrace of the Siesta Key house.

It captured me at first because my grandmother looked so alive, so in her element, her head thrown back, chin jutting as she took a jaunty drag on one of those little cigars she'd taken to smoking in Spain. She had a drink in her hand, and guests similarly equipped were arrayed about her. This terrace was such known territory to me. I could close my eyes and put myself right there, feel the tiles of black slate beneath my bare feet and smell the almost painfully sweet gardenia blossoms from the garden wafting on the breeze through the screening. I had observed, from afar, so many of these "adults only" soirees at my grandparents' home. At the time, they seemed a staple of life as I knew it. Now, of course, it was an antiquity, something I hadn't even thought about in decades. But it all came back, not just the memory, but the *sense* of it—the bustle of preparation, the approach of tropical evening, the smell of my grandmother's perfume. The recall came on sharply, a wave of longing for the irretrievable past.

I began to study the faces of the guests. Four were visible, seated, smoking and drinking around a wooden folding table. Three were women, all in full or partial profile. The fourth face I could see full on, and suddenly I had to catch my breath.

Hemingway?

I looked closer.

There was the broad brow; the sweep of dark hair plunging to a dramatic widow's peak; the huge, intense wide-set eyes; and the thick brush of a mustache—all characteristic of Hem before his hair turned white and his mustache became a full beard.

I knew that Mack and Irene had visited him in Cuba in the early 1950s. My mother told the story many times. I have a picture of Mack, Irene, my parents, and my uncle seated along the bar in Sloppy Joe's, one of Hemingway's favorite bars in Havana. My father looks all of nineteen, though he was twenty-four then. Mack had taken them all to the island for a vacation—on his dime, as always—and one stop on the itinerary was a day with the Hemingways at Finca Vigía, Ernest's rural homestead. My mom remembers seeing a chart on the bathroom wall by a doctor's scale where Ernest had recorded his weight every day for months, and staring goggle-eyed at a stack of manuscript pages by the black typewriter set on a worktable. When she asked him what he was working on he said, "Oh, it's just a small book."

My father said that he had watched as Mack and Ernest sat together on a couch beneath a variety of antlered animal heads, discussing their work, and after a time it became embarrassingly obvious to him that Ernest knew much about my grandfather's books, in fine detail, but my grandfather had not read much, if any, Hemingway. I later came across an article that quoted my grandfather saying that he hadn't been able to get through *For Whom the Bell Tolls*, Hemingway's famously readable novel about the Spanish Civil War. Hemingway meanwhile considered *Long Remember* among his favorite books by contemporary American novelists. I found it listed among the books he had kept in his personal library at his home in Key West.

My uncle gave his take on their relationship in his memoir: "Dad had avoided . . . friendship with major writers of the time. He knew many of them, he'd met them, but he tended to shun them, for it was important to him to be the center of any group of which he was a part. He *needed* to be the center."

My parents told the story of this visit to Cuba and the two authors' interaction as an object lesson in my grandfather's self-absorption and lack of humility, or at least that's how I heard it.

The truth is, I was never very clear on the nature of Mack's relationship with Hemingway—though I vaguely remember my mom saying they were really more friends of Mary's, Hemingway's third and final wife, who had been a correspondent in the war along with both Mack and Ernest. I assumed that's where they got to know each other.

I remembered, too, a summer day when I was seven years old. My grandfather had taken us to our front driveway to light off some of his folded-newspaper hot-air balloons when my mother called him from the front door to take a phone call. When he came back out, his face was pale and stricken as he put his hand on my grandmother's shoulder. I can't remember who said what, but I remember understanding that whoever had called—Mary, I'd always thought, but I can't say for sure—told him that Ernest Hemingway had shot himself.

This all came back as I looked at the photograph of that man having cocktails on the Siesta Key terrace.

Had they been closer friends than I realized? I never remembered hearing anyone say that Hemingway had visited them in Sarasota.

If only I could ask my mother.

Using my primitive photo-editing skills, I created a document with the face of the man on the terrace on one side and a dark-haired Ernest Hemingway on the other. If these were not the same man, the resemblance seemed uncanny.

I decided to send the image to a former *Washington Post* colleague, Paul Hendrickson, who had written a wonderful book with a great title, *Hemingway's Boat: Everything He Loved in Life, and Lost*. I explained my dilemma, and he responded: "For sure your grandfather visited Hemingway in Havana—that comes up in various places. I know nothing of EH going to Siesta Key. And if I had to guess, I'd say very close on the photo—but not him. But that is just and purely a guess. Hemingway could look different in different pictures. But I think the hairline is too high here. I could definitely be wrong. And it figures that EH could have stopped off in Siesta Key on his motor trips to Sun Valley—that would be roughly when he would have looked something like the man in this photo."

The next day he wrote back: "I have another idea. Try James B. Hill at the JFK library in Boston. He has a genius for faces. He was the primo A/V guy for the library and has committed to memory tens of thousands of images not only of the Kennedys, but of Hemingway."

As I was sending Hill the composite of the two images, I looked back at the original and saw something essential I had missed. On the bottom of the photo of the cocktail party was a small date stamp: 1957. This was all Hill needed.

"The fellow in question does resemble a younger Hemingway," he wrote. "Similar high forehead, cheeks, and chin—and it was enough to take a second look, but for 1957, think of the famous Yousuf Karsh 'fisherman sweater' portrait as representative of how EH looked at that time, with a full white beard and thinning hair combed forward."

So the man on the patio—not Hem.

Just when I was concluding that possibly the Cuba visit was a one-time deal, and maybe my grandparents were in fact mere acquaintances, I came across an article in *The Sarasota Herald-Tribune* from 1961, in which Mack was asked to reflect on Hemingway's suicide.

"Kantor said the last sight he had of the bearded author was as he strolled across the lawn of his Siesta Key home one day three years ago."

That would have been 1958, around the time the photo of the man on the patio was snapped. But Hemingway would have had the full white beard in 1958, as Hill noted. So he had been there, all right—certainly he'd had drinks on the patio—but apparently nobody had thought to take his photograph then.

I eventually found a more poignant reference to one of Hemingway's visits to Siesta Key in a letter my grandfather wrote barely a week after Hemingway braced his shotgun stock on the floor, put the barrels in his mouth, and pulled both triggers. "Last Sunday," Mack wrote, "when the news came about Ernest, I really went out and got drunk. I kept thinking of his coming in here two or three years ago."

Mack thought Hemingway was disturbingly obsessed with aging. "Don't ever get to be fifty-eight," he advised my grandfather, which of course was how old Ernest, five years Mack's senior, had been at the time.

Now I knew they were more than mere acquaintances, but I still didn't have a feel for just how substantial their friendship had been. Sarasota was on the way if you had to drive from Key West to Idaho with almost no interstate highways, as Hemingway did. So stopping there could have been mostly a matter of convenience. And I'd found a bit of hearsay that may have indicated Hemingway had a critical take on my grandfather. John D. MacDonald, a cult-favorite mystery novelist who became something of a protégé of my grandfather's, once claimed that Hemingway had said mockingly of Mack, "He would be a little bit better writer if he would resign his commission in the Confederate Air Force."

So the picture remained stubbornly foggy. I hoped I could clarify it in the Library of Congress files—the catalog entry for my grandfather's collection said it contained correspondence from Hemingway, but I couldn't find any. I'd assumed Hemingway, given his prominence, would have had his own folder. But maybe not. I began digging through all the files simply marked *H*.

And there it was. A single sheet of semitransparent typing paper stamped FINCA VIGIA in red on top and dated May 16, 1952, a time when my grandfather had put back on his correspondent's uniform to cover the air war in Korea.

The letter was typed rather roughly with some accent marks added in black ink, and signed in blue ink at the bottom: *Ernie Hemingway*.

I'd seen similar letters offered for sale for thousands of dollars. This was far more interesting than any of those. Instead of mundane items of business, it was a description of a social scene that might have jumped right out of one of Hemingway's novels. And it demonstrated an interest in, and concern for, my grandfather that went beyond the casual.

Dear Mac:

. . . We were talking about the last time we were together with you and your fine family. You brought out some wonderful champagne and we never opened it or drank it. You remember Mary wasn't here and we were improvising fast on a meal for quite a few people and it was my oversight that the champagne was not opened. But it wasn't truly all oversight because we drank a couple of dozen bottles of that Rose from the Hospice de Beaume and I remember thinking how that wine seems to have no strength at all when you drink it but actually it is about twice as strong as any other Burgundy. It tastes so light and simple like a health drink that you drink it fast and, when it is cold, like a thirst quencher. I remember thinking that if we served champagne it might be bad for the kids. You and I are supposed to be able to take anything but I can't stand running even a chance of making kids tight and that Rose from Burgundy is the most deceptive wine I know.

But I should have written you to thank you properly for the wine you brought out and for the book. Let's leave it this way: you have a credit of many bottles here and I will trade you even on books when mine comes out with Scribners on September 8th. Since it is shorter than yours I'll send you two copies.

Your book confirmed me more than ever in believing you shouldn't fly more combat missions. I don't like to have you do it anymore. . . . I don't think it is necessary and I wish to hell you would not do it. But if that is what you want to do ok and I will

sweat you out. But will have to classify you in prayers under cra-
zies and other ranks. That is a high classification. But I'd rather
know you were writing, not flying.

That short book Hemingway had promised to send in duplicate to measure up to my grandfather's larger book—probably an all-but-forgotten novel called *Don't Touch Me* (whose lead female character was based on his girlfriend of the time, Ginny)—was precisely the "small book" my mother had seen by his typewriter on their Cuba visit.

It was called *The Old Man and the Sea* and it would win the Pulitzer Prize the following year, and prompt the Nobel Prize the year after that.

If Hemingway actually sent those two copies he'd promised, they would have undoubtedly been signed first editions, and now insanely valuable. I couldn't help but wonder where they had gotten to.

By the time my grandfather visited Hemingway at Finca Vigía in the early 1950s, his money problems should have finally been behind him. He'd had a handful of best-selling books to his name, some extremely lucrative movie and screenwriting deals, and at least some credit for creating the story behind one of the most critically and financially successful American films of all time. He was famous, a frequent bold-faced name in newspaper and magazine celebrity coverage, and one of the first dozen Americans honored with the Medal of Freedom.

So I had to rub my eyes and check the date twice on a letter Mack had written aboard a ship sailing back to New York after he and Irene had spent the better part of a year in Spain: "We've made some strides toward getting out of debt, and even have part of my income tax paid for the current year—something I haven't been able to manage since the halcyon motion picture days."

In another letter in the spring of 1955 he wrote, "I haven't earned an outside dime since October 1953."

And yet he'd just spent a year traveling in Europe. He claimed that living there was so cheap "we can't afford to live anywhere else." But . . . really? In another place he wrote: "My funds were depleted by the year abroad."

My mother had often clucked about his lavish spending and his distrust of any sort of investment. When I thought about it, I could almost understand his motivation. He'd seen firsthand what had happened to stocks in the Depression, of course, but he also had a file full of letters from people who had been cheated out of their investments by his father. Besides, he had always believed the best investment was in himself. His personal history had given him faith that no matter how desperate his situation became, he could write something that would save him.

I couldn't help but admire the drive, the courage, that permitted my grandfather to live full bore, walking that tightrope with no net, trusting his talent and his ability to work hard while indulging his thirst for experience. Of course, he wasn't just exposing himself to the risk, but also Irene, who had consented to live as his dependent, and, in their childhood, my mother and uncle, who'd had no say in the matter. While I might have taken the chance on myself, I never could have put my family in that kind of peril. But Mack just kept on pushing all his chips on the table. Now he was about to hit the jackpot.

That incomeless year of 1954 would become the most significant of his life—and, in one indelible sense at least, of mine. Perhaps it's inevitable that the more you learn about an immediate ancestor, the more parallels you will find to your own life, and the more connected you will come to feel. Before I began this book, if I thought at all about any comparison between my grandfather and me, it would have been focused on the ways we were different—he a frothing extrovert, me an inveterate introvert; he a big drinker, me a two-beer-limit guy; he an archconservative, me anything but; and so on.

But I had come to believe that our connection—beginning but not ending with some of the odd and unanticipated synchronicities in our writing careers—went beyond the inevitable. One of the most trivial of these coincidences, but somehow still compelling to me, was that he had lived for exactly half a century (plus two months) when I began my own countdown of sunrises and sunsets. In his case, fifty was more than just a very round number: It was the year he began the work for which he would forever be best remembered—until there was nobody left to remember him, and no Internet to look up who won the Pulitzer Prize for fiction in 1956 (right there on the list, immediately following Ernest Hemingway and William Faulkner).

In many interviews and letters, my grandfather said he'd planned to write a novel about the Andersonville prison camp since the early 1930s, around the time he was researching his escaped Civil War prisoners novel, *Arouse and Beware*. I have to think that family stories about the Civil War captivity of his great-grandfather's brother Thomas Bone inevitably figured into his interest in the topic.

But he also said that his experience at Buchenwald—seeing the horror of what humans could do to defenseless captives in the name of war—was the trigger that, nine years later, compelled him to write *Andersonville*.

His desperate need for money also figured into it.

He had finished two novels during his time in Spain in 1953—one during a stormy passage in the 349-passenger Spanish ship *Covadonga*. In his annotations he says the ship went through the middle of one hurricane and skirted the fringes of a second, and that he finished the book in the mid-Atlantic, "to the tune of much smashing glass in the little barroom where I worked early each morning, storm or no storm. I had to hold the typewriter on the table with one hand and type with the other. Every now and then a whole shelf of bar glasses or crockery would explode behind me."

J esus. No wonder he ended up publishing forty-five books. I know from experience that completing any book, even under ideal conditions, requires an almost superhuman ability to focus and ignore distractions. Simply sailing the ocean on sedate seas would, for me, be a recipe for literary paralysis. The other passengers parading past, the endless vistas of sky and sea (not to mention the endless buffets), the constant rolling motion of both the ship and the roulette wheel in the onboard casino—all a conspiracy to prevent me from writing more than a paragraph or two. I get distracted by incoming e-mail messages. Hell, I *yearn* for incoming e-mail messages as an excuse to be distracted, to briefly muffle the pain—not so much of writing, but of the fear that what I am writing is irredeemable crap. I cannot even imagine what it would take to bear down against that pain and do serious work under the circumstances my grandfather described.

For the moment, though, his astounding focus and drive had gained him nothing. He'd also been working on the notes for an early version of what would later become part two of his autobiography, but neither the two novels nor this had sold.

His relationship with Tim Coward and Coward-McCann in ruins, he had followed his good friend and Hollywood agent Donald Friede to the World Publishing Company, where Friede had been hired as an editor.

Friede was an amazing character in his own right. The son of wealthy Russian émigrés, he managed between 1918 and 1920 to be expelled from Harvard, Yale, and Princeton. It happened that the final expulsion coincided with his father's death, and the thrice-failed scholar inherited a great fortune. He bought his way into a publishing career in which he had substantial (but not always mutually satisfactory) dealings with Theodore Dreiser, T. S. Eliot, Ernest Hemingway, and James Joyce. As one profile put it, "He co-founded a publishing firm that went bankrupt, and he left numerous places of employment under difficult circumstances." He spoke four languages and was married six times, including to the famous and famously beautiful food writer M. F. K. Fisher (a whirlwind romance, after which the newlyweds subleased Mack's New York apartment). He even had a much-photographed fling with Jean Harlow.

Mack gives an amusing account of meeting with Friede; his new boss, World vice president William Targ; and another World exec at the Plaza's Oak Room almost immediately after his ship docked in New York. Friede and Targ proposed that he write a book about the pre–Civil War South, and said they could pay an advance of $7,500— worth about $70,000 in 2015. For someone desperate for money, that must have been a huge temptation—comparing it to my experiences in twenty-first-century publishing—although it seems surprisingly low for a brand-name author. I am not remotely as bankable as my grandfather was at that point, yet the advances for my last four books have all exceeded that number. I did a little historical research and quickly discovered an excellent *New York Times* article from 2009 that shed some light on that puzzle: "The current culture of blockbuster advances really took shape in the 1970s," it said, when sales from reprinting hardcover books in high-quality "trade paperback" editions began bringing in serious money; before that, advances were much more meager. The advance for the 1971 blockbuster *Day of the Jackal*, for example, was only $10,000—even slightly less, in 2015 dollars, than what my grandfather was offered in 1953 for the proposed "southern book."

Mack immediately said no.

Not because he didn't think the offer was high enough.

"I wanted a good book contract and an advance most desperately, but still didn't wish to do the Southern book as outlined by the editors."

They asked why.

Mack said, "Because it would take away from *Andersonville*, a book I've planned to do for a great many years."

And then he excused himself to go to the restroom.

"I made a very leisurely session of it," he wrote. "When I got back to the Oak room, the three men still had their heads together, and only broke apart when I approached the table. Donald waited until I sat down to my coffee—or Southern Comfort, most likely, in those days—and said, 'Well, what's the matter with doing *Andersonville* now?' I exclaimed in pretended amazement, 'Why, I'm not ready to do it!' but all the time I knew that I was."

This provoked a flurry of persuasion, all three men chiming in with reasons why he should do the book now "while I still had the youth and strength to approach such a demanding task.

"They were all saying exactly what I had hoped and prayed that they might say, but I played hard-to-get for another half hour, and then we all went back to the office and a contract was promptly drawn up and signed."

He eventually got a $15,000 advance—think $140,000 in 2015.

I found multiple accounts Mack wrote detailing his writing of *Andersonville*. He began in Sarasota in the final weeks of 1953, and then decided that he and Irene would leave again for Spain in late March 1954 to complete the bulk of the book in Europe.

I read right over that twice before I saw it.

Late March 1954.

I was born on April 9, 1954.

I try to imagine climbing on a plane and leaving the country on a whim—and, no question, Mack didn't *have* to go to Spain to write his book, much less have to go in late March rather than postponing for a few weeks—while one of my daughters was in the final stage of pregnancy with my second grandchild. And then I try to imagine insisting that my wife board that plane as well. Neither of those things would ever happen. And if I tried to force the second thing to happen . . . I don't even want to think about that.

Irene was not the distant, unaffectionate type. She was an adoring mother and grandmother. We yearned for her visits. She was hardly through the door before she had an apron on, leading us through the delicious-at-every-stage process of making gingerbread men with chocolate-chip eyes and sugar-candy buttons. She'd tell us stories she'd made up when my mom was little about two bears named Molly and Bruin who sometimes misbehaved and had all kinds of adventures as a result. The stories were engrossing to us, and had been to my mother and uncle to the point where Mack sometimes stalked off in a huff because the kids wanted to hear Molly and Bruin stories rather than listen to Mack read one of his favorites.

It's difficult for me to believe she wouldn't have been consumed with regret at having to leave the country when waiting just a few more days would have allowed her to be there for her daughter and new grandson. But I can't know for sure how she felt; another unanswerable question on the long and growing list for those who are gone.

In Mack's view, the trip to Spain was no frivolous endeavor, but essential to accomplishing the herculean task of writing an epic, exhaustively researched, and historically accurate novel. Being abroad was the lubricant that allowed him to navigate the narrow passage between what was possible to accomplish and what was doomed to fail.

"I followed the same plan of work in Europe," he wrote, "writing daily wherever we happened to be. In all the hotels where we stopped I had a table in our room or suite—if weather or other circumstances precluded my going out in the car, as in London or Madrid. Normally, however, I worked in the car along roads and in lonely woodlands of Britain, France, and especially Spain, where we spent most of the year. . . . To suggest how these long books get written, you can conjure up a picture of me sitting resolutely in the Hyde Park Hotel before my typewriter all day long. Imagine—in London, one of my very favorite cities! However, I emerged from my cell each night and we went to the theater and had fun, saw friends at dinner. . . ."

I knew that feeling of resolutely sitting, lead-butted, before the keyboard, letting entire days pass, the world going on without you as you struggled along—all the while worrying that your sacrifice was for nothing. How much harder would it be with the enticing bustle of London or Paris or Madrid just beyond your door?

As I thought about it, I realized that the ability to force yourself to sit against all fears of failure and urges to flee is what separates those who can successfully complete a substantial work—of fiction or nonfiction—and those who, although possibly more talented, cannot. I began to remember things that I'd all but purged from my mind: for my first book, whose small advance demanded it be written while I continued my full-time newspaper job, I woke up every morning at two hours before dawn and sat grimly at a primitive computer in a closet-size room before a window that remained unyieldingly black against the harsh glare of a desk lamp. My eyeballs felt as if they had been rolled in sand, then reinserted in their sockets; bile bit the back of my throat. But somehow I kept forcing my fingers to move and the words to appear on the screen.

For another book, I had to complete the research and writing, start to finish, in four months. I worked seven days a week, often twelve hours a day, more as I crashed toward deadline with thousands of words left to write. My eyes would begin to close, my head would nod forward. I'd shake my head, but when that didn't do the job, I'd slap myself to wake up enough to keep going. If nothing else, I discovered, I did have a talent for endurance.

Though I would be unlikely to ever intentionally place myself in such extreme temptation as my grandfather did, perhaps I inherited, at least to a diluted degree, his ability to refuse to give up, or even get up, for long hours, day after day, week after week, month after month.

I also recognized in him my strange affinity for writing alfresco. For my later books, when I've been able to work at them full-time, throughout the daylight hours, I prefer to set up my laptop on the back porch. Feeling the breeze, hearing the birds and the fluttering leaves, I don't feel quite so cheated of the time that passes. I'm not hidden away from the day, but in it. And when my focus begins to break, I can simply stop and gaze at the clouds drifting, expanding, shape-shifting, or listen to far sounds of the wind, muffled car engines, and the nearer chirp of crickets or the tinkling of wind chimes. Sometimes my elderly neighbor, back behind a screen of trees, plays classical music just loud enough so that when the wind dies, the notes trickle in, more like something faintly remembered than an actual sound.

Mack did me one better: He rented a house on a cliff near Torre-molinos in Andalusia, Spain, loaded his car with a folding chair, type-writer, research materials, a woven market basket filled with fresh fruit, vegetables, cheese, bread, and a bottle of wine, then drove out into the countryside on a dirt track until he was sure only the braying of don-keys or the bleating of sheep could disturb him. Often, Irene would come with him and set up her easel and paints just out of eyeshot. The routine takes on flesh in a letter he typed on his folding desk chair on one such day. "I wish you folks could take your work on your laps, the way I can. I think I'll knock off for a minute, take a little stroll up the hill and see how Irene is making out with her picture."

Then he types a long ellipsis to indicate a few minutes have passed and resumes. "She says that the sheep are disconcerting. The whole flock is circulating over this hillside and the orchards adjacent to the hacienda, and are controlled by a lame shepherd who can't run after them, but who directs them by heaving rocks at them! Quite a literary renegade on the traditional Good Shepherd theme. . . ."

By the time they sailed back to New York in October, Mack had written 175,000 words. That would be long for most novels. Mack was barely half finished.

Around my first birthday, in April of 1955, World began to put the book into type to meet its May production deadline.

"I still had a great deal of work to do," Mack wrote, "and was at an almost unbearable point of tension. . . . I wrote 27,000 words in the last five days. My publishers were on the phone with me several times each day—listening, checking, advising, holding my spiritual hands and mopping my spiritual brow."

He finished the final paragraph on May 25. The last word he dic-tated to his secretary, sitting on the porch of his Siesta Key house, was *Andersonville*.

"It was a little after four o'clock. We yelled for Irene; there was a certain amount of kissing; I think the women shed some tears; then we hastily poured out drinks, and I called Donald."

For me, finishing a book has always been a private moment, a rush of exhilaration and relief—it tends to take me by surprise. One second I'm typing along, just as I have been for months, and suddenly—nothing left to type. It takes a minute to sink in, to believe that I've really written the final sentence. Then maybe I'll get up and find Lisa and tell her, "I'm done." I know she won't get it at first. Done for the day? Done as in "fed up"?

"No. With the book. It's finished."

Which she will be glad to hear, if only so she no longer has to listen to me whining all the time about how hard it is. Maybe we'll go out to dinner to "celebrate."

So I read with a mixture of amusement and envy Mack's description of what happened next.

"We telephoned friends who had been waiting around with bated breath, and they started appearing at the house within a couple of hours. A lot of the folks had been preparing gifts. . . . I remember that Dick and Patty Martin bought a stockade composed of upright cigars carefully laced together . . . a silver-plate tray for Irene, designating her as a survivor of *Andersonville*, and a desk-lighter for me, with the circumstance and date engraved."

The idea of a circle of friends waiting by their phones—"with bated breath," no less—for me to finish a book so they can rush over with elaborately themed gifts is beyond ludicrous. Though I have a handful of close friends, some of whom I've known for decades, only a few live nearby, none of whom are intimately aware of my writing schedule.

It is a documented fact that people of the twenty-first century tend to have fewer close friends than people in the latter part of the twentieth—surveys then and now show an average of three close friends has dwindled to an average of two. But that doesn't begin to cover this disparity. Forget an imagined swarm of admirers celebrating my accomplishments: I barely socialize at all. I regard party invitations with something close to dread.

Compare that to an excerpt from a 1940s profile of my grandfather:

It is impossible to convey through the medium of print the vivid and warm personality of MacKinlay Kantor. Upon first meeting, he communicates instantly his robust quality of mind and spirit and his entry into a roomful of people is a challenge to be gay and interesting. . . .

"If I can't be with the people I like best all the time, I'll take those I can get," says Mack. "I like people and I've got to have them around me."

It raises at least the possibility that Mack didn't like to be alone because he wasn't comfortable in his own skin, which could also help explain his serial affairs, or even his compulsion to prove himself in combat.

Another possibility: Maybe I am *too* comfortable in my own skin.

Rereading my notes I came across something my grandfather wrote in one of his story collections that hit me with a shock of recognition, and some regret: "I wish that all writers might have as good of friends as I have owned and still own. Writing is a desperately lonely business. It is scarcely worth living for in itself. But friends help to keep you going."

By any measure, though, the spontaneous outpouring that greeted the completion of *Andersonville* bears no comparison to my experience, and perhaps can be explained by a simple fact that would be proven out dramatically in the coming months. The book was in fact a huge achievement.

That's certainly how Mack saw it.

As he neared the end of his labor, he wrote this in a "Dear Everyone" letter:

I thought I had known exhaustion and depletion before, and here, at the age of fifty-one, I find myself struggling with a burden I couldn't have attempted to shoulder when I was writing Long Remember *twenty-two years ago! I suppose old men shouldn't get ambitious. And sometimes, wracked and sleepless at night, I wish to hell that I hadn't. Of course the book is so good that frankly it seems to me that I must not have written it. It somehow captivates everyone who reads it. . . . There hasn't been anything remotely resembling it in the annals of American historical fiction. Everyone has to go back to* War and Peace *for comparison.*

If he didn't say so himself.

But I have to wonder if that extreme faith in himself, bordering on egomania—*I believe in you as I believe in a supreme being*—wasn't precisely what gave him the power to push through all the monstrous doubts and fatigue that stop so many in their tracks, regardless of talent.

In this case, anyway, his absurd level of self-belief turned out to be not simply his own opinion, but the world's.

FIFTEEN

I have written or cowritten five books and have been the editor on three times that many. Over the years, dozens of my friends have published books. Some have big names, but most have been relative unknowns. I would say every single one of them has had dreams— dreams they wouldn't admit to—that their book would become a number one best seller. I know I have. I also know it will never happen.

A few years back, *Huff Post* media blogger BJ Gallagher ran a memo sent to her by a book publisher listing "ten awful truths" about book publishing. From an author's point of view, they were more like plot points in a slasher flick: More than three million new books are published every year, and every new book is competing with ten million existing books. Even including e-books, total sales of all book formats are declining. A hundred to a thousand books compete for every open spot on a bookstore shelf. The average nonfiction book sells fewer than 250 copies a year, and fewer than 3,000 copies in its lifetime.

And yet, the fantasy is that your book will be different, defy the odds, catch a wave, strike a chord, and somehow become a cultural phenomenon. In the dream, there might be a short drumroll, a few hints that something big is about to happen. And then—*bam!*—the book blasts off like a rocket, and there you are, sitting atop the best-seller lists.

As I began to wade through the voluminous correspondence concerning *Andersonville* from Mack's editor, publisher, and publicists at World Publishing, I felt as if I were stepping into my wildest fantasies.

"So *Andersonville* is finished, and ready for the ages!" World's publisher Bill Targ wrote on May 25, 1955. "I feel something historical about this day. . . . No matter what happens, you've written the biggest, the most moving novel I've read by any American (excepting perhaps *Moby Dick*)."

That's some drumroll. And then, blast off.

Paperback rights were purchased for $75,000. Book-of-the-Month Club paid $30,000 to make *Andersonville* its main selection. *Reader's Digest* bought the rights to one chapter for $35,000. Then the real money came in: Columbia Pictures paid $250,000 for the movie rights. That was very close in inflation-adjusted value to the $135,000 that Hemingway had gotten sixteen years earlier for the rights to *For Whom the Bell Tolls*, which at the time was the most ever paid for movie rights to a novel. Altogether, the various rights for *Andersonville* totaled $390,000— the equivalent of $3.5 million today—before the first book was printed.

In September, after Mack had labored through all the galleys, all 768 pages of them, he and Irene, soon to have what for them would be unimaginable wealth, went off to Europe, supposedly to recoup, though they both got terribly ill and had to hole up in a hotel. "Run down, weak, giving colds back and forth to each other—oh this has been the sheerest misery. We have not been able to enjoy one single solitary moment of contemplation of all the success won by Big A."

Not to worry, they'd have plenty of further opportunity to do so. By midmonth, finally on the mend, he was cheered by this note from Donald Friede: "There now begins a feeling of mounting excitement and anticipation. It's a wonderful feeling, and it cannot be counter-feited. . . . How we both live for things like this—and how rarely they happen. . . . We have the rare knack of enjoying and milking every last drop of excitement."

For once, a singular rarity in publishing, the giddy reading of pre-publication tea leaves barely measured up to the reality.

Look magazine wrote a glowing feature about the book, calling the outrageous-for-1955 quarter-of-a-million-dollar movie rights purchase "not too high a price."

By the end of October, Friede's wife and World's marketing director, Eleanor Kask Friede (Donald's sixth and last wife, who would gain eter-nal publishing fame as the person who saw something in an eighteen-times rejected manuscript about a spiritual seagull named Jonathan Livingston and ended up with one of the best-selling books of all time), wrote to Mack: "I hear that over at the *New York Times Book Review* office they have a pool, like a baseball pool where everyone gets a number, on which week you, or rather BIG A, will replace *Marjorie Fallingstar* as #1."

Marjorie Fallingstar was wordplay, a derisive reference to Herman Wouk's novel *Marjorie Morningstar*, what a twenty-first-century critic would call his "bloated but entertaining" novel about a beautiful young Jewish woman who discovers that a glamorous life is a life of sorrow, and that it was much better to marry a nice Jewish doctor after all. It totally captivated women readers of the day, who made it an instant best seller, until an unrelentingly bleak novel about man's inhumanity to man miraculously began to overtake it, just in time for the holidays.

On December 20, Donald Friede wrote to Mack, "And a Merry Christmas to you—oh best-selling author in the United States of America! For that is what you are today—even though the *Times* still has you at #2. All other papers—and all the bookstores—say that you are the #1 seller. We cannot stop shipping, or billing, long enough to run up daily totals, but you must be mighty close to 110,000 copies sold, if not over. . . ."

The last redoubt, the *New York Times* list, fell on the first Sunday of the new year, 1956, when *Andersonville* began a long reign at number one and remained near the top of the list throughout the year.

I found an earnings statement for November 1956 that detailed *Andersonville's* sales and earnings eighteen months after publication: 175,000 copies of the book sold, from which my grandfather netted $130,000, the equivalent of well over $1 million today. The sales would continue (at a steadily diminishing rate) for years to come—for the original edition and for subsequent paperback editions for which it might be impossible to get exact numbers. I do know that one day, sixty years later, I arrived home from my research at the Library of Congress to find in my mailbox a modest check for *Andersonville* royalties for a paperback edition that still sells about a thousand copies a year. Its sales numbers were indeed exceptional, especially considering the book's length and weightiness. But to put it in perspective against a book that remains, unlike *Andersonville*, world famous a half century after publication: Hemingway's *For Whom the Bell Tolls* sold three times as well, a half-million copies within months of publication. (*Andersonville* would eventually reach the half-million-sales mark—if I can believe my grandfather's own accounting in a 1972 letter, in which he claims 500,000 hardcover copies eventually sold and "in the millions" of cheap mass-market paperback books.)

At any rate, nobody involved with *Andersonville* was complaining. While the money poured in, so did the accolades. The superlative ("the greatest of our Civil War novels") on the front of *The New York Times Book Review* was echoed around the country:

> *"The best Civil War novel without any question."*
> —The Chicago Tribune

> *"Will give Civil War buffs their greatest hours since* Gone with the Wind."
> —Time

> *"No one who reads it will ever forget it."*
> —*The* Christian Science Monitor

Now, even in Europe, American tourists recognized Mack from his newspaper profiles and book-jacket photo and approached him for autographs. So many letters flooded in—fan mail, requests for appearances, people soliciting the newly rich author for investments or charity—that his sister, Virginia, volunteered to reduce the incoming post to the most interesting and important pieces before sending them on to Mack.

Already one of the country's best-known authors, Mack was boosted to a new level of celebrity by *Andersonville*. I got the biggest kick out of a full-page magazine ad that ran in *Life, Newsweek,* and *The New Yorker* at the height of the *Andersonville* frenzy. In it, five gleeful middle-aged white men in tailored suits are planted in a posh hotel room, smoking, drinking, laughing as if at some particularly wicked, off-color witticism, all turned toward a sixth man standing tall and straight in the middle of the frame wearing a sly grin and a double-breasted navy suit, and gripping a pipe in his fist. It is clear he is the one who has just expressed the aforementioned witticism. The headline says "Lord Calvert American Whiskey for Men of Distinction," and the caption: "When MacKinlay Kantor, noted author of the current best-selling novel *Andersonville*, entertains his friends, Lord Calvert helps to make them welcome."

I look at Mack in that image—fit and dashing at fifty-two, full head of still-auburn hair, immaculate tailoring, a starburst of good humor emanating from the pleasingly masculine lines of his face, officially a *Man of Distinction*—and can't help thinking of Tom Wolfe's coinage of thirty years later . . . *Master of the Universe*. Nothing could make it clearer than this piece of advertising art that Mack was most certainly the master of his. When you are a Master of the Universe (or a Man of Distinction), you are elevated in a golden light that seems to flow from some infinite source, naturally focused on *you*. Imagining that this moment in May 1956 would be the absolute pinnacle of his career, and that the golden glow would slowly dim to a shadow from that moment forward, is too much to ask of anyone in such exalted circumstances.

Not long after I discovered the Lord Calvert ad, I happened upon a classic 1950 *New Yorker* profile of Ernest Hemingway by Lillian Ross. It was an account of a Hemingway visit to Manhattan during which Ross shadowed his every move. At the very end, a phone in Hemingway's room at the Sherry-Netherland began to ring. "Hemingway picked it up, listened, said a few words, and then turned to us and said that an outfit called Endorsements, Inc., had offered him four thousand dollars to pose as a Man of Distinction. 'I told them I wouldn't *drink* the stuff for four thousand dollars,' he said."

On the heels of that weird irony came immediately another: As I was learning more and more about Mack it made me think about how little I knew about my other grandfather, my father's father, Millard Shroder. As I began casting around, I found a digital copy of a promotional book, one of only 210 copies printed, titled *Accomplishment*, containing photos and descriptions of Millard's many building projects around New York. One of them, the highest profile perhaps, was the 1927 Sherry-Netherland.

There is no Library of Congress collection concerning the life of Millard Shroder, and almost nothing else online. My father and his sisters are all dead. So I sent a message out to my six cousins on that side of the family, and managed to find only two salient facts about his background. He was an eighth-grade dropout who somehow—nobody knew how—managed to become one of the top builders in New York before he was thirty-five. On the day of the stock market crash in 1929, he returned home to say, "I lost a million dollars today."

From an entire lifetime biography, up to the time I knew him as a sweet old man willing to get down on the floor and wrestle with his small grandchildren, that's pretty much all that remains.

One late December a few years ago, exhausted by the masochistic ordeal of parking-shopping-paying-wrapping-stressing-and-overindulging that is sadly at the heart of the twenty-first-century Christmas experience, Lisa and I rented a house in the rural hills just outside the small Spanish city of Ronda in Málaga province.

We'd always dreamed of living for some extended period in France or Spain, and this little peek at that fantasy did not disappoint us. The house had a vine-draped trellised porch on which we ate breakfasts of fruit and creamy yogurt and drank thick, dark coffee while listening to roosters crowing, dogs barking, and somewhere just out of sight a donkey braying. The ancient city—Phoenicians were the *second* people to inhabit it—consisted of narrow streets rising to a peak, then descending steeply to a spectacular, craggy-sided gorge that split the town down the middle, plummeting 330 meters to a cascading river that meandered through a valley spotted with olive groves and rimmed by mountains. Crisp mornings warmed gradually through the afternoon under relentless sunshine. We felt almost miraculously at home, and sorely tempted when we learned the property was for sale. Tempted . . . but unable to pull it off financially. Imagining that under somewhat more prosperous circumstances we might have bought the place only made it more heartbreaking to leave when the holidays were over.

In the several years since, I've thought of that house frequently, and with longing: the fantasy that got away.

With all the odd coincidences and parallels I'd encountered researching my grandfather's life, it shouldn't have come as a surprise when I learned that the cliffside cottage he rented in which to write *Andersonville* was near Torremolinos in the province of Málaga, a short drive west of Ronda. He even wrote a book, *Lobo*, about his time in Spain, his first book after "the Big A," which I had never read. Now I did, and it was like an exclamation point on a growing theme: What I fantasized, my grandfather had lived.

I know it's hard to believe, but the idea that I wanted to emulate him never entered my mind. My dreams seemed to arise organically, without reference to anyone else. I didn't even appreciate the full scale of similarity until I came across his book about living in Spain.

Actually, it was only secondarily a book about a lifestyle. Primarily, it concerned a dog, Lobo, whom my grandparents encountered at a swank hotel-restaurant complex on the Mediterranean coast. Lobo was a Basque shepherd dog, owned by no one, known by everyone, and a fixture around the restaurant at dinnertime, where he feasted nightly thanks to indulgent staff and customers alike. Apparently, Mack was even more indulgent than most, an attribute Lobo quickly fastened upon. One evening after dinner, Lobo trotted in the open door of my grandparents' room and hopped up on the couch, not budging until breakfast smells wafted past his nostrils. When my grandparents left the hotel for a house down the road, Lobo waited by the highway exit—for two days, the locals attested—until my grandparents reappeared, at which point Lobo sprinted toward their car and leapt through the open window into Mack's lap. From that moment, Lobo was Mack's dog. When they sailed back to the United States, Lobo sailed with them to New York, then motored in the backseat all the way to the house on Siesta Key. An agreeable orphan and mild-mannered beggar all his life, Lobo had suddenly become a family dog of considerable property. It went straight to his head.

He became, wrote my grandfather, "more avaricious than Hetty Green, more savage than Simon Girty, less charitable than Ebenezer Scrooge." And more territorial than Genghis Khan. Or as my grandfather recounted it: "'Good grief!' he would roar at the top of his lungs, dashing out to the porch, slashing the rugs as he came. 'Look out there on the beach! There's an old man walking on *my beach*. I can't *stand* this. He needs to be torn limb from limb! Please open the door and let me out! I want to go down there and *assassinate* him.'"

My mom and uncle Tim always used to say that Mack overroman-ticized Lobo's viciousness. They called *Lobo* "a pretty good book about a very bad dog," and threatened to write a sequel called *The Truth About Lobo*. In reality, Lobo's aggressiveness became a huge problem, epitomized when Irene became ill while Mack was away and Lobo almost dismembered the visiting doctor, which was probably the beginning of the end of house calls.

In my memory, Mack always had a dog. The first I could recall was a black mutt named Bill Dog. Bill was my father, and whether that name was in honor or in mockery of him, we were never quite sure. As I read *Lobo*, I found myself wondering if I ever had met the Basque shepherd (mourning, as had become my habit, the fact that here was yet another question I could have asked my mom, but never had). I had nearly finished the book when I arrived at this passage:

Our two small grandsons came with their parents to spend the Christmas holidays, and we watched Lobo narrowly. I heard him growl just once. He had an ear infection and Mike, the elder, pulled his sore ear. I explained to Mike, and he did not do this again. On the other hand, I came in one day to find the smaller boy in his playpen with Lobo lying just outside the wooden bars. Tommy had fastened his grubby mitts on Lobo's muzzle, and was kneading flesh and nostrils energetically. Lobo was not uttering a sound, nor was he trying to move away; he was just taking it from the baby. We breathed more easily after that.

Even if others believed Lobo's bad habits outweighed all else, Mack would never be persuaded of it. As he labored to complete *Andersonville* on deadline—the type for the first part of the book being set in the printing presses even before he'd finished the last—he struggled to find the energy required to meet an unforgiving pace. Every day he would flee the house with his typewriter to drive far into the woods to avoid any possible interruptions. But "there came a day when I thought I could work no more. My head ached, my eyes hurt. . . . *You can't finish*, evil voices were crying."

That was when he began to find Lobo in the car, waiting for him each morning. "He sensed I needed help," Mack wrote. After that, Lobo remained by his side, steadfastly, until he typed the last word.

Or so Mack says in the book. Overly sentimental, perhaps, to attribute those motives to a dog. More than likely he just wanted to go for a ride. Yet I found myself choking up when I read it.

When I was writing the acknowledgments for my previous book, I meant to say in them that I should have given my dog, a yellow Lab/ hound mix rescue dog named Sally, a coauthor byline, if only for the fact that her butt time in my office as I wrote the book just about equaled my own. As soon as she realized that I'd headed upstairs to work each morning, I'd hear the scritching of her claws on the wood stairs and then see her pad into the office and plop down on a cushion in the corner, staying there hour after hour until it was time to start bugging me for her walk, a distraction I was both irritated by and grateful for. This continued day after day over the eighteen months I labored, from the time she was thirteen and a half past her fifteenth birthday, even as she aged dramatically, her rear quarters growing progressively weaker, making that climb up the stairs ever more difficult. I tried whenever the weather permitted to work on the back porch so that she could lie out on the deck beside me and avoid the climb. When it got too hot, too cold, or too wet to work outside, I always felt guilty for climbing back up those stairs, because nothing could dissuade her from following me. She stuck it out to the end, far more patient with the damnable immobility of the process than I ever could be.

It was almost as if she were waiting to die until our work was done. We had to put her down just two weeks after publication.

Immediately after my grandfather had finished *Andersonville*, he and Irene visited us in New York as he met with the publishers to smooth out the final small-print details of publication. I didn't remember this, of course, having just turned one at the time, but I was surprised to learn in the book that they brought Lobo with them— possibly encouraged by the evidence of our playpen rapport in Florida. During the visit, Mack took Lobo to our family vet and discovered that he had heartworm. Lobo was left for what was supposed to be a safe and effective series of shots. After the very first injection, he dropped dead for no reason anyone could discover.

Mack arranged burial in a nearby pet cemetery—a cemetery whose existence I was aware of growing up without ever knowing that a visit there would reveal a headstone for my grandfather's dog with the inscription ADIOS, AMIGO.

We buried Sally in our backyard with her favorite toy in a hole I dug myself, covered with a thick piece of slate from the garden path she loved to run along. I've had to write this book solo.

By spring of 1956, Mack and Irene were both back in fine health and enjoying their *Andersonville* victory lap of Europe. They'd arrived in Paris, staying in the elegant Prince de Galles Hotel across the Seine from the Eiffel Tower. On April 19, a telegram arrived from my mother with two bits of news. "Novel accepted. Hurray! John Kantor died last night."

The novel referred to in the telegram was not another of my grandfather's works, but something my mother had knocked out between changing diapers and making dinners for four, meaning she would soon be a third-generation published author. The "Oh, by the way" news of John Kantor's death, reduced to five words at the back end of a message about something else, was a stark but fitting end to his career as a lousy father. The next morning Mack sent a return telegram through his publisher. "Inform Layne we had champagne last night for two reasons."

My uncle said that Mack told him that his first words after reading my mother's telegram were "At last we're rid of him."

Almost.

When he returned to the States, Mack found a rather desperate message from the billing department of the hospital that had treated John in his final illness. It seems upon admission, John had persuaded the hospital intake staff that his son, the famous novelist MacKinlay Kantor, would be paying the bill. (*By God! How I love to burn him up.*)

Mack confessed feeling only righteous indignation when he disabused the bill collector (no doubt colorfully) of that hope. But how could he have not felt a pang of loss as well? Not the loss of John, but the loss that had haunted him his whole life—the loss of the last slender filament of a chance that he'd ever have a father capable of love.

I encountered many surprises in my research, but possibly none less expected than evidence that John Kantor did not go entirely unmourned. To the end of his life, there were still family members who found him impressive and desired his company. I knew this because one of Mack's first cousins was yet another in the family who became a journalist and a writer. His name was Seth Kantor, son of John's brother Arvid. Seth had a small role in a large historic event himself. Covering a presidential visit to Dallas on November 22, 1963, Seth rode in a press bus behind the limousine carrying John Kennedy. He heard two of the three fatal shots that rang out from the Texas School Book Depository, and was one of the first reporters to get to Parkland Memorial Hospital— there in time to see the president's blood pooling on the ground beside the hastily parked and vacated limo. Still unsure what had happened, Seth talked his way inside the hospital. As he was walking down a hall he felt a tug on the back of his coat. In Seth's testimony before the Warren Commission, he said, "I turned and saw Jack Ruby standing there. He had his hand extended. . . . He said, 'Isn't this a terrible thing?'"

Seth Kantor is probably best known for the book he would eventually write on Ruby—the mysterious nightclub owner who, two days later, would walk into the basement of Dallas police headquarters and fatally shoot Lee Harvey Oswald. But the assassination and the book were both years in the future when Seth wrote a piece for *The Dallas Times Herald* that began:

The last time I saw my Uncle John, my father's brother, he was in his 74th year. He had business in Dallas, and had taken a suite at the Adolphus. He was still a massive man with a mountainous memory. . . . He still wore spats. His voice still came like articulate cannon with a volley that could be heard for hours. . . . He talked to my wife and I at our dinner table for a little more than eight consecutive hours. It was not so much that he talked for such a fantastic span of time . . . it's that each of us sat transfixed by John Kantor's words and wished for more.

Late in this marathon monologue, "Uncle John" began to trace the Kantor family history, all the way back into Europe, telling "what he knew of the family's outcasts and successes. 'It is a fact,' he said, munching a slice of cheese at nearly midnight, 'that in our family alternate generations are full of achievement and alternate ones are not successful.'" Then he looked at Seth with his intense, hooded eyes and said, "You are in the wrong generation, you know."

"He was wrong," Seth wrote. "Three weeks after Uncle John's death in his 77th year, his son, MacKinlay Kantor, of the 'wrong generation' won the Pulitzer Prize for *Andersonville*."

Oh, that.

Mack was still at the Prince de Galles two weeks after he learned that his father had died when he happened to run into an old friend. Mike Cowles had hired Mack as a columnist at *The Des Moines Register* a quarter century earlier, and had since gone on to found *Look* magazine. Now, by coincidence, they were staying at the same hotel.

"We met at the bar for drinks, Irene arriving a bit late. Mike had said, I suppose you've already been given the inside dope about your getting the Pulitzer Prize." Mack's heart flipped somersaults in his chest. He had no such dope, and with great effort refrained from leaping for joy. "I said without batting an eyebrow: . . . I never count on anything until official announcement is made. . . . And he smiled and said, Well, I guess I ought to know—I'm on the jury—and may I add that it was unanimous."

Actually, Mack's memory of the conversation must have been a little off. Cowles was on the Pulitzer board, which ratified the jury's recommendation. The jury consisted of Francis Brown, the editor of *The New York Times Book Review,* and Carlos Baker, a renowned literary critic and Princeton professor who later wrote the best-known biography of Ernest Hemingway. Discovering that Baker was half the Pulitzer jury rang a loud bell. I had earlier found a letter to Baker from Bill Targ, *Andersonville's* publisher, describing "a private conversation" the two had had on the day earlier that winter when they learned "Big A" had been passed over for the National Book Award in favor of *Ten North Frederick* by John O'Hara. According to Targ, he and Baker had vehemently agreed that a far less deserving book had won, and consoled each other with the notion that "justice" would prevail "in the long run." A few months later, Baker was in a position to administer that justice himself. In their report to the Pulitzer board, he and Brown wrote, "*Andersonville,* a historical novel in the grand manner, recaptures the tragedy and drama not only of the prison stockade from which it takes its name, but of the Civil War itself. Here is a panorama of the war years and of the divided nation which fought the war. Here, described with moving compassion, are the men and boys who fought and lived or nobly died. Here are those who knew in the Confederate camp at Andersonville man's inhumanity, and humanity, to man. For sweep of subject matter, for depth of understanding, for skill of narration, this novel would be great in any year and surely in 1955 was unsurpassed."

They concluded, "In the better than average fiction year, then, these three—*Andersonville, Ten North Frederick* and *Band of Angels* [by Robert Penn Warren]—stood forth, but in our view, as we have stated, the chief of these was, and is, *Andersonville*. We urge it again for the Pulitzer Award."

As I read my grandfather's letter, I could picture Mack, Irene, Cowles, and his wife sitting in the bar, Cowles quoting the jury report from memory and Mack floating along on a high unrelated to the no doubt top-shelf whiskey in their glasses. I felt astonishing good fortune to be holding in my hands the actual account, written on the day after it happened, of what had always been a mythic event in my family. As an adolescent, I remember staring, fascinated, at the surprisingly small piece of parchment, about half the size of a sheet of typing paper, hanging in my grandfather's study in a distressed gold frame. It surprised me that something so insignificant-looking could have had such an impact. I have said often here that I grew up discounting my grandfather's importance as a literary figure, understanding first and foremost that his vision of himself as such had been disproved even before his death. But there was one thing that had always impressed me, and would always impress anyone who heard of it, and it was there, inside that frame—a document appearing to be nothing more than a bit of bureaucratic inconsequence, a preprinted form with spaces for a name and a title, which were typed in as if an afterthought.

Just looking at it now, I recall the comforting musk of mildew and moldering books and cedar that had always surrounded it in the eternal twilight of my grandfather's study. And I can look at it anytime I want: it hangs on the first floor of my home, not far from another similar, though somewhat larger and more professionally constructed looking version of the document, an "honorary" Pulitzer presented to me by my staff when I left *The Washington Post*. It was a kind gesture, intended to recognize my role in the Pulitzers awarded to articles that I had edited. I gushed my thanks, of course, and never told anyone that in fact I found the document humiliating, a consolation that failed to console. My name was not on any of those Pulitzers, the real ones, a reminder that there were things I had wished to achieve that I never had.

I could well imagine what it would have been like—those moments of pure satisfaction that occur after recognition on a grand scale, ratification for all the world to see that your best efforts were, in fact, good enough.

And now I didn't have to imagine, because Mack's letter allowed me to come along for the ride:

> We had our drinks. . . . Irene and I wandered out to a cab, rode clear down to St. Germain Blvd. at the Odeon, sat, had coffee, walked, had wine, walked slowly, ate mild dinner in a small cheap café but GOOD, walked all the way up to the Seine under stars on the first warm night of the year in Paris, walked through the Tuilleries gardens, walked home, sat in a bar, I had TWO yellow Chartreuses, Irene had TWO tomato juices, came up to bed, read magazines idly, went to sleep before one a.m. . . . Is that a way to celebrate a unanimous Pulitzer Prize?

Yes, most definitely, it is.

In fiction, climaxes so often consist of a nexus point, where dramatic resolutions to crucial but seemingly unrelated plot points occur simultaneously. This contrivance would not feel as satisfying as it does if the phenomenon did not occur so often in real life. How odd, I thought, that within two weeks in the early spring of 1956 my grandfather would receive news of both the final resolution to his lifelong bedevilment by his sociopathic father and the pinnacle achievement of his career.

Throw in, as icing on an already rich cake, the evidence that his talent and passion for writing had been successfully transmitted to his progeny—the sale, simultaneous to all the above, of my mother's novel—and it all seems a little *too* contrived.

And that was my first thought. The odds of a random housewife successfully selling a first novel are astronomical; but perhaps considerably less so if her father happened to be the current best-selling author in the country.

I had grown up with my mother's novel, *The Four of Them*, always visible on the bookshelf in our living room. It was a fact. My mother had written a novel. But it was something, like her eye color, that existed without consequence. I didn't remember her writing it, and she never talked about it, or published anything further.

I never even removed it from the bookshelf until I was in eighth grade, when I read *The Four of Them* and wrote a book report on it for school. I pretended not to be shocked or embarrassed that my mother could have written a novel that revolved around sex—the unmet needs, physical and emotional, that drove a sensitive, alienated young woman enduring suburban wifehood to have an extramarital affair and the bleak consequences ensuing. This was just at the point in time when I began to fantasize about being a writer myself. I wish/don't wish that I still had a copy of the book report. I'm sure it would be excruciating to read. I can only remember that I had smugly and obnoxiously given it a mixed review—as if my fourteen-year-old self knew better.

Reading the novel now for the first time since then, I still give a mixed review, though with somewhat more nuance and superior credentials. The prose is occasionally overcooked and the plot, certainly by today's standards and quite possibly even by 1956 standards, is a little trite. But the writing itself has signs of real talent—a feel for language, a knack for imagery, and the ability to make trenchant observations that ring true. The handful of reviews the book got after publication were—you guessed it—mixed. "In an exuberant first novel, Layne Shroder reveals herself as a talented writer, but one whose gifts and enthusiasms occasionally lead her away from her story rather than into it" was the first sentence of one review, whose almost every sentence contained a bit of praise followed by a "but."

O f course, I am not a casual reader, but someone searching the pages for insight into my mother, who never revealed herself this intimately in a lifetime of conversation.

I had been poleaxed to learn for the first time, as I was sitting in the manuscript room reading a letter my grandfather wrote to an old friend, that my parents came within a breath of divorce when I was seven years old. ("This is the real thing this time. Layne told me that she plans to go to Mexico for a divorce in the fall.")

Their marriage would survive that moment without any of us ever realizing how close the end had come. Divorce did come, but a decade later when I was a sophomore in college, after which I discovered that adultery had been an issue for one, or possibly both, of them. So in this clearly autobiographically influenced fiction, I expected to find some insight into the forces that ultimately unraveled my parents' relationship. In the book, the main character, called Sarie, decides in the end that her difficulty feeling passion for her husband—a passion briefly ignited by another man with bitter aftershocks—is ultimately less important than her feeling of deep affection for him, and that perhaps by focusing on that feeling one moment at a time, she can manufacture a lasting love. "She managed, for the moment at least, to make it true," my mother writes in the novel's penultimate sentence, "and futures are composed of present moments."

So there was that.

I was also looking for a sense of a writing style that resonated with my own. I had seen that echo in my grandfather's writing, and even in my great-grandmother's, and by now I expected to find it here. What I didn't expect was this passage, in which Sarie is reflecting on natural beauty: "She immersed herself in it, until she felt she might burst with the pressure, the hurtfulness it caused."

An interesting idea not all that commonly expressed—that beauty, deeply felt, can cause pain. I certainly hadn't been thinking of my mother when I wrote of a moment of personal epiphany in the conclusion to my most recent book: "I felt the pain in the joy, the unbearable beauty of the world. . . ."

I suppose that it should not be surprising that a son could absorb even unspoken attitudes—but I never would have associated that sentiment with my relentlessly optimistic and not particularly outdoorsy mother. And then there were the inevitable similarities of her heroine's life to her own, and the possible insights it provided; like the passage in which Sarie remembers crashing her bike as a girl and confronting her father as she stumbled home. "She remembered anger in her father's face. . . . 'Jesus Christ, Sarie, haven't you any sense? . . . Do I have to take your bicycle away from you? God damn it, Edith, do something!' he appealed to her mother. 'Why do I have to be presented with all these problems when I'm working?' He'd stormed back to his typewriter. . . ."

That squares with the disappointingly little I know—because I never asked—about how my mother regarded her upbringing. As best as I could reconstruct from stray statements across a lifetime, she had no doubt her father loved her. When he was away, which was often, he would write amusing and affectionate letters to her, and no doubt he could be the same when they were together. But he could also be prickly, distant, and unavailable. As Tim put it in his memoir, Mack "wanted to be the best father in the world," but "what model did he have?"

There were times when having us grandkids around irritated him into shouts of "Jesus Christ" and "Goddamnit!" just as in *The Four of Them.*

But as I've said, he could also be sweet and charming and generous to us, and it had been the same with my mom when she was little. What surprised me in the letters Mack wrote to friends was how highly he spoke of my mother's talent as a writer—and how fiercely he wanted her to make use of it. I found a three-page letter he wrote praising her talent and counseling her at length in the practical matters of advancing her career, even suggesting topics for a second novel. Between the lines, you could sense how much he dreaded the idea she might not write one. In one letter I discovered that he had even underwritten the cost of a full-time maid in our house so my mother would have time to write. When he thought my parents were about to divorce, he unloaded on my father in a surprisingly progressive screed about my dad's very typical 1950s attitude about separation of domestic duties and my mother's career aspirations:

"He never did learn to give her the slightest cooperation in the actual running of the house . . . and flew into a rage if he thought she was taking any time out for her own writing, when she should have been waiting on him."

Shortly after Mack got his Pulitzer, when he was delivering family news to his old chum Dick Whiteman, he crowed about my mother's unassisted sale of her book in the same breath he announced the birth of a new granddaughter: "Layne-o has presented the world with a girl for a change: one Susan Irene, who is a calm and meditative baby. She is also going to present the world with a new novel, to be published by

Houghton Mifflin next year. They never guessed who Layne Shroder was, which of course filled her with delight; she did the whole thing on her own. I'm reading the book now; it really is fine."

Parental pride, of course, is to be expected. But somehow it surprised me, given what I believed about his self-obsession, and I was moved to see this clearly heartfelt praise.

And then he had this to say about the theme: "The subject bores me though. I told her that I couldn't get interested in a gang of young people just discovering for the first time that there is such a thing as marital infidelity, and Layne says haughtily that a few million people may disagree with me; which I hope is true. Marital infidelity is just as sure to be persistent in the world as the sun, moon and stars. In every case except your own of course!"

I had managed to stifle the impulse to snort thus far, but then he came up with the capper.

"Come to think of it," he wrote, "I believe I only made one pass at your dear wife in all my existence, and when she said No, I retired gracefully."

Something tells me he wasn't joking.

My mother wasn't wrong about a few million people being interested in adultery in the mid-1950s. Sexuality in suburbia, adultery in particular, powered *Peyton Place* to near the top of the best-seller lists, alongside *Andersonville*, for much of 1956 and 1957, the year my mother's book was published. Even so, like the immense majority of first novels, *The Four of Them* sold sparsely—more likely in the hundreds of copies rather than the thousands. I had long known that she'd begun a second novel, and then abandoned it with, as far as I knew, no regrets. I'd wondered about that. With all the promise and encouraging critical reception of her first novel, why didn't she keep going?

I stopped wondering when I started writing books myself.

There come just too many soul-crushing moments when all you've written seems gibberish and all possible paths forward look to end against an unclimbable wall, or over the edge of a cliff. I never would have completed anything if I hadn't already been paid an advance I would have had to pay back.

I was amused when I came across this quote from my grandfather, basically saying the same thing: "Most good writers, and most bad ones too, are poor people. Their earlier stories get written because they need food and shelter. Their later stories are written because they want . . . Cadillacs or want to go hunting moose."

He also wrote, "When you've been a writer as long as I have . . . nothing inspires you except a check."

Of course, Mack had managed to keep writing, completely checkless, contract or no contract. On my bookshelves, I found something I didn't even realize I had: a ledger book he had kept from the 1930s in which he scribbled notations in tiny script—the title of a submission on the left, and the fate of the submission on the right. Page after page have but one word, repeated again and again, in the right column: *Rejected.*

But he didn't stop. He couldn't stop. For him it was write or starve.

In the years after my mother's first novel, Mack's letters always had the same two comments about her writing; he believed she was truly talented, and he feared the comfortable, distracted life of a suburban mother threatened her deserved future as a writer.

I thought his analysis was as good as any explanation of her abandonment of writing: absent the threat of starvation and legal obligation to whip her along, she simply got stuck and couldn't find sufficient motivation to unstick herself.

It wasn't until I began looking through the documents I'd collected in a file marked LAYNE-O that I realized something startling: of all the letters she wrote exulting about signing a book contract, only some were from 1956. Another, I noted, was dated 1957. This was for the *second* novel, signed shortly after publication of her first. She'd had a contract after all, which must have made it exponentially more painful to quit in the middle—especially for a woman who wrote in her alumni magazine, "After my first son was born I told myself and the world that I was so busy and contented that I would probably never write again, but I soon began to feel restless. . . . It seemed it was impossible to discard my ambition without discarding a part of myself. Writing is for me almost like a drug. I doubt I will be able to stop for more than a short time."

After her divorce from my dad, my mother went to law school—the oldest person in her class by about twenty years. She passed the bar in her mid-forties, and practiced for thirty years as a public defender in juvenile court—a job she considered a calling and approached with indefatigable passion, despite the fact that it was one of the most taxing, depressing, and thankless tasks imaginable. At the end of her long life, when she was heroically refusing to yield her spirit to rapidly advancing lung cancer, I reopened the topic of her writing career.

"Even if you couldn't finish the book you started," I said, "didn't you ever have the urge to write some other book?"

"You know," she said, "night after night when I got you all to bed, I would sit there and struggle to write, because I had always thought I was meant to do it. But eventually I realized: I *hate* writing."

SIXTEEN

———

The first sign of even an inkling of self-awareness by my grandfather that he had a drinking problem came in a letter from Europe in those first weeks after finishing *Andersonville*, when he and Irene were both sick as dogs: "I'm still coughing, still sneezing, still nose-blowing. I've taken the last desperate step, and am now On the Wagon—for how long I don't know but certainly until I'm better. Perhaps that's not literally true, but I mean no cocktails. . . . In Spain it would be almost impossible to go completely On."

So he was aware, but unaware.

Both Mack and Irene came from nondrinking families, and they'd learned to drink together as a release and a modest rebellion, staking out territory they saw as the proper ground of creative types. It may have helped, in Mack's case, that John Kantor made a very ponderous point of disdaining all drink. Whatever John didn't like, Mack would love.

In his autobiography, Mack said he'd always felt alcohol was benign, even helpful, as a contrast to drugs of any kind, which he abhorred. "I had visions of becoming a groveling monster under the influence of drugs," he wrote. "Liquor was something else. It was fun, it could be indulged in at the end of a hard day's work if one had the price."

Anyone who has watched the TV series *Mad Men* can easily picture the drinking culture Mack enthusiastically participated in as a rising writer with an overactive social life.

No doubt, there had been embarrassing scenes and alcohol-fueled regrets aplenty during those years. But it took a persistent case of flu on the heels of the exhausting finish of *Andersonville* to make Mack think of taking that "last desperate step"—not even of stopping drinking, but just cutting back.

By then, according to my uncle's memoir, Irene was already seriously concerned, as were their closest friends. If anyone said anything about it, Mack bellowed, "How the hell do you expect me to come down from that labor, this excitement, overnight?"

Being on the wagon, such as it was, clearly didn't much outlast the sniffles. Back in the States, now a certified literary lion and for the first time in his life having the economic liberty not to immediately harness himself to another weighty writing project, he sloshed his way around the country.

My uncle described post-*Andersonville* visits to New York that resonate deep in my memory: "Sometimes during their stay in the city, they'd go up to Scarsdale, to visit Layne and Bill Shroder and their children. Mother would be anxious and warm and eager, a youthful, sweet-scented . . . grandmother. Dad would usually drink too much, and always he would want to perform and preside—singing songs, reading to Layne and Bill the latest chapters of the manuscript he was working on, reading to the kids excerpts from children's books he had written. . . . And always, back in New York, there would be ritual . . . drinks in their suite at the Algonquin, then cabs summoned, and then the grand procession to a table, with greetings from the manager or owner and a scurrying of waiters, and drinks and dinner and laughter, at this favorite restaurant or that. And at the end of the evening, he would insist on picking up the check for everyone, and tip quite grandly. . . . He moved through some of those days in a bright alcoholic fog. Sober as a stern, demanding judge in the mornings; foolishly benign, foolishly angry, late at nights."

I remember how, after his third or fourth cocktail, his face would seem to tilt sideways, his jaw shifting beneath slightly unfocused eyes as he brayed out a joke or a song; how he looked around for approbation, but more easily found something to irritate or enrage him.

When I showed my sister the above section as I was writing it, she reminded me of something I'd forgotten, a story my mother told us: At one big alcohol-fueled night out with her father at a dinner theater performance, deep into the post-meal drinking, the emcee of the event announced to the crowd that the famous author MacKinlay Kantor was in attendance. A spotlight waggled its way around the tables searching, settling finally on Mack, passed out facedown on his dinner plate.

The drinking had gone well beyond even the most liberal definition of moderation. I found a 1957 letter from Mack himself that paints the picture quite clearly:

Made a nice acquaintance on the airplane . . . quite a drinker. We both were to have a little time in Dallas, so we killed a bottle of champagne in the bar, and then my flight got delayed . . . so we went back to the bar, more champagne. Our flight was called—engine trouble. Back to the bar. More Champagne. I think this went on two or three more times, but I can't remember very well. . . . It took me two days to recover, but now I am drinking almost nothing, and feel grand.

The key word in that last sentence: *almost.*

I can only imagine what Awful Incident made Mack grasp that his drinking had gone well beyond supplying the occasional amusing anecdote and was something that needed to be addressed. Was it a hideous public explosion? A bad fall? A near miss on the highway? All three in one night?

I'll never know. But within months of the party in the Dallas airport bar, he wrote again to Dick Whiteman:

I had a great deal of trouble with liquor ever since I saw you. When abroad usually I don't drink too much, although there have been notable exceptions. Back in the US, with the pressure mounting on me from every angle, I found my only relaxation at the end of a day in about a thousand Gibsons, which of course necessitated further treatment next morning. So it went; I was on the wagon three different times, during one period of which I joined AA and was bored stiff with the people and their utterances, if not their practice. Finally I decided to seek divine guidance from the former head of the Yale Plan Clinic. He studied the thing from every angle—physical, chemical and psychological—and came up with the not too unexpected verdict that I could not drink like an ordinary human being, at least not at this moment in my life. The funny thing is that I find no difficulty ever in quitting. It's just that I would prefer to drink and have liquor in my life. In the past I have gone a month on two different occasions, and nearly three months on another without trouble during the duration of dryness, but with the firmly-arrived-at intention of practicing moderation when I returned to drinking again. No soap—couldn't be done. Thus I went dry on the 17th of Sept and will be dry until the 17th of March. My own hunch is that it will be like that from now on, punctuated with an occasional happy fling.

The problem, as Mack would put it exactly halfway through his time On the Wagon in a letter to Hark:

I'm having trouble re-establishing connections with my novel. I am far away from it just at present—intellectually I am eager to return to the fray; emotionally, I still recoil. This is a tough business in a creative existence—trying to adjust to a creative life without alcohol when it has determined one's pattern of conduct for so long a time. However, I am willing to spend six months in trying.

It happened that, during this brief dry spell, Hemingway showed up with his longtime companion and confidant Toby Bruce, whom my grandfather described as their "mutual friend."

I told Ernest I was on the wagon for six months and couldn't join them in a drink. Ernest looked at me sadly and said, "Mack, I have a crushed kidney, and you can't drink with a crushed kidney." So I asked Toby what he'd have. He said, if the two biggest drunks in North America weren't drinking then he wasn't either.

I found nothing directly calling his experiment with not drinking a failure, but I didn't need to. Instead there was this, from early 1958, exactly two months before his dry period was supposed to end: "We talk about going to Mexico in the Spring; I am hoping to be working on my novel again. I certainly don't feel like it now, or feel like much of anything else. This life of sobriety is not for me, but I must maintain it as scheduled until the 17th of March; then the hell with all such attempts."

In April he wrote a long letter to the Yale alcoholism expert arguing the necessity of drink to his creative process. "The point I wish to make," he wrote, "is that dreams of complication and clarity almost never occurred to me during the times when I was on the wagon. I am prone to regard these as evidences of a creative force and ambition."

I think that was the end of his attempts to stop drinking for a number of years. For me, the most moving part of my uncle's memoir had to do with an incident in the summer of 1962. Tim, then a freelance photographer, was in New York when he got a long-distance call from Mack: "I'm out here in Webster City. . . . I've been drinking my way across the country—the booze had started to build up before I left Sarasota—and I've been drinking here, and last night they had a party for me. At six o'clock this morning I woke up and found that I was staring at the goddamn trees. I'd passed out on the lawn and so, I decided it was time to climb back on the wagon. The trouble is I've got the shakes, bad. I'm due in NY in a few days . . . but I don't dare drive the car. I wondered if you could possibly fly out to Des Moines. . . . I can get the car that far."

When Tim met Mack at the airport, he handed him the car keys, hands shaking. "I damn near didn't get here, even though I only went at thirty miles an hour all the way," he said.

Tim started out cross-country, his father, diminished, beside him. When they stopped for dinner, Tim hesitated before ordering a drink. Mack said, "Go ahead, you earned it. The booze is my problem, not yours."

That's where the story ends in Tim's telling, but I winced. I knew what Tim, in the writing of his book, either didn't know or wouldn't admit. Mack's alcohol problem was most definitely his problem, too. Despite tremendous talent—he was a brilliant photographer and a fine writer himself—after a hitch in the Air Force, which no doubt pleased his dad more than himself, he modeled a career based on his father's—in independent pursuit of artistic success in one medium or another. Though Mack was fiercely proud of Tim and believed in his talent, even he urged him to take a more practical course. "If he would just take some part time jobs, say, and work three days a week at something remunerative, which he could easily find to do—even if he had to go into a factory—then the problem would be solved," Mack wrote to a friend. "But he stubbornly refuses."

Tim had some success with photography, but never enough to live comfortably or support a family. He eventually gave up that pursuit to become a writer, which wasn't as loopy an idea as it may sound, considering his true talent. He published *My Father's Voice* to some good reviews. This was a high point for him, a moment of hope: Now that he was a published writer himself, things would change. "I have a novel to do," he wrote in the book's final chapter, "and I hope books after that. . . . I am eager for the future."

When the book didn't sell, he blamed the publisher, as writers so often do, for failure to adequately publicize it or bring out a paperback edition. He had interest from publishers in another book, but that stalled when his health began to degenerate, mostly due to a lifetime of heavy drinking and smoking. He ended up flat broke, and too often drunk, living in an ancient Florida apartment house that had been charming in the era when Mack built the house on Siesta Key, but was now disintegrating around him.

"He never had the money for bills—although always, mysteriously, for alcohol and cigarettes," my cousin, his daughter, Lydia remembered when I showed her Mack's letter. "In response to my often begging him to get a job, even if it was working as a cashier or bagging groceries, he always told me that the very reason he couldn't have a 'normal job' was the fact that from a young age, Gramp had told him that a regular job was simply not acceptable: only greatness counted. Given this letter, apparently that was not the case, and Gramp and I had very similar attitudes towards Daddy's situation."

I knew that my mother was constantly tormented by the worry that Tim might end up on the street if she didn't lend him money, and that she might be enabling him if she did.

In the end, he discovered he had lung cancer only because he fell down—no doubt when drinking—and busted out some teeth. A checkup at a charity dental clinic revealed he had worse problems than a broken smile. I loved him dearly, which only made it more painful to see his decline and the relentless vise grip that drinking had on him.

Which brings me to . . . me.

Both my mother and my father drank all their adult lives. Based on what is now known about how alcohol impacts physiological health, they undoubtedly drank too much. They may have been partially psychologically dependent, with negative emotional consequences. I'm not talking falling-down, getting-the-shakes, tragedy-level consequences. It was more things said and done that couldn't be unsaid and undone. By some definitions, *any* negative consequences of frequent alcohol use qualify as alcoholism.

According to Robert Morse, MD, the former director of Addictive Disorders Services at the Mayo Clinic (and a million other sources), "the single most reliable indicator for risk of future alcohol or drug dependence is family history. Research has shown conclusively that family history of alcoholism or drug addiction is in part genetic."

The relationship between individual genes and alcoholism is intensely complex and far from completely understood. Research with mice, though, has demonstrated one fascinating genetic link. Deficiency in a specific gene has been shown to increase anxiety behavior of mice in a maze, and those mice with increased anxiety go for alcohol over water when given a choice, while mice with sufficient quantities of that gene prefer water. In fact, when the gene-deficient mice drink alcohol, their anxious behavior diminishes—so drinking is an apparent attempt at self-medication.

Even if there is a human equivalent gene or combination of genes that could create a higher risk of alcoholism, not all offspring of parents with those genes would be at risk. Inheritance is always a roll of two dice, and it's the combination that ultimately matters.

Ironically, my own genetic predisposition—or lack of it—would colorfully express itself one night when I was fifteen . . . on my grandfather's beach. Mack had said a friend and I could camp overnight. He came by at dusk, as he almost always did when I camped there, and chatted for a bit. I can't remember a word of what was said, but I would now pay a small fortune for a tape, or better yet a video, of that conversation. Most likely it would have been a monologue by my grandfather. When he'd said his piece, he shuffled back up the lawn toward the house, fragrant clouds of smoke from his pipe lingering behind as he disappeared into the growing darkness. We set to digging a pit in the sand for our campfire, using as a scoop one of the baked-bean cans we'd already emptied into the frying pan. We'd scooped only a few canfuls of sand before we hit something metallic. With a small thrill of discovery, I reached down and pulled. It was an even greater find than I could have imagined: a completely full six-pack of beer still lashed together by its plastic harness.

In order to appreciate our glee, I have to reiterate that we were fifteen and had a long night of sitting on the beach with absolutely nothing to do. Without so much as phony IDs to our name, it was as if the booze fairy had waved her magic wand over our campsite and, presto chango, the brewskis rose from the earth, right into our eager hands.

I brushed off the sand on one of the cans, popped the tab, and took a big swig . . . then gagged and spit. God knows how long that six-pack had been buried, but based on the degree of flatness and staleness of the liquid it contained, I would have guessed Late Jurassic.

I grabbed the can out of my friend's hand as he began to tilt it toward his mouth. "Don't do it!" I shouted. "It's completely foul."

We settled for shaking the cans and spraying them on each other. Even that was disappointing due to the lack of fizz.

I thought nothing more of the incident until many years later when my friend, whom I hadn't seen for some time, was telling me about his terrible descent into, and struggle to recover from, alcoholism.

"In fact," he said, "I first glimpsed that I might have a problem with alcohol because of you."

I told him I had no idea what he meant.

"It was that night we were camping at Mack's beach and we found the six-pack."

What about it? I said.

"Well, you took one sip and spit it out, and then started pouring all the cans out on the ground, and the whole time I was thinking, 'Wait a second! It's still alcohol!' The taste of it, which is what mattered to you, was completely irrelevant to me. The only thing I cared about was the buzz."

I did have a handful of incidents of binge drinking in college, and just out of it, but only enough to learn in a way hard to forget that what heavy consumption of alcohol made me was not creative but, first, stupid, and second, sick as a dog.

Most likely I had my genes to thank for that ultimate aversion to drunkenness—certainly not Mack's, but, who knows, maybe . . . John Kantor's.

Mack ultimately got off the wagon—he didn't fall, he leapt off—and continued to drink, as he would for the rest of his life. Once again, five o'clock cocktails and refills throughout the evening fueled his self-confidence and ambition. On top of the literary world and barely into his fifties, he began thinking big, bigger than ever. Given that he was always puffing on his pipe—new pipes and pipe tobacco were pretty much what us grandkids gave him every single birthday and possibly every Christmas for good measure—it would have been clever to call them pipe dreams, if he hadn't already succeeded so grandly. Certainly his editor took them seriously, possibly even prompted them. Soon after the news of the Pulitzer, Donald Friede wrote Mack a "What now?" letter.

> *It is the damndest challenge any writer ever faced. You've got to follow* War and Peace *with* Moby Dick. *And you can do it. Here's why. For the first time in your life—this was not the case while you were writing Big A—you have security for years to come. You don't have to worry about anything financial—not even what you'll have to do when you finish* Son of Andersonville *and are waiting for it to ring the cash register. . . . You can write as well as you can as slowly as you must. . . . You have hit your full writing stride at your young age. . . . Everest, hell. Stratosphere! And it's yours for the reaching.*

Not only his editor but the world at large kept telling him he was a Great Man and had no limits. Paul Reynolds, his agent for foreign rights, whispered seductively in his ear, "If *Andersonville* can get a wide enough foreign distribution you might get a Nobel Prize. I know you think I'm crazy but there is that real possibility."

Mack didn't think it crazy. He was beginning to believe he deserved it. Why not? Nothing seemed denied to him.

Drake University, where Effie McKinlay met John Kantor, granted him an honorary doctorate. To celebrate a powerful new set of beacon lights beaming from the ninetieth floor beneath the world-famous spire of the Empire State Building, Mack was commissioned to write a poem to be cast in bronze and installed on the observation deck. His effort, a tepid echo of the inspiring Emma Lazarus poem for the Statue of Liberty (*Bring me your tired, your poor . . .*), was soon forgotten (*Whence rise you, Lights? From this tower built upon Manhattan's native rock. Its roots are deep below forgotten musket balls, the moldered wooden shoe, the flint, the bone*). Still, his writing was now literally on top of the world.

Nicholas Ray, director of *Rebel Without a Cause*, even cast him in a speaking role in a filmed-in-Florida movie—*Wind Across the Everglades*.

"At first I thought I would do it only for kicks," Mack wrote friends. "But to you I will admit privately that I now entertain the glimmering of ambition along this line." During the glacially paced filming, he got to hang out with celebrity pals Burl Ives—the future Oscar winner whom Mack had helped get national recognition when he had been a little-known folksinger—Peter Falk, Christopher Plummer, Emmett Kelly, and Gypsy Rose Lee. All great fun, feeding his glimmer of Hollywood ambition, until he saw the movie's premiere and discovered to his horror that all his lines had been dubbed in by another actor.

So forget acting. Mack had serious writing to do, Great Writing, and he set to it, this time on his own timetable and employing researchers to help lighten the immense task. He'd written *Andersonville* in a year and a half; for this new book, he took five years, the entirety of his mid-fifties.

"Yes dear ones, it is all done," he wrote to Dick Whiteman and his wife in July of 1961. "The word length approaches five hundred thousand. I suppose that makes it the longest historical novel ever to be published in America."

He said it with pride—without a thought for how readers might react to a book that would run just short of a thousand pages. He'd quite intentionally doubled down on the success—and excess—of *Andersonville*. *Son of Andersonville*—its real title was *Spirit Lake*—was intended to do for the conflict between white settlers and Native Americans what *Andersonville* had done for the clash between North and South. Only more so. Scores of characters, each drawn in minute, historically accurate detail from their points of origin to where their fates collided in a grim little massacre that brought out the beastliness in all. Each individual became a tile in a grand mosaic of the westward expansion, complete with abundant lore and verse and song and customs elaborately described, for both whites and Sioux—who were depicted unromantically, but not without some sympathy and densely realistic detail. A columnist for the Sarasota paper recounted with awe that Mack not only read everything written on the Sioux, he made repeated visits to reservations in South Dakota and lived with tribe members, even learning their native language. In fact, all the characters in *Spirit Lake* spoke in archaic dialects and vehemently inhabited vanished worlds of the American past.

Everyone involved with the book was giddy with excitement. If *Andersonville* had been big, this was bigger, and the bigger the better in all their estimation. The most tangible evidence of this enthusiasm was a first printing of one hundred thousand copies. Even before Mack had finished the book, paperback rights were purchased for a guarantee of $100,000 against future royalties—"an absolutely history-making deal," Mack crowed, certain that the eventual earnings would be even greater than the guarantee once the book became a perennial best seller. A Book-of-the-Month Club endorsement, which would account for thousands of sales, seemed almost assured. (Mack reported: The book club manager called asking when the final proofs would be ready, saying, "No, we haven't got any good novel for November, *but we think we know where we can find one.*")

This wasn't just Mack self-enthusing. Friede told him that *Andersonville* had "just been a finger exercise" on the typewriter compared to *Spirit Lake*. World Publishing was committing a $50,000 advertising campaign—absolutely huge in 1961 terms—to launch it. Mack boasted that a war correspondent buddy had called some of the book's passages "the greatest prose ever written in the English language."

As to *Spirit Lake* surpassing *Andersonville* in success, they were all deluded; blind to the currents of the new decade, the first trickle of what would soon be a torrent rushing toward the next century, an era of sound bites, BuzzFeed, and instant messaging, and the ubiquitous meme responding to anything extending beyond a few bytes of text: *TL; DR.* Too Long; Didn't Read. Throughout the rest of the twentieth century, prodded by the growing ubiquity of light entertainment on television, attention spans would shrink, as would patience for ornamented language and weighty subject matter.

In the five years of terrible toil it took my grandfather to write *Spirit Lake*, the world had become a different place. Instead of the critical ecstasy that greeted *Andersonville*, major reviewers openly mocked the new offering. *Time* headlined its review "Wordy Way West," and sneered, "Wordier even than *Andersonville* . . . *Spirit Lake* is distended by a cast of more than four dozen major characters cursed with total recall and the folksiest dialect since *Mr. Dooley.* ('Well sakes!' says one.

'Course, I ain't had a touch of shakes since two years agone, and I do firmly believe that it was because I et three hard-boiled eggs on Good Friday.')"

The *New Republic*'s premier critic, Stanley Kauffmann, seethed at length about the novel's verbosity, its "carbonated lyric gush."

The verdict, though not unanimous, was damning. There were some raves. *The Chicago Tribune* called it "a massive and magnificent novel." The New Orleans *Times-Picayune* said, "If the Great American Novel can be written, this is it." But even positive reviews tended to linger on the book's ponderous length. "Much of the telling is sheer poetry—in the old saga tradition," concluded *Kirkus*. "Some of it is legend and myth. There is variety, and pace and a zest for story telling. That sometimes it drags could be forgiven were it not unduly long—at times unnecessarily tedious. But in the main immensely rewarding."

And, for Mack and his supporters, immensely disappointing. The Book-of-the-Month Club endorsement failed to materialize—by one vote of the selectors, Mack claimed—dooming *Spirit Lake* to mediocre performance.

The hardcover edition sold barely more than half of its optimistic first printing—enough to get it very briefly to number three on the best-seller list but hardly enough to justify the huge ad campaign and the astronomical expectations.

Unlike *Andersonville*, which I had at least attempted (and failed, three times) to read through, I'd never even considered cracking open the massive *Spirit Lake*, which, picking up on the between-the-lines implications of family lore, I'd always assumed was a face-plant of a failure, dense and unreadable.

Now I've gone back to both books. I'd read no further than page 34 in *Andersonville* before I recognized the passage that had stopped me every time. To put it in cinematic terms, Mack had been doing a

close-up on one of his characters—Henry Wirz, the eventual commandant of the prison—while he was on medical leave in Paris, before
his assignment to Andersonville. At the end of the scene, he pulled the
camera of his mind's eye back to an ever-wider perspective; first taking
in the Parisian environs, than all of Western Europe, then the cresting
waves of the Atlantic, then zooming in again on the pinelands of
Georgia. A younger me thought it impenetrable. But now I can't
fathom why I reacted that way. It's a bit purple perhaps, but only a few
paragraphs long, after all: "One might then have gone far beyond
Henry Wirz, through darkened bricks of the tall old house . . . past the
spires of Versailles . . . and spread across the thrashing coasts. . . .
Away, away, going in thought or imagination above the long black
swells. . . . Above estuaries and over camps the fast wild thought might
have gone fleeting, born in a brain which truly had no power to bear
it; for this moment became a part of the future where a man can never
dwell, and where gods are merely invented, and where the new unseen
sun gives off its roaring, and new unseen stars are intact."

So yeah, dense *and* purple. But this time I found I admired it as
poetry, understood my grandfather meant to evoke a feeling of sweep
and grandeur. And it's not as if equally windy passages constantly pop
up throughout the book: this is a rare flight of fancy. Most of the novel
is granular and gritty to a fault.

I was equally surprised by *Spirit Lake*. Mack wasn't wrong. *Spirit Lake*
was, at least, on a par with *Andersonville*, and of the same quality. I was
surprised to discover that even now, if you look up both books on Ama-
zon or one of those reading community websites, they still get some rave
reviews from the handful of contemporary readers who take them on.

One such review of *Andersonville*: "This is one of the most remarkable books that you will ever experience. It has a reputation as a 'tough
read,' but the effort is more than worth it."

Of *Spirit Lake*: "This historical novel is a literary feast. It is a true readers' read."

My own assessment is that there is something close to genius in both novels, an obsessive attempt to paint the most painful, defining moments of America's past in a gigantic, inclusive mural, a Sistine Chapel version of the historical novel bristling with intimate knowledge of everything from how people talked to how they smelled. Not even half a chapter into *Spirit Lake*, you learn a folk remedy for fever involving a pound of fresh-butchered beef, a few quarts of human urine, and a black dog—and you just know from the feel of authority with which it is written that this is no figment of my grandfather's imagination, but a true historical fact.

The books' failing, the reason *Andersonville* especially did not retain its prominence into another century, is that the authenticity of detail serves to make these characters from the past seem alien. They not only look different but think different and feel different. Which is probably true, but it is also true for Tolstoy's countesses and generals from early nineteenth-century Russia. And yet, reading *War and Peace*, the overwhelming impact is not how different the characters are from you, but how eerily the *same*. (See also: William Shakespeare.) It would be unfair to compare any writer to Tolstoy, the Einstein of the human soul, but that's who Mack compared *himself* to.

Even failing Tolstoy's immortal alchemy, Mack would have helped contemporary readers, and possibly even readers half a century ago, if instead of dozens of characters equally weighted, there were one or a few in whom we could become supremely invested, and whose path through the novel, from beginning to end, kept us turning pages, desperate to know how it all turns out.

Hemingway, Fitzgerald, Nabokov—the great twentieth-century novelists who are still part of the conversation today—all employed that strategy to keep 'em reading, a strategy especially important if you wanted to go on for 951 small-print pages. It might not have hurt to tighten things up, either.

In the unobstructed view looking backward from the present, justly or unjustly, *Spirit Lake* was the turning point, the beginning of the decline of my grandfather's career and reputation.

My grandfather could be forgiven for not seeing it that way, at least not immediately. Why focus on the negatives, when instead you could focus on *Life* magazine calling *Spirit Lake* "a gigantic sweeping symphony," on the sixty thousand copies sold, or the acquaintances from Sweden who'd heard it was being mentioned for the Nobel. . . .

Publishers still believed in Mack and waited eagerly for his next pitch. Invitations to appear on television were floating in—he even got paid for strumming his guitar and crooning on a variety show with Burgess Meredith. He could make headlines just by visiting a city. The Air Force brass still loved him, drafting him—very much to his satisfaction—to fly to Europe and write up top secret assessments of new NATO installations. And Hollywood was still stumbling around, threatening to make a huge budget *Andersonville* epic, which, unlike *The Best Years of Our Lives*, would be unambiguously about his novel—and named for it. This of course would stand to reinvigorate sales and add to its place in history.

I pieced together the narrative of his life in the early 1960s as if it were a ten-thousand-piece jigsaw puzzle. It occurred to me that this was precisely the point in time when I made my first clear memories of my grandfather: the life I glimpsed on our Christmas visits to Sarasota, and their trips to see us in New York—the cocktails, the limos, the fancy restaurants; that penetrating, nasal midwestern voice rising above all background din and asserting itself as the center of every-thing through recitation or song, personal anecdote, or off-color joke.

In 1963, Mack flew my father, my brother, and me to Missouri—the hill country where he'd wandered as a young man and set *The Voice of Bugle Ann*, his most popular novel save *Andersonville*—to join him and Tim on a float trip down the James and White Rivers. I have indelibly pungent memories of the smell of catfish frying in fat in big black iron skillets, of skipping rocks across the rock-dimpled shallows, of sitting up late playing poker with Mack and the guides, using a can-vas cot as a table and smooth river rocks for chips. Late in the proceed-ings, I felt my brother nudge me beneath the cot, darting his eyes at one of the guides, who instead of buying in when he grew low on chips, was simply and not so stealthily picking rocks off the ground.

One afternoon, mid-expedition, I was fishing with worms and a bubble float from the bank when I blundered into a school of hungry fish. My pole jerked forward with shocking urgency. There was a pull, a brief struggle, and exultation when the shiny wet creature splashed out of the water into dappled sunlight. As soon as I could unhook the wriggling catch and toss the rebaited hook back in the water, the pole lurched once more. At first I was thrilled, but as I reeled the flapping and gasping creatures in one after the other and the catch bucket began to fill, my rapture turned to nausea at the slaughter I was perpe-trating. Stricken, I grabbed the bucket and upended it, sending my victims back into the swirl of the current. I had a brief moment of hope, then my stomach churned as, one by one, the liberated fish turned white-belly up in the black water and drifted away.

Fifty-two years later, as I was standing in my Northern Virginia living room, it took me a while to spot it. High on a bookshelf, nearly hidden by the much larger volumes beside it, was the diminutive November 1963 issue of *Pageant* magazine (cover stories: "Must We

Die? A Major Report on Medicine's Startling New Frontier"; and "Sex in the Office—Why It Happens"). The back of the issue features a half-dozen photographs from that trip ("How to get away from it all? A prize-winner's prize-winning secret"). In retrospect, I think Mack came up with the whole idea of the trip as a way of furthering Tim's freelance career—for he was the one who took the pictures. It had been at least thirty years since I'd last looked at those photos—my brother skipping rocks and sucking on a grapevine cigar, me diving naked into the current (visible only from the waist up, but I remember the skinny-dipping), my father, twenty-five years younger than I am now, shirtless, balding already, with surprisingly powerful arms and shoulders and a bit too much flesh at the belly. And there we are playing poker, just as I remembered, my grandfather, all business, dealing up the cards, my brother slyly sliding a rock into the pot in the center of the cot. The *Pageant* story says Mack "told pioneer stories and traded tall tales with the guides." I remember the fish and the poker.

I would soon discover a surprising backdrop for that trip. Three months earlier, Mack had returned from a secret project for the Air Force and tried to start on a new novel—one he only described as "modern." He got nowhere. This wasn't ordinary writer's block. On May 8, he wrote to a friend: "Everything I've done . . . is wooden, uninspiring, uninviting. . . . I have constantly entertained the feeling that I was stricken speechless, that my tongue was actually torn out by the roots, that I was paralyzed, calloused. . . . I've managed to work myself very close to a state of utter mental, spiritual and physical collapse. For the first time since I was in my twenties, I didn't even wish to go on living. The tension grew to exemplify itself in the fashion of another monster dwelling inside my own body and soul—a creature made perhaps of wire-mesh or wire rings laced closely together, and extending from my fingertips to my gullet and up into the aching recesses of my skull and down across my chest and into every organ and extremity."

Five days later, he discovered the identity of that monster. Doctors diagnosed an episode of congestive heart failure. He didn't use that term in another letter, describing it as a "strained left ventricle," complicated by high blood pressure. He said he was taking digitalis, and mourned the fact that his doctor ordered him to stop chopping wood: "My arms are falling away into nothingness."

What he didn't mention was the most relevant factor, which these days can be found with a simple computer search: chronic heart failure "is characterized by left ventricular dilation, increased left ventricular mass, and reduced left ventricular wall thickness among patients with *a long-term history of heavy alcohol consumption.*" The italics are emphatically mine.

It would take him another fourteen years to finish the job, but my grandfather was already well along the road to drinking himself to death.

M ack's health slowly returned, at least in the sense that he could work again. But the new decade asserted itself, and his perception of himself began to change. No longer was he a hero of the age, but a victim of it, a holdout against the foolishness of contemporary enthusiasms—television, liberal politics, communism, homosexuals.

Here's a typical lead from a news story on a college lecture he gave (and there were many such speeches) in that period: "Pulitzer Prize–winning author MacKinlay Kantor took verbal pot shots at everything from women's fashions to American foreign policy here Tuesday night . . . leaving little doubt in anyone's mind that he not only remembers but prefers 'the good old days.'"

Exhausted from *Spirit Lake*, and shaken by its failure to renew the torrent of respect and cash generated by *Andersonville*, he began sending out bits and pieces of repurposed and repackaged work from the past. And to his horror, he began to accumulate rejections.

When he pitched a paperback reissue of a 1938 novel about the extinction of passenger pigeons, New American Library replied with a dismissive "We talked about the book this morning and agreed that it would stand very little chance of doing sufficiently well today."

He tried to peddle an old, never-published short story to *Good Housekeeping*, whose editor responded, "It's clearly too bucolic for us."

The frustration accumulated. When he got nowhere trying to pitch a 1949 novel to Hollywood producers, who called it too old-fashioned, he lashed back with a horribly cringe-inducing letter sarcastically proposing "real modern" stories. The first involved "a physical type (homosexual) and an embittered intellectual Lesbian" who "get swept into a sewer" together.

Another was an elaborate mess about a hotel filled with "pansies who pick men up at night" and "bare-bosomed, short-skirted whores" who get into trouble with the law and decide to go straight. The "pansies" become fashion designers who use the whores as fashion models, and they become a huge success.

The last is about "an American university commie" who falls in love with a beautiful Cuban communista and commits murder and treason just to have a tryst with her in front of the gates of the Guantánamo Bay U.S. Marine base, where they both get riddled by bullets from both sides.

All of this is elaborated in four painful-to-read single-spaced pages seething with bitterness. My heart sank even lower when I saw that he credited my sweet grandmother as co-creator of these vile parodies.

Mack was flailing, sensing a loss of contact with these new times, and no doubt feeling his mortality. This panic-tinged bitterness began to build just when I was getting old enough to notice my parents—both Adlai Stevenson liberals—rolling their eyes at Mack's latest pronouncements, and to see for myself and wonder at the bold FUCK COMMUNISM placard prominently placed near the entrance to his study.

In the Library's files, I discovered to my surprise that Mack hadn't always been this way—he'd once been a raging New Deal Democrat. In 1936, during the presidential race between FDR and Republican challenger Alf Landon, he wrote to his sister and her husband: "I want to tell you how gratified Irene and I are to hear of your change in political sentiment. I feel so violently on this question that I could scarcely admit to myself that you folks might vote against the President."

I was even more shocked to discover a note from just three years later when he mentions being invited to Hyde Park to picnic with Eleanor Roosevelt. "Irene got a fine note from Mrs. Roosevelt yesterday, asking us to come and suggesting that we bring our bathing suits so that we could all go swimming."

He saw the Roosevelts socially more than once. I later found a photograph of a laughing group surrounding a seated FDR on a summer lawn, probably at Hyde Park, and there was Mack standing right behind the president, unmistakable in a double-breasted white suit with the ever-present pipe clenched in his jaw. As late as 1958, Eleanor even wrote an endorsement of a rather patriotic story in one of his collections: "We all need a simple, uplifting philosophy. . . . In this saga, which is really a saga of America, we can see ourselves more clearly and live more happily because of it."

By 1967, Mack had developed a revisionist view of his relationship with Eleanor. "To be perfectly frank," he wrote, "she and I never got on very well together. We met first during the 1930s and quarreled immediately on the question of the WPA writers' projects. . . . I thought it was a boondoggle pure and simple like a lot of the Kennedy and Johnson stuff these days. Nonetheless, we threw back and forth a little mutual respect; but no affection. When it came to sitting down and talking about almost any conceivable subject, Mrs. Roosevelt and Uncle Mack always were arrayed on opposite sides."

This from a man who in 1933 wrote: "As for our economic system, I think it's all shit. Any formula which, naturally or unnaturally, can bring the ghastly tribulation which has come to this country, ought to be wiped out. Communism, anything would be better."

By 1974, a newspaper article could sum up his views, which depicts the "grandpa" I knew and rolled my eyes at, this way:

He believes in the American Dream, in George Wallace and Curtis LeMay, that Watergate is "a lot of crap" and President Nixon is the victim of a conspiracy. He hates the Kennedys, hippies, the anti-Nixon press. Anything written after WWII he just does not read. "America hasn't changed at all," he declared from his cabin on the American ship, the Monterey, *in Sydney yesterday. "It's just the young riff-raff and the anti-Nixon extreme Democratic press—they're angry that Nixon swept all the states and they've conspired to get him and use every bit of ammunition they can get."*

There was a far coarser side to his fear-fed reactionary views.

In 1961, he wrote to Dick Whiteman, "I wish that you were with us. I would sing you the song that I began work on at five o'clock this morning, knowing that you are just as disgusted as are we with the whole dratted mess which makes up our nation and our world today."

And then he reproduced a stanza of lyrics, and I really wish he hadn't:

Freedom Riders, hummin on the happy Greyhound Line / Off to Mississippi with that little coon of mine. . . .

I can't even quote any more of it. Thinking of him waking in the Siesta Key predawn to labor on this swill is heartbreaking.

I remember hearing similarly awful stuff from him when I was a teenager, just when I was developing a polar-opposite political sensibility, and now I recognize that the recoil fueled my tendency to assess not only his politics but his career achievements and the writing itself skeptically and negatively. Even then, though, I knew there was another side to him, and I saw it confirmed while digging through the files.

In the 1940s, Mack was friendly with a more or less openly gay couple to the point that they occasionally babysat Tim when Mack and Irene were away. Friends would say, "How could you let Timmy be with them alone?" And Mack would explode, "Oh, bullshit! Jake and Harry are about as eager to attack Tim as I am to rape some twelve-year-old little girl."

In 1939, he published a surprisingly nuanced story in *The Saturday Evening Post* about a young black boy who watches enviously from afar as an all-white Boy Scout troop tramps about the woods, learning merit badge skills. He finds an old discarded Scouting manual, and secretly teaches himself all about woodsman skills and first aid. When a white girl carelessly crashes her bike into the wagon he sells turnips from, he recognizes that she's severed an artery in her wrist and insists that her panicky parents let him apply a tourniquet. This saves the girl's life. When the Scout troop hears about it, they crowd the sudden hero, asking why he never joined the Boy Scouts.

The final lines, recognizing how blind even well-intentioned whites can be to the racism all around them, are sophisticated even by today's standards. For 1939, they are astounding:

"He grinned at last, feebly, but he could not offer a coherent explanation. Perhaps he would never be able to explain to them how different he was from them all—how different he would forever be."

In 1956, Sarasota was still a Deep South town, complete with Jim Crow laws. With all its miles of beach, there wasn't one foot of sand its black citizens were permitted to trod. Using his recent Pulitzer as clout, Mack conducted a campaign of interviews, letters to the editor, and the threat of writing a critical article for a national magazine to force the local politicians to create a public beachfront for blacks. One of his letters concerned a dream he claimed to have had in which the ghost of a black soldier, killed in the war defending American freedom, was wondering why he couldn't so much as wade in the ocean back home.

The Ku Klux Klan threatened to stage a demonstration on the road in front of the Siesta Key house. "I announced that that was fine," Mack wrote. "I said they'd find me sitting on a chair on the lawn with my 30-30 on my lap. A few cars did come by, with idiot faces glaring from windows, but they took off fast when I picked up the rifle."

The campaign was successful, a black beach was created, but I also noted that Mack made it clear that he wasn't "like some Yankee" insisting on integration of the beaches, just that blacks should have a beach of their own.

Perhaps the most ironic political switcheroo became evident in a 1934 feature on Mack, one of the first newspaper profiles ever written about him, shortly after the publication of *Long Remember*, in which the hero is vehemently antiwar amid the prowar fervor that surrounds him. When asked if he was a pacifist, Mack said: "I don't see how any intelligent person could be anything else."

Ten years later, Mack was initiating an intimate and lifelong association with one of the least pacific, and most significantly bellicose, figures in American history, Curtis LeMay.

LeMay was the architect and commanding officer of the World War II bomb group that Mack had adopted as his own. Robert McNamara, who would become the secretary of defense under Kennedy and Lyndon Johnson, said of LeMay, "He was the finest combat commander of any service I came across in war. But he was extraordinarily belligerent, many thought brutal."

When too many of his bomber pilots were pulling out of formation to avoid heavy flak and missing their targets as a result, LeMay announced that every pilot who did so in the future would be court-martialed, and that he would personally lead the next mission.

LeMay later designed and commanded the massive firebombing campaign against Japanese cities that did as much as the atomic bomb to bring Japan to surrender, and killed as many as half a million civilians in the process. He once said if the U.S. lost the war, he fully expected to be tried as a war criminal.

In mid-October 1962, Soviet nuclear missiles were discovered in Cuba. LeMay, then Air Force chief of staff, fiercely argued for bombing the silos—an argument Kennedy resisted in favor of a naval blockade of the island coupled with negotiation. We now know what Kennedy suspected was true, that silo commanders had been given authority to launch the missiles if attacked. LeMay's plan would almost surely have triggered World War III.

Mack's devotion to LeMay and the Air Force was a fierce passion, and he seems to have absorbed LeMay's hawkish view of the world, and especially the Soviets. When Mack won the Medal of Freedom he told friends this was "the only medal I am apt to receive, ever, unless we hurry up and hit those sour-pussed s.o.b.'s beyond the Volga River before I get too old to fly."

In 1963, an Air Force jet landed under heavy security at Sarasota airport, and Mack was waiting on the tarmac. The local paper reported:

"A red and silver jet Star streaked down through a storm cloud. . . . At the controls was Gen. Curtis E. LeMay, Air Force Chief of Staff."

The paper said he'd stopped by "for a chat." The truth was, he wanted to persuade Mack to act as the ghostwriter for his autobiography.

Mack was flattered. Here was a universe in which he was still a hero. "Curt said that no one else could do a decent job with the book, and he had always supposed I would be the one to do it. I wouldn't do it for anyone else in the world. I'm no ghost writer—never have been or wanted to be."

The book, *Mission with LeMay*, came out in 1965—after Lyndon Johnson had forced the general to resign as chief of staff, and as LeMay began preparations for a political career of his own. That career would consist entirely of running as vice president on the third-party ticket of Alabama segregationist George Wallace. (LeMay had never considered himself a bigot, but wasn't bothered so much by Wallace's racial views that he refused to join the ticket. Most likely he saw the campaign as a chance to step up on a national platform and preach an aggressive, militarily powerful response to the Soviets.)

The reviews of *Mission with LeMay* were once again mixed, and largely dependent on how the reviewer felt about LeMay's career. But to my delight, I discovered that the book had been reviewed retrospectively in *Foreign Policy* magazine in 2013 by Thomas Ricks, a Pulitzer Prize–winning expert on military affairs and a former colleague of mine at *The Washington Post*. Presumably, a half century after publication, Ricks would have the capacity to view the book with dispassion and perspective. This is what he wrote: "I recently picked up the memoirs of General Curtis LeMay, partly out of guilt that I don't know more about the history of the Air Force. My problem is, I still don't. The book is mostly pablum . . . much of the rest of it is the type of claptrap that H. L. Mencken made a living destroying. I had expected that having MacKinlay Kantor, the author of the Pulitzer Prize–winning *Andersonville*, as co-author of the memoir was a recommendation. I didn't realize Kantor was a hack."

Harsh. But something else I found in the files, written before the book was even published, must have struck Mack even more harshly. Through three decades after the breakup of their affair, Mack had stayed in polite and respectful touch with Peggy Pulitzer. As he began work on the LeMay book, Peggy, now seventy and the possessor of twice as many Pulitzer Prizes as Mack, responded to a letter from him this way: "I enjoyed your budget of news. Sorry about the heart trouble, and hope it is gone for good. But I'm sorry, too, to hear you are doing a biography of LeMay—autobiography you say? Does that mean ghost-writing, for Pete's sake?"

It did.

"I had to learn to think like Curt," Mack had said in his letter. "Irene says I already talk like him."

Indeed, I came across a letter he wrote to my mother that colorfully demonstrated that, like LeMay, Mack insisted on looking at nuclear weapons as just another tool of war.

"You may remember my old and oft-stated theory: a blunt sword, as used by some inept but fervent murderer in Genghis Khan's time, killed people just as dead as a hydrogen bomb. . . . I don't want Mike and Tommy and Susan to die suddenly, killed in a meaningless historical demonstration, any more than you do. But I should just as soon to have them die as a result of modern machinery as to have their heads lopped off with a sword."

It was in this state of possession—thinking and talking like Curt—in which Mack wrote the infamous phrase advising the North Vietnamese to "draw in their horns and stop their aggression, or we're going to bomb them back into the Stone Age."

LeMay's later insistence that this was a sentiment he didn't endorse—"overwriting" by his ghostwriter, he claimed—is of course absurd, unless we are to believe that he didn't even bother to read the page proofs of his own autobiography. The more relevant point to me is not that LeMay really thought that way, but that Mack no doubt did as well, and not just about the North Vietnamese. In his increasing dread of modernity, I have no doubt he would have longed, if only it were possible, to bomb the whole relentlessly changing world into its previous condition, in which he had felt so at home.

Mack may have sensed his turn of fortunes with growing anxiety, but only in retrospect is it clear that his career was now in irreversible decline. In fact, in 1965, it may have seemed like the beginning of a great crescendo. Early in the year Mack crowed about signing a deal for three more books, including an anthology of old stories, a sequel to his autobiography, and a novel literally to be named later. "Between the LeMay book and these other projects of my own," he wrote, "Doubleday will have committed themselves to an advance of $270,000, which could be a world's record in confidence reposed in an author by his publisher."

It was a brag, of course, but the defensive whine echoes within, especially when you know that recent rejections of a handful of his books by his previous publisher, Bennett Cerf at Random House, had singed his confidence badly. In a childish pique, he said he was temporarily titling one of the proposed new books, a collection of "sentimental journeys into the past, which we think will sell like crazy," *While Cerf Burns*.

So who needed Random House? The money spigot was flowing again. More good news:

In August, Columbia Pictures announced that, after a decade of delay, *Andersonville* was finally set to film, directed by a real cinematic heavyweight, Stanley Kramer, or as the news release put it, "a man who gets things done."

Indeed, Kramer had one of the best track records in Hollywood, having made huge critical and financial successes like *Death of a Salesman, The Wild One,* and *The Caine Mutiny.*

I, of course, knew that no film of my grandfather's book was ever made—so when I came across this clip, saying that the script, casting, and even location scouting were all under way, I was baffled. I could find nothing in the files, or in quick searches online, to explain how such a high-powered film project simply vanished without a trace.

I finally learned the answer in, of all places, a biography of Spencer Tracy by James Curtis. In 1962, Kramer had signed a three-picture deal with Columbia. The first of the three, *Ship of Fools,* performed poorly at the box office, and Columbia decided to rein Kramer in on his next film, which happened to be *Andersonville.* By this time, construction on vast sets of the prison camp was already under way in Georgia. When the moneymen saw the initial bills, they pulled the plug. "It was too expensive for them," Kramer said.

So *Andersonville* was abandoned, for the final time. Instead, Kramer made a less expensive movie with Tracy, opposite the inimitable Katharine Hepburn and a young African American actor named Sidney Poitier. It was a huge hit.

I'm old enough to remember watching—and loving—*Guess Who's Coming to Dinner* in a first-run movie theater when I was fourteen, never dreaming that this groundbreaking movie on interracial dating existed at the expense of a significant part of my patrimony.

I came across an interesting postscript to the whole situation by accident, when I stumbled on an interview with Daniel Taradash, who had won the 1954 screenwriting Oscar for *From Here to Eternity.* It turns out that Kramer, gung ho to make *Andersonville* an Oscar-worthy project, had hired Taradash to write the script. When the project was canceled, Taradash had apparently been far enough along to have sent the script to my grandfather for comment.

"MacKinlay Kantor was a strange fellow," Taradash said in that interview. "He got the Pulitzer for fiction . . . but he wanted to get it for history because of the research. He wrote me a six-page letter about inaccuracies in the script—uniforms, regiments, that sort of thing."

But Taradash remembers *Andersonville* for more than that minor annoyance. He called the failure to produce his script "the biggest disappointment of my writing life."

M ack was now sixty-one, my age as I write this, an age I am keenly aware is the beginning of a relationship with mortality that can only be guessed at in earlier decades. In Mack's case, old age came on like gangbusters. The heart problem led the way, a bursting of the dam. His bad leg formed another abscess and required an umpteenth surgery. A suspicious mole had to be removed from his thigh (benign, it turned out) and precancerous tissue scraped from his mouth (a result of the constant pipe sucking). Irene woke up one day in April 1965 with fever and abdominal pain, and ended up in the hospital undergoing an emergency appendectomy—only, when the surgeon got it out, the appendix didn't seem sufficiently inflamed to explain the condition. Back home she went. The next morning she awoke "in utter agony, her abdomen distended, the toes of her left foot turning blue, the leg as white as alabaster," Mack wrote. Classic signs of an embolism. She was rushed back to the hospital, where surgeons, fearing they could lose her at any moment, discovered five massive clots in her left femoral artery. Worse, the artery itself had degenerated to the consistency of cheese. Just a year or two earlier, she would have died on the operating table, but the then-new technique of replacing the artery with a Teflon tube saved her life.

Exactly a month later, in the first hours of Memorial Day, the phone rang in my grandparents' bedroom at 2:30 a.m. Donald Friede, Mack's agent/editor for exactly twenty-five years, had died of a sudden heart attack.

"To say that it was a crushing blow to me is to put it mildly," Mack wrote.

I find it odd and a little disturbing that, though I had been eleven years old during this deluge of ill tidings, old enough to be aware—at least of my mother's anguish about her father's heart issue and her mother nearly dying—I have no memory of any of this. My sister doesn't remember, either—but she was only nine, so maybe that's to be expected. My brother, who was thirteen, has no good excuse, but, like me, remembers nothing. Possibly my mother thought she was shielding us from upset by not telling us the scary news. But I have an uneasy feeling it is at least partially due to our self-absorption, a tendency to lack empathy, even for our grandparents, when the pain is offstage, out of sight. Yes, all children may share that tendency to a varying degree, but I have often wondered if I tended toward it a little more than most.

When my parents separated in 1961, they gathered the three of us— nine, seven, and five—together on the living room couch. Sitting opposite us, across a Danish modern coffee table, in mismatching armchairs, they launched into a shaky but obviously rehearsed speech. They loved us and still loved each other, but they were going to live apart—just for a while. What I remember most about it was this: I looked from my brother to my sister, and both were crying. I wasn't crying, and decided that said something about a way in which I was different from them.

I don't want to overdramatize. What I felt could just be a valuable inner confidence, an innate self-reliance, or simply a streak of pure practicality—what good would crying do, after all? But emotional distance is also an element in the extreme kind of sociopathy exhibited by my great-grandfather John Kantor. As is true with alcoholism, geneticists believe sociopathic disorder is about half due to genetic makeup through production of proteins that affect the way the brain operates. Could the tendency I've noticed in myself be some thankfully watered-down inheritance from John?

Or, to consider it from a less fraught angle: Do I at least wish that I had been more aware, more attuned, to the suffering of people I loved?

Yes.

Judging from his letters, and his subsequent production, Mack rebounded from all of this adversity with admirable stoicism. He went back to work on another big historical novel, an idea he'd played around with not very successfully before he'd set it aside to plunge into the whirlwind that was *Andersonville*. Now he outlined the whole project—a story told through the eyes of a southern widow before the Civil War who buys, and becomes fascinated by, a slave.

Once again, despite the relative disappointments of the recent past, his name and ideas seemed to make magic. The proposal for the novel, *Beauty Beast*, provoked a bidding war between two publishers. The winner agreed to an advance of $250,000 for the book rights alone—an astonishing $1.7 million in inflation-adjusted dollars.

"We signed the contract a little before the noon hour in the Putnam office. . . . It was the first deal of this kind, and the largest, ever made in New York—at least according to the editors and agents involved," Mack boasted. Any intimation that he might be past his prime must have simply blown out that conference room window.

Mack finished the book in less than a year.

"Then the trouble began," he wrote. "It was turned down by all of the book clubs."

Now that the bloom was off the prose, the publisher "objected to certain things in the book. Then everyone at the office started raising their little voices, and saying the book would be better if written this way or that way. Of course I was adamant. . . ."

He probably shouldn't have been. *Beauty Beast* came out to a maelstrom of criticism, and worse, disinterest.

The *Kirkus* review began, "This turbid novel in which almost no story is embedded in a splotchy style . . ." It didn't get any better from there, concluding, damningly if not accurately, "Mr. Kantor spent fourteen years writing this novel and perhaps it was as difficult to write as it is to read."

The cover blurb begins: "This rich sensual novel of a woman's forbidden love for a magnificent young slave . . ." and you don't have to read much of the book before agreeing with a contemporary online review that says, in its entirety, "Wrong, on so many levels."

Beauty Beast reached the open doorway [of the bedroom]. . . .
"Missy, you— You said that I was to—"
"That you were to come to me here."
He took a cautious step beyond the doorway. Stopped.
"Missy . . . You said that you had something which you wished
 to offer me?"
"I wish to offer you myself."
She heard the long intake of breath, and lay pulsing in natural
 expectancy, knowing how she desired him. . . .
He came springing. . . .

And when it wasn't like a bad romance novel, it was just plain bad writing. Mockingbirds "sang out the miracles of their latest brooding," and the morning light "congratulated the woman on her restrained beauty."

If I look hard, I can find faint intimations of these tendencies in my grandfather's earlier books, but he had nearly always veered away from the cliff. In *Beauty Beast*, it seemed, the critical mechanism that had ruled against my grandfather's worst tendencies as a writer—we all have them—had simply deserted him.

Bottom line: A man who made jokes in which Dr. Martin Luther King Jr. was referred to as "Martin Luther Coon" had no business writing about a white woman lusting after an enslaved black man— even if his writing hadn't tipped into a pothole the size of the Ritz.

In the half century since publication, *Beauty Beast* has been blessedly forgotten. I don't think I could have even recognized the title as one of my grandfather's works. But as the pieces from letters and newspaper clips and Internet searches began to fit together in my conception, the book built from a curious footnote into a smoking gun. *Beauty Beast* was no simple misstep. It was a catastrophe.

As to the scope of the damage, Mack seemed entirely deluded, blaming the mess on the publisher's lack of support and uneasiness with the edgy subject matter. "It could easily become the top best seller in the Nation," he wrote. "But I fear they are chickening out."

Today, in more sensitive and socially connected times, Mack would have become an Internet punching bag and punch line. In 1967, he was simply shunned. The spectacular failure, combined with the fact that Putnam had paid a record-setting advance *and* invested in a big advertising campaign, left upon Mack an ineradicable stench he refused to acknowledge.

"I wrote the best book I am capable of writing. . . . Whatever happens, I'm satisfied. . . . A quarter of a million dollars is a quarter of a million dollars, even if we don't sell the picture rights." And then, pathetically, I thought, he closed with this: "Several people close to the deal have remarked that *Beauty Beast* would make a marvelous play."

SEVENTEEN

———

Beauty Beast was my grandfather's last big payday.
It seems ironic to me now, but it was almost immediately
after that disaster, in 1968, that my family moved from New
York to a modest home on a canal on Siesta Key, less than a mile from
my grandparents' house. I had no sense of Mack as having endured
some dramatic change of fortune. He was as he'd always been. He still
had money—that quarter mil was flowing in bit by bit. He still presided over his stretch of subtropical paradise; still convened weekly
cocktail-sodden lunches of Sarasota's most notable writers, his braying
voice rising above all others; still opined colorfully for profiles written
by mostly respectful newspaper columnists and feature writers.

And he still closed the door to his memory-stuffed study and wrote.

In proposing another three-book contract to his agent (which would be his last), he wrote: "I have never learned to live without writing, and I never shall."

Willfulness, and egotism, had pushed him through a ledger book filled with his handwritten record of a thousand rejections and carried him from nearly hopeless desolation of a coatless winter in the depth of the Depression to the ascendancy of a Pulitzer Prize and riches beyond his imagination. It pushed him still.

But the vessel had weakened. "There's another doctor whom I wish to consult about my general health," he wrote. "A specialist in energy, so to speak. I so long to recapture the physical energy which has driven me on through the years."

In this diminished state, he lacked the stamina for a big new project. He began to cobble together bits of his past for repackaging and recycling—a collection of already published short pieces called *Story Teller*; *I Love You, Irene*, the sequel to his 1947 autobiography, which was already mostly written; and *Hamilton County*, the mishmash of essays and stories—mostly written long ago—combined by slim pretext with my uncle's photographs taken in a dozen counties of that name. None of these sold well, and the reviews ranged to the vicious.

"MacKinlay Kantor's subject matter and techniques are sentimental, unsophisticated, and old-fashioned," began an all too typical review.

Another concluded: "As a stylist and a thinker Kantor had gone as far as he was ever going to go back at the point of time when Edward VIII was deciding that he wanted Wallis Warfield Simpson more than Britain's kingship."

Yet another: "He manages to sound as garrulous as Polonius in his cups and as self-conscious about it. And worse: as bigoted as a Wallace and as belligerent as a LeMay. . . . And even worse: as cantankerous as a retired Midwesterner a-settin' on his front porch in Sarasota retirement, which is exactly what and where Kantor is."

As a writer, I know you can claim to be unconcerned with critical opinion, to trust your own judgment above all else—and indeed my grandfather said just these things. But I also know negative reaction is like sand poured into that delicate engine of motivation, the self-belief that allows you to push through the appalling swamp of the writing process.

Add declining health, disappearing energy, and the ever-increasing skepticism of publishers to the toxic mix, and it's amazing my grandfather was able to keep working at all. Yet he did.

With all his vanities, prejudices, and arrogance creating a kind of fog around him, I'd never appreciated just how heroically he kept pushing on. A passage in one of his "Dear Everyone" letters particularly moved me. "Work," he wrote, "has been our atmosphere, our sky, our planets. Work has been the earth between our feet. Work has been the fire where we warmed ourselves and it has been the blast which froze us. . . . Work is our lunch, our agony, our inheritance, our God, our monster."

If work was the monster, he was its Dr. Frankenstein, bringing it to life each day before dawn behind that big desk with its heavy freight of memorabilia, manuscript pages, and unpaid bills. Even as his prospects diminished, he refused to yield. He pumped out a little novel about a Korean vet and his wife on a cruise ship tour of Asia (of course, he and Irene had to take a cruise to Asia so he could write it) that earned little money and even less benediction from critics ("A long way from *Andersonville* and still some distance from modern times, even if it takes place in the present").

In what must have been an especially galling concession to his circumstances, the man who less than a decade earlier vowed he was "no ghostwriter" hired himself out to a rich widow of a man who made a fortune in the insurance business, of all things, to ghostwrite a vanity memoir. She paid him $85,000 to do it, but of course he had to spend God knows how many hours of his dwindling energy and take an extensive and expensive Alaskan cruise (because the subject had a fascination with Alaska) to get the thing written.

And then he made one last thrust, a final attempt to recapture the *Andersonville* magic in a novel about the American Revolution called *Valley Forge*. It was clearly an exhausted rather than an exhaustive effort—more a collection of sketches than a proper novel. The dialogue was even more arcane than in *Spirit Lake*. The publisher who originally bought the idea rejected the manuscript, and Mack scrambled to find another, off-brand publisher.

The advance was tiny by comparison to those past, and the extended cruise on which he wrote the book was even more fabulously expensive than the Alaska one, through the South Pacific to Australia. But he had hopes the book would break through, like *Andersonville*, like *Long Remember* and *The Voice of Bugle Ann*, changing the equation once more. Despite the downward shift in publishers, the publicity department managed at least a small advertising campaign—increasingly rare in publishing even then—and the book attracted some advance press, in which Mack was still talking about his chances of winning a Nobel Prize. ("Should win me the Nobel," he told one interviewer "in his staccato, telegraph like syntax. 'Shoulda won it for *Spirit Lake*.'")

One of the photocopied newspaper articles on *Valley Forge* in the Library's files snapped me to attention. It was a feature column in the Fort Myers *News-Press*, the inaugural column of a writer named Randy Wayne White. Two years later, I would get my first newspaper job at this paper and get to know Randy, having no clue that his first column had been about my grandfather.

"Physically, age is catching up with him," White wrote. "You notice it in his short shuffling gait and in the wisps of white hair which cover his head like hoar mist. When he lights his pipe, the broad, wrinkled hands shake slightly. . . . But Kantor, the ageless MacKinlay Kantor, lies just behind the speckled green poet's eyes. . . . You don't believe him when he says, 'Why have I succeeded as a writer? Well, it's like the old prostitute who was asked, "Why are you a whore?" And she said, "Just lucky I guess."' . . . With Kantor, luck begins at 4:30 in the morning."

But now no amount of work would change his luck.

Valley Forge earned respect from a few reviewers like Robert Kirsch of *The Los Angeles Times*, who saw in the book "a powerful sense of personal witness . . . convincing human voices and emotion . . . the American Revolution itself."

But some were actively hostile, even mocking my grandfather's insistence on using authentic period spelling. *Kirkus* sneered, "The novel shows contempt for everyday narration and proceeds, fragment by 'smoaky' fragment, as the author's heart dictates."

The first printing was advertised at thirty-five thousand copies, but it didn't sell nearly that many.

Now Mack was branded by failure, and he knew it. What he didn't know, couldn't imagine, was that his life's work was finished. The last word of *Valley Forge* was the last word of the last book he would ever publish. That word was: *pride.*

I was twenty-one when *Valley Forge* came out, and I remember visiting him at his house while home on my final college winter break. He shook my hand as always, and there was something extra in his smile, a little gleam in his eye, as he pulled himself erect and limped over to the bookshelf to pull out a fresh copy of the book. He turned, the smile growing wide enough to reveal the full upper plate that so often plagued him, and handed it to me. It is the book that now sits beside me on my desk while I type these words, its cover jacket scuffed and torn at the binding. I must not have looked at it too carefully back then, because only just now, as I opened it to find the publication date, did I notice the dedication: to his grandchildren.

———

Mack included in his bequest to the Library of Congress even his tax returns, so it was depressingly easy for me to see the horrific details of the transition from record-setting advances to . . . almost nothing. In 1972, his total earnings barely topped $8,000. And yet he continued to live as he had become accustomed to living, which is to say, grandly. His "professional expenses" that year, including the extended Asian cruise that he deemed necessary to lubricate his writing process (along, no doubt, with uncounted Gibsons at onboard watering holes), totaled more than three times his annual income.

For a man who had made, over the course of his career, the contemporary equivalent of tens of millions of dollars, this should not have been a huge problem. But, incredibly, except for the beachfront land and the home—updated and expanded with *Andersonville* money—he had no investments and no assets, and soon his once prodigious savings had dwindled to the point where he had to retake mortgages on his home to pay his bills.

In files of letters from the 1940s, I found a particularly telling passage in which my grandfather is talking about an earlier time when an early fortune earned by his writing had evaporated.

"Oh, well, said Grandpa Vanderhof, you can't take it with you. But you can take the memory of the Panama jungles, the heather of Inverness-shire, the rocky lakes of Killarney where you can drink cold water that you dip up over the boat-side—you can carry along the picture of the blue-and-violet glass in the Cathedral of St. Germain, and the hot wet rain of the Cuban mountains, and the sound of music on Regent Street, and the flashing water off the coast of Nicaragua. If I had fifty thousand dollars worth of Treasury Bonds right now, I wouldn't have the rest of it; I'll take the roads of France, thank you, the whip-crack of Toscanini's baton, and the pale orchids Irene has worn now and again and the taste of good scotch instead of rank green liquor; and all the rest of it."

I have no question now—how could I, after learning all that I've learned—that my grandfather lived an extraordinarily rich life, the kind of life I have aspired to. But it's one thing to face an empty bankbook when you are in your prime, talent and prospects undimmed, and quite another when age and health and a changing world conspire against you.

I could find no letters from this period in which Mack addressed his dire circumstances. I did find this particularly depressing passage in my uncle's memoir:

> He blamed his lack of success in this current world to fashion. He believed that since he had had no major commercial success since Andersonville, editors and reviewers might be prejudiced by the sight of his name. . . . In a sad, elaborate scheme, which he revealed to none of us, he submitted—over and over again—the manuscript of what he thought to be a "contemporary" novel to various publishers under a pseudonym. The novel was short and bad, and it was rejected again and again. He went on humming and smiling and walking his hound dog Maury, working endlessly, staving off creditors.

My mother told me that, as his finances became increasingly desperate, she spent hours going through his bills and his accounts, trying to persuade him of the necessity to cut back. He insisted on continuing on as he always had, eating at expensive restaurants every night, even though, increasingly, "eating at expensive restaurants" consisted primarily of *drinking* at expensive restaurants.

"Honestly, Daddy!" she said. "I think you believe in miracles!"

"Oh, yes!" he said.

When Tim was going through my grandfather's desk after he died, he found a folded piece of notepaper under the blotter. On it, Mack had transcribed a quotation: *When we are born, we cry that we are come / To this great stage of fools.—Lear, IV:6.*

Beneath that he had written in a shaky script: *Jan.–April. No income.*

I have a photograph of my grandfather from this period. My last photograph of him. It is from December 1976, at a wedding reception for my first marriage, a union that lasted, legally at least, nine years to the week from that day—eight years and three months longer than my grandfather would last. He is standing between my two grandmothers, Irene to his left, and my father's mother, Mildred—we called her "Gackie"—to his right. The navy blazer looks two sizes too big, its collar curving around the empty space where robust shoulders and a strong neck used to be. On the breast is some sewn-on regimental insignia from the Air Force, dominated by an imperious eagle. He has that same pencil-thin line of a mustache he'd worn in photos from 1944. His eyes are drilling into the camera, revealing too much. He has those extra, hooded folds of eyelids, just like his father, beneath which are dramatic bags eloquently describing sleepless nights. His cheeks are sallow and sunken, his mouth thin and pressed, as if in grim determination, or pain. He is holding his chin up high.

It kills me to remember that this is the party when he told his too long, too unfunny story, and my friend made a much funnier joke at his expense—"Great story! You remember the first half and I'll remember the second half!"—humiliating him and making me laugh. What would I give to take that back? Name a price, please.

If only I could have spent a few months at the Library of Congress in the fall of 1976. It wouldn't have been impossible: The material was there; I was already a professional journalist. I'm sure I could have sold that story to someone. But the idea never occurred to me, and even if someone had suggested it, I would have shrugged it away. My grandfather had always simply been there, an eccentric part of the landscape, and I had long been in the business of believing he was unremarkable, and would continue on believing that until these last eighteen months, when I discovered just how *not* unremarkable he was.

In fact, there's little use pretending here that my grandfather represents a kind of Everyman—how many Everymen have childhoods out of some Dickens tale, write themselves into Hollywood history, and American history, sup with Papa Hemingway, make and lose fortunes. . . .

Still, I have no problem asserting that the most singularly remarkable thing about him is how much of himself he left behind in the hundreds of thousands of words in his books, and in the documents in those file boxes. Everyman, so revealed, would become remarkable.

In 1973, when he was sixty-nine—three years before that last photograph of him, and when he still believed in miracles—he speculated in a letter to Burl Ives that somehow he could contrive the perfect death. "I'll take airplanes, and so will Irene, and we plan to be aboard one—when we're eighty-something years old, and tired of working—when it hits a mountain while we're sound asleep. Curt LeMay agreed succinctly, 'That wouldn't be bad,' so I'll see if it can be arranged."

God, when we are still strong, still astride life, waking up every morning pulsing and planning and pushing forward, we feel such control. Arrange the perfect death? Why not?

Unfortunately, dinners of martinis and vichyssoise—always vichyssoise—starved the body and fed the slow destruction of his heart. What remaining strength he had drained away like a broken wave washing back to sea across the stretch of sand just beyond his door. Now it was the grinding, methodical, relentless process of death, begun years earlier, that gained strength and took control.

Within weeks of the photograph taken at my wedding reception, Mack's heart and mind slipped away. On a day of gentle breezes in early April, the doctor examined him, then retreated to the side porch of the house, surrounded by jungle and the sighing of fronds sliding against the screen. This was where Mack had spent countless hours on fine days like this one, writing one word, and then the next, and the next. Out of words now, he remained inside the house, reclining blankly in a big chair, wrapped in a white sheet, groaning. The doctor sat before Tim and Irene and delivered the grim prognosis . . . ten days to two weeks. No more.

But Mack defied him, held on for months. Or at least his increasingly emaciated body did, wasting into dispiriting shapes ever more like those living dead he'd witnessed at Buchenwald.

Mack was now beyond worrying, beyond hoping, beyond miracles. But Irene was not that fortunate. The financial situation, so desperate to begin with, threatened to evict her from this home that had been refuge for forty years, a constant in a life of inconstancy. Mack's endless array of friends had dwindled and disappeared. In May, a letter from a man he'd been closely associated with professionally and personally since 1934 and *Long Remember* put the situation so well into words:

Dear Irene,

 I was shocked to hear the news about Mack. I wish I could do something to lighten your burdens, but of course I cannot.

In the end it was another Sarasota writer of more recent acquaintance who found he could do something, and did it. This was a fellow participant in those gin-soused Friday repasts of local authors they called "Liars' Lunch," which Mack had dominated from the start by reputation and inclination. It was also a man Mack had for years belittled in the guise of advising him to abandon the genre books he wrote so he could write "a real book."

Mack was the literary lion, the Great Man, so John D. MacDonald simply took the needling, over and over, until late one night in 1960, he sat at the typewriter that would produce seventy-eight novels, many of them best-sellers featuring a memorable private detective named Travis McGee, and more than 450 short stories, and wrote:

Dear Mack,

It has been your habit (over the years I have known you) to make snide remarks about the work I do which is of importance to me. They have stung. I have been unable to laugh. You speak of "that mystery stuff" with a slurring indifference.

"That mystery stuff" had made him millions, was still making it when my grandfather's royalties had dwindled to insignificance, and it afforded John D., as everyone called him, the ability to not only forgive my grandfather but to save him—or Irene, since Mack was beyond salvation—by donating enough cash to keep the deeply mortgaged house on Shell Road out of default. The fact that John's literary reputation would remain substantial decades after my grandfather's had all but disappeared would be a fitting reward for his magnanimity.

Through all of this, I was absent, just seventy-five miles down the road. I had reasons—a new and demanding job, a new baby on the way. I'm sure my mom wanted to spare me seeing my grandfather as a wraith, hollowed of the spirit that had always burned so fiercely. But I needed to not be spared.

In September, Maury the dog, blind, lame, incontinent, had to be put down. My grandmother, desperately trying to maintain in grief and disbelief, fell while walking along the beach and broke her wrist, and the last strand of her resilience broke with it.

I'd always thought of it as grief and worry alone that strained her to the limit, but now I can see that it was more than that. She'd loved Mack, but she'd also put up with him. Put up with his multiple and unapologetic meanderings, his compulsion to hog the spotlight and suck up all the oxygen in any room they shared, his insistence on living a narrative that could barely spare a footnote for her. In exchange, she had gotten travel, fascinating conversation, constant adventure, and economic security. And now she'd been betrayed—by Mack and circumstance. After keeping to her bargain for half a century, her payoff had been denied, revoked without appeal.

She went to the hospital for surgery on her shattered bone and came out with a shattered mind. In the same heartbreaking week, Tim and my mom decided they could no longer handle the physical care of my grandfather and moved his spent shell of a body to the hospital as well. He hadn't spoken a word for days, I was told. Time was short.

I drove the two hours north from Fort Myers, fearing what I would encounter. Finding neither Tim nor my mom when I arrived, I asked the hospital receptionist for MacKinlay Kantor's room. She wrote a number on a slip of paper, handed it to me like a summons I had no choice but to obey, and watched me make that lonely walk down the nearly empty corridor.

When your number's up, your number's up. I remember my grandfather telling me that's what the airmen flying those deadly bombing raids into Germany always told one another before missions, a fatalism permitting them to ride a hurtling tube of metal into frozen clouds of flak. But that hadn't turned out to be true in my grandfather's case. His number had come up, and yet he lingered in some state between life and death, a shrunken man, tethered to tubes, lying curled and insensible as in the womb behind that numbered door.

I've always wondered if he even knew I was there beside him, lightly touching his arm; if he gathered the power for those final words as a reflex or a warning.

I have pondered those two words that were really one, a thousand times, ten thousand times, in the four decades since. "*Horrible! Horrible!*" It's a hell of an epitaph for a life of such spectacular and varied accomplishment, of such passionate use and celebration of the gift of being alive. Forgive me for taking it personally.

The features of his remarkable life had emerged, phrase by phrase, as if I were excavating that mountain of documents with a teaspoon. Throughout, I could never stop comparing my life to my grandfather's. For all I had accomplished, he'd accomplished more. For every memorable experience I'd had, he'd had two. For all the sparkling, witty, unforgettable people I'd known, he'd known three. I would never write a book as big and important and successful as *Andersonville*. He had, but in the end it stood only to remind me, like the "shattered visage" of Ozymandias buried in the endless stretch of desert sands, to look upon his mighty works, and despair.

All of it had brought him to that ultimate destination; the stark room and those bleak syllables, jagged cliffs against which all hopes and dreams and sparkling memories dashed themselves to bloody bits. So what hope was there for me?

This is what I've been pondering as I've worked, sorting through the sometimes eerie similarities and the stark contrasts of our two lives. On my side of the ledger, and I see now that I have my grandfather to thank for this, I have managed to live a rich life without leaving myself and my family in penury. As his financial disaster unfolded in Sarasota in 1977, I was beginning my own career. My grandfather's nightmare example made me fiscally cautious, debt averse, eager to save and invest. When, thirty years later, the world changed out from under me, as it had from my grandfather, I was able to walk away from a profession that no longer fully valued what I valued, or at least was no longer willing to pay for those values. And though I, too, would face filing tax returns in some of these later years with disturbingly slender bottom lines, I had spent weeks in Spain instead of months, eaten grilled fish on the back porch instead of filet mignon at Delmonico's, drove a budget rental car along the Pacific coast instead of sailed a luxury cruise ship across the Pacific. As a result I had also accumulated enough of a cushion—retirement accounts, pensions, annuities, extended-care insurance, and all the other tedious and unlovely instruments of responsible money management—that those lean years caused barely a shudder.

Despite my grandfather's spectacular paydays, I ended up more financially secure than him when it counted, and felt no poorer for the moderation of my spending—in part because I had also conserved my most important treasure, the love of my wife.

Mack always insisted—to the point of titling his autobiography *I Love You, Irene*—that Irene Layne was the great love of his life, and I don't disbelieve him, despite all I've learned. But I also have no doubt he'd squandered that love, as he had his other fortunes, through questing after the extravagant adventures of serial affairs. As his fame leached away, perhaps he understood that the same diminishing force had worked on the sustaining connection with Irene as well. When he was most alone, Irene's affection was stained with bitterness.

Was that what was horrible?

Maybe, in part.

There's still that second "horrible," and that's the one that had worried me most—the physical destruction and permanent obliteration of the body and all the thoughts and memories it contained; the end of which no amount of anticipation, no manner of good living, no wisdom, no generosity of spirit, no love, not even the kind of immortality attained through fame or genius, could prevent. One day, it might well be me curled and tethered on that cart, croaking out grim tidings of my own.

What my grandfather said in his hospital room that day has haunted me for years. It's only been in these past months, reading through his life, that I've begun to think about it differently; to consider that, maybe, last words are less important than all the words that came before.

EIGHTEEN

———

That "little book" on the writing table at Finca Vigía on the day in 1951 when my grandfather visited, *The Old Man and the Sea*, won Ernest Hemingway the Nobel Prize. In his acceptance speech, Hemingway said: "Things may not be immediately discernible in what a man writes . . . but eventually they are quite clear and by these and the degree of alchemy that he possesses he will endure or be forgotten."

Hemingway had a high degree of that alchemy. His work can be picked at, kicked around, reconsidered, but it is a long way from being forgotten. Even John D. MacDonald, a writer of the genre fiction my grandfather sneered at, produced enough alchemy that, thirty years after his death, Random House decided to republish his entire oeuvre.

In early 1956 when Mack, still number one on the best-seller list, learned that he had lost out to John O'Hara for the National Book Award, he fired a message off to my mother.

"Forget about that book award," he wrote. "I ain't worrying. Fifty years from now everyone will know Big A, and forgotten John O'Hara."

The literary legacy of O'Hara is debatable. But that's the point. It *is* debated. Some may diss, or dismiss, him, but he is still a part of the conversation.

I thought of that when I went searching for contemporary mentions of my grandfather, which are few, beyond the smattering of online reader reviews of a handful of his books. I came across a video of a 2008 Oprah interview with novelist Cormac McCarthy, who has won both the Pulitzer Prize *and* the National Book Award. Oprah asks McCarthy about his trademark refusal to use quotation marks in dialogue.

McCarthy responds that if you wrote something well enough, quotation marks were unnecessary. The first writer who showed him that, he says, was MacKinlay Kantor in "a very good book" called *Andersonville*. McCarthy pauses reflectively, then adds, "Now, there's a writer people don't know anymore."

Don't tell that to the people in Webster City, Iowa.

On the first day of my research trip there—I'd been coincidentally and conveniently invited to speak as part of a civic effort to "bring more awareness to MacKinlay Kantor in this area"—Lisa and I took a walk down the main street of the local business district, which looked eerily unchanged from the circa 1910 photo I had found in the Library of Congress files. In the first couple of blocks, we almost literally ran into a huge historical marker, suspended from steel girders thrusting from the sidewalk, featuring multiple images of my grandfather as a boy and a young man. Later, we were driven thirteen miles south of town to a lovely, tree-shaded park in a valley along a bend in the Boone River. Another historical marker informed us that we were on the grounds of what had been a grain mill purchased by Joseph Bone in 1867. The name MacKinlay Kantor once again figured prominently. As I read the small print about the history of the place, I skimmed over the names of the pioneer mill family—Joseph Bone, Evalyn Bone McKinlay, Adam McKinlay, Effie McKinlay—reading along casually until it struck bone.

Every name on that plaque belonged to a direct ancestor. Some fragment of the essence of all those named there, the sequence of chemical compounds that program the production of everything that makes a person who they are, from cuticles to cerebellum, was now running in my blood, pumping through my heart, inhabiting every cell of my skin. Across the water up on a hill, the sign said, was the original family homestead built by Joseph Bone. I later found a photograph of that house from the 1870s in which, from a distance, you could see a lone male figure standing somberly to the side and a small girl playing on the porch. It had to be one of the earlier photographs of such an iconic American scene. How strange that the man was my three-times great-grandfather Joseph Bone, and the little girl was my great-great-grandmother Evalyn Bone.

I've always thought of myself as an East Coast kind of guy. But here I was now, in the heart of the heart of Middle America, standing on ground sacred to those who had brought me into being. This quiet spot on the banks of a brown river was as much my place as any place in the world.

It doesn't make much sense at first, does it? Before I began doing this research, I didn't even know most of these people existed. So why was I feeling such a powerful connection? I spent a lot of time casting around through the research heavily featuring that tidbit about genealogical research being second only to pornography in Web hits.

Caring about our ancestors may be ubiquitous these days, but it sure isn't new. In Chronicles of the Old Testament, lineages are detailed back twenty-three generations. Matthew and Luke went to great trouble—complicated by the Virgin birth doctrine—to trace Jesus's lineage not only to God the Father, but through Mary to the Jewish King David. Throughout history, and prehistory, humans have benefited or suffered for the deeds or sins of their ancestors—inheriting not only genetic traits but wealth or poverty, social standing and reputation. In language after language, the family name contains a prefix or suffix meaning "son of": -*fitz* in Irish, -*son* in English and Swedish, -*ovich* in Russian, *ibn* in Arabic, *Mc-* or *Mac-* in Scottish, -*ides* in Greek, -*ez* in Spanish, -*wicz* in Polish, -*oglu* in Turkish, -*zadeh* in Persian. Even preliterate societies—with no Bibles to write down the names of past generations—often had individuals specializing in memorizing lineages, if not full-blown ancestor cults. The idea that relations were somehow "in your blood" predated by centuries the biological understanding that DNA was passed along through the union of sperm and egg cells.

As with the claim that Jesus descended from King David—a prerequisite for the prophesied Jewish Messiah—knowing your ancestry has always been a potential leg up for the current generation, whether to legitimize royalty or just ownership of the lower forty.

But we all know the feeling is at least as much emotional as practical. It's easy to speculate that the origin of the bonds of family predate even modern humans; a connection initially forged by the flood of powerful hormones surging in the brain and body—of both mother and father—set off by the birth of a baby and the process of caring for it thereafter. The hormone cocktail incites feelings of closeness, trust, and bondedness that can last a lifetime, making the parent-child nexus a focal point of safety and trust in a hostile world. That love and dependence is projected both into the past in our caring for long-dead ancestors, and into the future, in our concern about descendants not yet born.

The profound psychological impact of ancestry has been cleverly highlighted by recent research at Emory University, where randomly selected children were tested on how much they knew about their ancestors. Then researchers gave them a wide range of diagnostic tests. The overwhelming result: The more children knew about their family history, the better they scored on measures of psychological health, well-being, and adaptability. Perhaps even more impressive, children who learned about their ancestors during the study improved their test results. Other research shows that adult subjects randomly assigned to think about their ancestry before taking a test performed better on it than control groups given no such instruction.

But standing there on an Iowa patch of green grass, watching that brown river flow, I didn't really feel smarter or more adaptable. What I felt was . . . peace.

I could have stayed there for hours, but our tour guides were urging us on, back into town to the main attraction—a stone monument in the middle of the city's largest park. Set in the stone was another plaque, this one bronze, containing quotes from my grandfather expressing his love for Webster City. It ended, *In my own time, let my ashes prosper in my own good soil.*

As I looked down on the embossed bronze plaque, set in a table-size slab of concrete, I thought of a letter Irene had sent to a friend in Webster City sometime after the monument had been dedicated in the summer of 1976. "It was grievous to remember the services held at the dedication, for Mack was a very sick man and I wondered whether he would be able to finish his speech."

Now I realized that I was standing in the same spot he had undoubtedly stood during that speech, so ill and struggling to keep upright. I felt a sadness that seemed somehow to emerge from the ground beneath my feet and seep through my body.

My whole life I've had the feeling that the physical location of significant events somehow retained some of the energy of what had happened there. I'd discovered Mack felt the same way. I remembered the letter he wrote about getting the inspiration to write *Long Remember*, the "emotional wallop" he said he'd felt when he stood on the battlefield at Gettysburg and how the image of his headlights sweeping across the gravestones of the fallen kept him from sleeping that night.

As it happened, gravestones were the next stop on our tour. Graceland Cemetery meanders along a wooded creek bed for three-quarters of a mile, a gentle slope of lawn studded with mature pine trees. I'd recently found a note Mack had written in one of his story collections talking about a visit to Webster City when he'd stopped at Graceland: "I went back there at sunset one June evening, tired and sick at heart. I had spent the week in Des Moines looking after the funeral services of one of my best friends. When it was all over, instead of catching a plane back East, I drove seventy miles to the plot of ground where my mother and grandparents lay. I stopped beside the lot, then walked over to the hilltop and flung myself flat on the grass, gazing through the dusk at the little bed in the creek where we boys used to swim. . . . I can swear to it: there was an actual force, a comforting vigor that flowed out of that soil into my body as I lay there."

In a letter about another Webster City visit, he said, "I strolled through Graceland Cemetery as I always love to do when I'm there. One of these times, I suppose I'll go to Graceland *without strolling*, but Jesus please wait on that one."

Jesus waited only a distressingly brief eleven years, but Irene delayed things for two more. Mack was cremated after a grim ceremony in Sarasota of which I remember very little. My daughter had been born just three days before Mack died, and I was in a fog of sleep deprivation and emotion. My only clear recollection is sitting beside Irene in a front row of folding chairs, uncomfortably aware of her lack of presence. She had been released from the hospital barely in time for the service. In the hours leading up to it, she had railed about "Mack's desertion" and shuffled around pitiably, lost and uncomprehending. The shock of surgery and her emotional collapse had set her up to fail. Overmedication in the hospital did the rest, precipitating psychosis. A new doctor, horrified by the combination of pills my grandmother had been given, stopped the medication cold. We hoped she might come out of it then, but weeks went by with no improvement. When it seemed past the point of hope, my mom and Tim had to make another awful decision, this time to put their addled mother in a nursing home.

Irene had no reaction when her children explained what they had decided. They arrived at the home and she shuffled obediently into the lobby on Tim's arm. It was a clean but clearly institutional place. Her head swiveled to the left, then the right, as if noticing her surroundings for the first time. She dropped Tim's arm, turned around, and shuffled back to the car.

The next morning, for the first time since she'd broken her wrist, she made breakfast for herself in her own home. Three weeks later, because she disapproved of the stuffing Tim intended to make, she cooked the Christmas turkey and all the fixings using her own recipes.

She progressed from there, but it took two years before she could deal with arranging the gravestone engravings and shipping Mack's ashes. Now, presumably, they lay beneath my feet by the marker that said, MACKINLAY KANTOR, SINGER OF SONGS, TELLER OF TALES, "FOREVER WALKING FREE."

I thought that last was a nice sentiment, but wasn't sure why it was in quotes. Turns out it was even more fitting than I imagined, and in an unexpected way.

"Forever Walking Free" was the name of a short story Mack had written during the war, about an American airman meeting a pretty, blond English girl named Joan during a German air raid in London. When the bombs fall silent, he invites her to an off-limits supper club called the Blue Polly, with "swell liquor, swell food, and doubtless plenty more of those peppery American cigarettes"—all items hard to come by legitimately in wartime London. There's music, dancing, and lots of drinking. Joan's resolve not to be an easy pickup is dissolving when she realizes that the name of the "base" her American said he was stationed at— Brookwood—was actually a cemetery, and that he's dead, and so is she.

In his notes on that story, Mack conceded that some readers might be offended by the idea. "Would this author have us believe that heaven is a *saloon?*" he asks on their behalf, and immediately supplies the answer. "Indeed, even heaven may assume the form of the Blue Polly on occasion; possibly the seraphim are sometimes named Joan, and have beds in Bloomsbury. If so, I can think of no future satisfaction more agreeable."

So perhaps Mack now rests with a bottle and a babe in a bed in Bloomsbury, forever walking free.

Returning to downtown Webster City, we stopped into the Mornin Glory, a surprisingly lively coffee shop in this Starbuckless city where it seemed the entire citizenry met to plan or recap the day. Yes, thank God, they had espresso drinks. It turned out that, in the reflected glory of my ancestry, and because I had spoken at the community auditorium the previous evening, even I was a minor celebrity here. After the talk, an eighty-six-year-old woman approached me to say that, when Mack had returned to Webster City for a summer in 1938, she had come around to play with my mom and Tim. Well—she corrected herself—really, it was just Tim. My mother wouldn't have much to do with her because she was older. I did the math. "But she was only eleven months older than you," I said.

"Well, she was *much* taller."

During this conversation she had been nervously fidgeting with a manila envelope. Now, hesitantly, she handed it to me. Inside, she said, were clips of my grandfather's that her even older neighbor, now ninety-one, had been keeping since she was a little girl, impressed by the local boy who'd made good.

"She's just held on to them all these years, but she thinks that you might make more use of them now," the woman said, sounding personally unconvinced.

I unsealed the envelope and gingerly slid out the brittle newsprint. I stared, disbelieving. It was a ninety-four-year-old section of *The Des Moines Register* featuring the winner of its 1921 short story contest: "Purple," the very first story my grandfather ever published.

The next morning at the café, another woman who recognized me from the talk wanted me to know that, every Memorial Day, she put flowers on my grandfather's grave, because that's what her late father had always done.

I'd noticed a group of women in their fifties talking and laughing at a large table in the middle of the shop. From what I could overhear of the conversation, they were planning a fortieth high school reunion. Now one of them, a slim, youthful brunette, got up and came over. "Your grandfather put me in a book," she announced.

Really? I said. What book?

"It was called *Hamilton County*. I have the picture here." She opened a box sitting on her table and pulled out an image of a group of teens standing in a school hallway. One of them, a cute brunette with the exact same short bob haircut as the woman holding the photograph, and obviously her younger self, was talking and gesturing with animation.

I recognized it instantly as the image for which my grandfather had commissioned me to write imagined "teen" dialogue in 1970. I even remembered the first line, and why wouldn't I? They were the first words I was ever paid to write: "You should have heard what Barbara said. . . ." I hoped that forty-five years was not too long to wait to apologize for putting words in her mouth.

Not much later, yet another citizen sought me out—an older man who wanted me to know that his former business partner hosted Mack on one of his triumphant returns to Webster City. "They got roaring drunk, as usual," he said, smirking slightly. "Mack went out to piss and passed out on the lawn, and in the morning there was a knock on the door. The garbageman . . ."

I knew the end to that story.

Apparently, however, Mack's public drunkenness didn't stop the county from naming a road after him. It's a ruler-straight highway on the edge of town lined by fields of corn—which would have tickled the 1970s critic who had called Mack's short stories "boiled-and-buttered native corn, fresh from the can."

And it didn't stop one of the teachers at the fine new high school from assigning this unlikely scenario as an essay prompt:

"You're on the subway in New York and you begin talking to your seatmate. You exchange pleasantries, and you've just informed them that you are from Webster City. Your new friend says, 'Isn't that the town that MacKinlay Kantor is from?'"

In the New York subway system, do people really exchange pleasantries and have ready knowledge of my grandfather?

As Hemingway put it at the end of his first novel, "Isn't it pretty to think so."

For sixteen years, my brother and his family have lived in a home he built in Sarasota, just two minutes from where Mack and Irene lived. I've visited frequently, but never once looked in on the old house—I wasn't sure I wanted contemporary reality to intrude on memory. Now, curiosity, plus the fact that I was writing this book, made me feel I had to.

I looked up property records and found a phone number for the current owner, a woman living there alone. When I called and told her who my grandfather was, she immediately said, "He was mean as a snake."

I was more amused than offended. I knew my grandfather, and all his moods, pretty well by now. It turned out this wasn't her firsthand opinion, but commentary from an elderly tradesman she'd met who had done work for Mack in the day. Plus, and this would have annoyed my grandfather spectacularly, she was a raging liberal, unforgiving of what she knew about his politics.

In any case, she was gracious enough to invite me to stop by, which Lisa and I did on a warm September morning. The address is Shell Road, but Shell Road no longer exists, thanks in part to my efforts. Mack had for years railed in letters to the editor and to county officials about the annoyance of tourists driving through what he considered his backyard—Shell Road, which indeed was made of crushed shell, ran across his property, separating his lawn from the beachfront. Heavy rains and erosion caused potholes to form, which the county was habitually slow to repair. Mack decided that it was his prerogative as a homeowner to declare the road abandoned.

One afternoon—I must have been home from college—I had a message from him, asking me to stop by. When I arrived, he had a posthole digger and some palm logs stacked up, each about four feet long. I dragged the logs out to the road. Mack took a few bites with the digger, then apologized for his bad back and handed it to me. When I'd dug down deep enough, we both wrestled the logs into the hole—making sure that at least two feet of each log end stuck up from the surface. *Et voilà*, a sturdy palisade blocked the road on either side of his property. From that moment forward, not another car would ever pass behind my grandfather's house. He offered me a beer and fixed himself a cocktail. We sat on the patio, toasting the success of our rebellion.

I was remembering this, wishing we'd had more moments like it, as Lisa and I turned off Higel Avenue—the main road heading south on the Key—onto the still jungle-canopied driveway. This had always been how I'd approached his house, and at first it was surprisingly and reassuringly familiar, until we slammed to a halt at a structure I didn't recognize. It took me a while to get my bearings, to realize that encroachments from the new homes to either side, where the buffer of untouched jungle had been sold off piecemeal, had pushed the entrance drive to the wrong side of the carport. The driveway I remembered, the one where I rode my first two-wheeled bicycle early on a Christmas morning more than fifty years before, no longer existed. Neither did the screened entrance terrace, which had been covered with a roof and enclosed, as had the back terrace overlooking the Gulf of Mexico. The living space, always filled with frond-filtered light and open to the outside, now seemed dark, hunkered down, cluttered. His den had been chopped up, with a bathroom and storage closets intruding on what had once been an expansive, regal rectangular space. It all felt so shrunken. But for the coquina rock fireplace and the black slate floors, I would have doubted it was the same house.

At least the ocean was still there. We walked out the back, across a lawn half as wide as I remembered, toward the beach.

There was no trace of the old road. And there was no beach. Instead, a concrete seawall, fronted by a pile of riprap boulders, held a perilous line in a war against rising sea and sweeping tides. I stood at the edge of the seawall and looked out into the shallow water, imagining the stretch of sand where I had played with my toy trucks, built camp-fires with friends, made love for the first time.

Gone.

I thanked the woman for her hospitality, knowing it would be the last time I ever saw the house, or wanted to. There's always a last time for everything, of course, you just don't always know when it's arrived.

Irene had lived on in that house for some months after my grand-father's memorial service, slowly coming back to herself, but strug-gling with the precipitous rush to sell off the mortgaged property, first the buffer lots, then the house itself.

My mother said she kept asking, "How could your father have done this to me?"

Unfortunately, it couldn't have been a worse time to sell, a low ebb in Florida real estate. Waterfront acreage that would have been worth millions today was sold off for just enough to pay off the second and third mortgages and build a modest bungalow on an inland canal. There was only enough for that because my father, no longer married to my mother but still very fond of Irene, built it for her at cost.

Irene had never learned to balance a checkbook—but with my mom's help, she learned to manage her reduced but stabilized finances. The new house was small but comfortable, wrapped around a pretty screened patio shaded by palms and flowering sea grape trees and over-looking the peaceful tidal canal. This is where Irene set up her easel.

From time to time I'd drive up from Fort Myers to visit with her. Whatever bitterness she felt seemed to have simply vanished, replaced with a powerful serenity that infected me with calm as soon as I walked in the door. There was something new about her, an agelessness I'd never seen before. We'd sit out by the canal, watching boats drift by. Sometimes she'd paint, but mostly we chatted—more like old friends than grandmother and grandson—sipping the sweet tea she'd spritzed with juice from Key limes that grew just outside the screen. I remember thinking that she might be the sanest person in the family.

In her mid-seventies then, she was still working at her art, taking lessons with an internationally respected painter in a little cottage studio just a few miles away.

One June morning in 1982, Irene had been painting in her teacher's studio when he stepped out for a minute. He returned to find Irene sitting rigidly on the floor, a paintbrush still gripped in her hand. She could talk, but could not stand.

Tim raced to the studio, helped carry Irene to the car, and drove her to the hospital. She had been planning to fly to New York in two days to visit an old friend. As my mom left her hospital room for the night, Irene said, "This is a hell of a time for something like this!"

Isn't it always.

Sometime before dawn she had another stroke and died.

I've often thought in the years since that, if my grandfather's death was a model of horror, my grandmother's may be the best imaginable scenario in an array of unattractive options.

After the memorial service, I went with my mom to the little bungalow to help sort through my grandmother's possessions. As I was opening drawers in her bedroom, I came across a note scrawled in Irene's looping script:

> Vivid dream. Mack had been up
> doing something—he jumped back into
> bed—his top bare—solid chest as when
> young against me.
> A happy dream.

For the first I could remember, I cried.

POSTSCRIPT

———

In the weeks after I completed the first draft of this book, I had free time on my hands for the first time in nearly two years. So of course my wife pressed me into service to help her sort through the overwhelming collection of junk that accumulates in a basement after fifteen years of family living. We saved the worst for last—the unlit irregular space beneath the basement stairwell, every inch of which was crammed with God knew what. When we finally got it all out—boxes filled with toy soldiers, stuffed animals, paintings that hadn't seen light in a decade, and miscellaneous mementos that had bled out of all memory, I crawled back into the farthest reaches one last time with my flashlight just to be sure we hadn't missed anything. In the darkest corner, my hand touched plastic—a ziplock bag filled with papers of some kind. I grabbed it and backed out into the light to inspect the final haul. The first thing I looked at was a yellowed piece of paper beginning "Dear Grandpa." There were other letters, too, from my grandfather to me, and from me to my grandfather. One of the latter, signed "Tommy," is undated, but I have no doubt it is from the late 1960s, when I was in my early teens and soon after we had moved to Sarasota.

It reads in its entirety:

> You have always been a grandfather. Sometimes you brought me presents. Sometimes you told stories. I have given you the love assigned to grandfathers. But you have never been a person until this year. And I am very happy to meet you.

With the advantage of a half century's hindsight, I can say now that, though I appreciate the sentiment, I was incorrect in my conclusion. It is only now, after this long labor of love, that I truly know MacKinlay Kantor as the brilliant, selfish, loving, complicated, damaged, unforgettable person that he was. And I am truly happy to meet him.

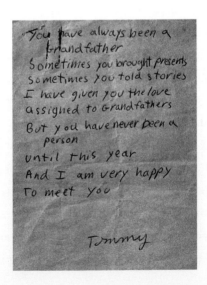

ACKNOWLEDGMENTS

I would be remiss if I didn't first thank the Library of Congress, its curators and the staff of the manuscript reading room for storing, indexing, and preserving my grandfather's papers with such uniform professionalism. I also want to thank my cousins Lydia Whitney and Melissa Pop-Lazarova, my brother Michael, and my sister Susan, my coheirs to my grandfather's literary estate, for blessing, encouraging, and actively assisting in this project. I need to add a special note of gratitude to my sister for having the foresight to insist on keeping and storing multiple bins filled with hundreds of letters, files, and photographs when I might have, in the name of decluttering, consigned them to oblivion. Not only did she go to the trouble of boxing and storing the material, but she also graciously hosted me when I finally recognized them for the treasures they were.

Exploring the entirety of a life that ended forty years ago is a daunting project. I was lucky to have a leg up thanks to the poetic 1988 memoir *My Father's Voice*, written by my late uncle, Tim Kantor, also a gifted photographer whose portrait of my grandfather and a five-year-old me graces the frontispiece of this book. Paul Juhl's meticulously researched volume *MacKinlay Kantor's Webster City, Iowa* was also a great resource.

I also want to thank April Witt for not only taking my photo for the book jacket but reading an early draft of the book and offering great encouragement, as did my old friend David Klein, my beautiful, brainy (and long-suffering wife), Lisa Shroder, and my daughter, Jessica Shroder. And then there's Gene Weingarten, who got me started on the whole shebang with a simple request: "Write me one paragraph on what you know about your grandfather."

I owe a special debt of gratitude to the city and the people of Webster City, Iowa, for their loving efforts to keep my grandfather's memory alive, and specifically to Paul Juhl, Nancy Kayser, and Angie Martin-Schwarze, who showed me I was a Midwesterner after all, and proud of it.

Finally, this book never would have happened if my publisher, David Rosenthal, hadn't instantly seen the potential in a casual conversation over Mexican food, and it would not have been the book it is without the inspired advice and direction of my editor, Sarah Hochman. Last and certainly not least, I am forever indebted to my dear friend and agent, Gail Ross, without whose understanding, support, and superlative instincts my career would almost certainly be moribund.

INDEX

Page numbers in *italics* indicate the Kantor family tree.

INDEX

ABOUT THE AUTHOR

TOM SHRODER is an award-winning journalist, editor, and author of *Old Souls* and *Acid Test*, a transformative look at the therapeutic powers of psychedelic drugs in the treatment of PTSD. As editor of *The Washington Post Magazine*, he conceived and edited two Pulitzer Prize–winning feature stories. His most recent editing project, *Overwhelmed: Work, Love, and Play When No One Has the Time*, by Brigid Schulte, was a *New York Times* best seller.